Gustave Louis Maurice Strauss

Men Who Have Made the New German Empire

A Series of Brief Biographic Sketches

Gustave Louis Maurice Strauss

Men Who Have Made the New German Empire
A Series of Brief Biographic Sketches

ISBN/EAN: 9783337031008

Printed in Europe, USA, Canada, Australia, Japan

Cover: Foto ©ninafisch / pixelio.de

More available books at **www.hansebooks.com**

MEN WHO HAVE MADE THE NEW GERMAN EMPIRE.

A SERIES OF

BRIEF BIOGRAPHIC SKETCHES.

BY

G. L. M. STRAUSS.

IN TWO VOLUMES.

VOLUME I.

London:
TINSLEY BROTHERS, 8, CATHERINE STREET, STRAND.
1875.

CONTENTS.

I.

	PAGE
WILLIAM I. . .	1
THE LATE QUEEN DOWAGER OF PRUSSIA	. 33

II.

FIELD-MARSHAL GENERAL VON ROON	42

III.

FIELD-MARSHAL GENERAL MOLTKE	54
THE "VÆ VICTIS!" OF DONCHÉRY	72

IV.

PRINCE BISMARCK .	88
THE ROMISH EPISCOPATE AND THE OLD CATHOLIC MOVEMENT . . .	. 258

ERRATA TO VOL. I.

Page 15, line 5 from the top, *for* "statesman," *read* "statesmen."
,, 17, ,, 1 ,, ,, *for* "Bronnzell," *read* "Bronzell."
,, 23, ,, 6 ,, ,, *for* "definitely," *read* "definitively."
,, 24, ,, 5 ,, bottom, *for* "memoirs," *read* "memoir."
,, 33, ,, 3 ,, top, *for* "(Joseph of Bavaria)" *read* "(Joseph) of Bavaria."
,, 43, ,, 12 ,, bottom, *for* "Alt-dabum," *read* "Alt-Damm."
,, 58, ,, 1 ,, ,, *after* "after," *insert* ", in 1859,".
,, 59, ,, 7 ,, ,, *for* "Steihle," *read* "Stiehle."
,, 60, ,, 10 ,, ,, *for* "that," *read* "this."
,, 61, ,, 6 ,, ,, *for* "von," *read* "of."
,, 78, ,, 10 ,, top, *for* "heart," *read* "hearts."
,, 82, ,, 12 ,, bottom, *after* "face," *add* "to "; *for* "finding," *read* "find."
,, 95, ,, 3 ,, ,, *for* "manors," *read* "manor."
,, 130, ,, 12 ,, top, *for* "question," *read* "questions."
,, 131, ,, 8 ,, bottom, *for* "similar," *read* "German."
,, 136, ,, 5 ,, ,, *after* "granted," *dele* ",".
,, 140, ,, 6 ,, top, *after* "day," *dele* "of the new session."
,, 142, ,, 12 ,, ,, *for* "She," *read* "Austria."
,, 155, ,, 14 ,, bottom, *for* "Mioks," *read* "Macks."
,, 159, ,, 9 ,, top, *after* "who," *insert* "had."
,, ,, ,, 5 ,, bottom, *after* "Falckenstein," *dele* "Voigts-Rhetz."
,, 163, ,, 13 ,, top, *for* "Kendell," *read* "Keudell."
,, 180, ,, 9 ,, bottom, *for* "knights," *read* "kings."
,, 201, ,, 13 ,, ,, *for* "Fulde," *read* "Fulda."
,, 210, ,, 13 ,, top, *after* "than," *insert* "was witnessed."
,, 214, ,, 3 ,, ,, *for* "give," *read* "gave."
,, 215, ,, 7 ,, bottom, *for* "essential," *read* "executed."
,, 243, ,, 11 ,, top, and in other places, *for* "Kamecke," *read* "Kameke."
,, 249, ,, 14 ,, bottom, *for* "as," *read* "more;" *after* "plastic," *dele* "as ever."
,, 252, ,, 9 ,, ,, *after* "Cologne," *dele* "who is already in prison."
,, 263, ,, 12 ,, top, *after* "occurs," *dele* "in this protest."
,, 266, ,, 8 ,, bottom, *after* "Munich," *dele* ",".
,, 282, ,, *dele* lines 10 and 9 from the bottom.
,, 293, ,, 4 ,, top, *after* "speakers," *insert* ",".
,, 313, ,, 8 ,, ,, *for* "truly," *read* "very."
,, 318, ,, 10 ,, ,, *for* "by," *read* "to."
,, ,, ,, 11 ,, ,, *for* "bidding," *read* "bid."
,, 325, ,, 4 ,, bottom, *for* "the," *read* "its."
,, ,, ,, 2 ,, ,, *for* "anti-actional," *read* "anti-national."
,, ,, ,, 1 ,, ,, *for* "their," *read* "the."
,, 334, ,, 11 ,, top, *for* "man," *read* "men."

MEN WHO HAVE MADE THE NEW GERMAN EMPIRE.

I.

WILLIAM I.

History tells us of some kings of men, leaders of nations, and founders of empires, who themselves in great part achieved their own greatness.

Such were, for instance, Cyrus of Persia, Philip and Alexander of Macedon, Cæsar, Charlemagne, our own Alfred, Henry I. of Germany, the founder of cities; Gustavus Adolphus, the saviour of the Protestant faith; Oliver Cromwell, the true founder of England's power and glory; Czar Peter, the wonderful Colossus, who with his giant stride spanned the wide chasm between barbarism and civilization, kneading and moulding hordes of wretched serfs into material fit to form a future nation; the great Brandenburg Elector and the unique king, who between them laid the foundation of the new German empire of our own days; and George Washington.

Also of some who had the greatness of others thrust upon them, and shone chiefly with the reflected lustre of their brilliant surroundings. Such were, for instance, Octavianus Augustus, the second Justinian Alp Arslan and Malek Shah, the two Seldschuk Sultans, who owed their reputed greatness chiefly to their famous vizier, Nezam el Mulk; Henri Quatre our own Queen Bess, Louis XIV., and, in our own days, Victor Emmanuel of Italy, and William I. of Prussia and Germany.

Still, to be thought worthy to figure even in this second category requires a certain innate greatness, an elevation of mind that will not grudge to afford free play to the actual workers of illustrious deeds. For history tells us also of some rulers upon whom even the greatest men bestowed upon them by kind Fortune have been more or less thrown away.

Poor Frederick William III. of Prussia, the father of King William, was a most striking and pointed example of this kind. Stein's vast genius weighed so oppressively upon the singularly small mind of that "military-tailor king," as the first Napoleon contemptuously called him, that he would rather continue to grovel in his own congenial dust than be dragged up to the most exalted height of greatness and glory by the stern Iron Baron.

And the late brother and predecessor of King William, brilliant, feeble-minded Frederick William IV., could never bear in his cabinet men above the intellectual standard of an Eichhorn, or a Manteuffel, or, at the most, a Radowitz.

It is one of the most convincing proofs of King William's immense superiority over both his father and his brother, that he has been able to get along so far with Bismarck and Moltke, and the other great men who have made his reign one of the most illustrious in the annals of the world's history.

King William I. of Prussia, the first emperor of the new German empire, was born on the 22nd March, 1797. His father was the then Crown Prince, afterwards King Frederick William III. of Prussia; his mother, the beautiful, good, and accomplished Princess Louise (Augusta Wilhelmina Amalia) of Mecklenburg-Strelitz.

He was the second son of his parents. He was born at a period when the glorious creation of the second Frederick was fast disappearing in the worse than unskilful hands of Frederick William II., the great king's very little nephew and successor, to whose name in this world's historic records plainspoken Clio has irreverently affixed the unflattering cognomen of *le ventru*, as we choose to express it here from due regard for delicate ears.

This corpulent ruler of Prussia, whose immorality in every way was on an exact par with his intellectual incapacity, had shortly before out-Heroded the disgraceful peace of Bâle of the 5th April, 1795, by the infamous convention of the 5th August, 1796, which vilely trafficked away to France the left bank of the Rhine, in exchange for some fancied, ill-understood aggrandizement of Prussia in Germany.

A few months after the birth of the young prince, this cowardly and selfish policy of the second state in Germany bore its disastrous fruit in the bitter humiliation of the then first state in Germany — Austria, which had to subscribe the harsh conditions of the peace of Campo-Formio (the 27th October, 1797).

A few brief weeks after, on the 16th November, 1797, death removed Frederick William II. from the political stage. His son, the infant prince's father, succeeded him on the throne of Prussia.

The new king, Frederick William III., then in his twenty-eighth year, was much more moral in his private capacity as a man than his late father and predecessor had been, but he was equally base and incapable as a king.

Of this sad fact he gave convincing proof when, a few months after his accession to supreme rule in Prussia, he turned a deaf ear to Count Cobenzl's warmest and most urgent appeal to abandon the cowardly and cruel policy of his predecessor, which had already done so much harm to poor Germany, and was now threatening to hand that unhappy country over, bound hand and foot, to the tender mercies of France. The disgraceful peace of Lunéville, of the 9th February, 1801, to which Austria, coolly abandoned to her fate by Prussia and Northern Germany, had to submit, was the crowning point of this equally dastardly and blind policy of the Berlin cabinet.

But had not Frederick William III. his reward? Did not the "Deputation of the German Empire," by resolution of the 28th February, 1803, sanction the transfer to Prussia of some 5,000 English square miles of land, with 600,000 head of human cattle upon it, in exchange for about 1,000 English square miles and some 125,000 souls, ceded to France on the left bank of the German Rhine? Oh, these were brave times for Prussia and her young monarch! Was there not a large increase of territory and souls? Was not Prussia becoming very rapidly a "powerful" state, and her ruler a "great" king? And did not a promising opportunity offer soon after to make Prussia still more powerful, and her king still greater?

In the summer of 1803, the French stole Hanover from the King of England, and the noble-minded Frederick William III. looked on inactive, and rejected the overtures made to him by Russia for an Austro-Russo-Prussian alliance to chastise the insolence of the French, because, forsooth, Napoleon had opened to the dazzled sight of the Prussian envoy, Lombard, the seductively-enchanting vista of the possible incorporation of Hanover with the Prussian States.

The same immoral bait held Frederick William back in 1805 from throwing his sword into the then much oscillating scale between France and Austria and Russia, and made him actually sanction the disgraceful convention concluded with the French emperor by his wretched envoy, Haugwitz, on the 15th December, 1805, which handed over to France the Lordship of Neufchâtel, the Principality of Ansbach, and the Duchy of Cleves, with the important fortress of Wesel—all in exchange for Hanover, stolen from the King of England by the French, and handed over by the thieves to the receiver.

However, the measure was now full to overflowing. The year 1806 came, and brought with it the great Prussian cataclysm.

Prince William was nine years old when this crushing misfortune befell his family and his country. All this time his mother, good Queen Louise, whom history represents as having struggled in vain against the criminal folly of her husband and his vile advisers, had bestowed the most tender and assiduous care upon the education of her children—a care which had borne rich fruit, so that the stricken lady might well find her truest consolation in the promising bevy of children growing up around her. A few brief years after, on 19th July, 1810, death removed this most exemplary wife and mother from the midst of her sorrowing family. Prince William, her second son, had then entered upon his fourteenth year.

Happily it was not all dross in King Frederick William III. There was a sound substratum in the man, with some sterling qualities, which shone forth with a steady light after the overwhelming military and political calamity that had fallen upon him and upon his kingdom, and this latest heavy domestic bereavement had purified his moral nature.

The school of misfortune is a hard but good school to pass through, and Prince William has shown in after-life that he really profited by the bitter lessons learnt in that school.

As a son of the House of Hohenzollern, Prince William entered the Prussian army at an early age. That army was then in the course of re-organization upon Scharnhorst and Gneisenau's plan, which was admirably adapted to the requirements of the time.

The young prince, who was from boyhood of a serious turn of mind, embraced his new career with ardour, and devoted all his talents and energy to the study of the military service in all its branches. He attended his father through the first campaigns of the Liberation war.

After the final overthrow of Napoleon on the field of Waterloo and the conclusion of peace, young Prince William pursued his military studies again with the same ardour as before. His advancement in the army was rapid, owing as much at least to his real merit as to his princely rank. He pursued the even tenor of his way as a sober-minded, studious young officer, affording people very little occasion indeed for talk or comment.

In 1829, he married, on 11th June, Princess Marie Louise Augusta Catherine, one of the daughters of Grand Duke Charles Frederick of Saxe-Weimar, his younger brother, Prince Charles, having two years before married the other sister, Princess Maria of Saxe-Weimar, whose son is the famous Red Prince (Frederick Charles).

There are two children of this marriage of the present Emperor-King and the Empress-Queen Augusta, to wit, the Imperial and Royal Crown Prince Frederick William, born 18th October, 1831, who is married to the Princess Royal of England; and Princess Louise Marie Elizabeth, born 3rd December, 1838, who married, 20th September, 1856, Grand Duke Frederick William Louis of Baden.

In 1840, after the death of King Frederick William III. (7th June), Prince William became Prince of Prussia and presumptive heir to the crown, as his elder brother, the new King Frederick William IV., had no issue. He was also raised to the rank of general of infantry, and appointed governor-general of Pomerania.

It was at this time that his strongly-pronounced military predilections gained him the unenviable reputation of harbouring absolutist tendencies. His brother, the new king, full of his mediæval kingship notions, and guided by his Bavarian and Romanist wife, Elizabeth, in the narrowest path of anti-liberal retrogression and repression in religion and in politics, still would not disdain to court a little spurious popularity at his honest, straightforward brother William's expense. So the court and the *camarilla* were exhorted to encourage the popular delusion of poor Prince William's absolutist tendencies, and many were the dark charges and insinuations whispered against the "people's great enemy," the king's brother, who would not permit the excellent monarch to pursue a more liberal path.

Strong in the consciousness of the perfect integrity of his conduct throughout, the prince would not condescend to defend himself against these lying calumnies.

So when, on the 18th March, 1848, the king had treated his beloved Berliners to a few discharges of grapeshot, and had failed in overcoming the citizens' victorious outbreak against his Christian kingdomship, and had been compelled to humbly salute, hat in hand, the victims of the street fight, it was but natural that he and his *entourage* should bethink them of the excellent chance offering to turn Prince William to account as a scapegoat.

Accordingly these worthy people suddenly got

anxious about the prince's personal safety, and they urged him, therefore, to leave the country for a time and seek a refuge in London. It is probable that the prince in his heart despised the wretched intrigue and the vile concoctors of it, but he gave way to his brother's wishes, and left for England, to the intensest joy of the hoodwinked Berlin mob. The new Camphausen ministry, however, who were a little better informed upon the subject, soon recalled the exile to the Prussian capital. He returned to Berlin in June.

Some time after he was elected a member of the new National Assembly of Prussia. He took his seat, but he took no part in the debates.

In the autumn of 1848, the new system which the March revolution of the same year had inaugurated in Prussia was completely overthrown again, and the reaction set in with full force. Queen Elizabeth and her ultramontane and feudalist supporters were again in fullest ascendency. The king had put his hat on again, but he could not forget how he had been compelled to take it off, *coram populo*, and he could not forgive those who had made him do it. The "Christian kingdom" was now being established with a vengeance, and it was a wonder that Frederick William IV. would even graciously condescend to grant his "beloved people" a Brummagem charter.

The Prince of Prussia held aloof from the reactionary manœuvres and doings of these sad days. This, however, did not prevent bitter revilings of him among the people, in which many joined who were well enough acquainted with the true facts of the case to know the utter falsity of the imputations cast upon his character.

In the summer of 1849 he was appointed to the command of the army sent to put down the revolution in the south-west of Germany (Baden, the Palatinate, &c.) On his way there an unsuccessful attempt was made to assassinate him (12th June) at Nieder Ingelheim.

The revolutionists, who disposed of a by no means contemptible army, with a very fine artillery force, were commanded by the Pole Mieroslawski, who had for adjutant-general Francis Sigel, a young Badish officer of great promise, who actually managed to engage the Prussians opposed to him successfully at Wiesenthal, and might have succeeded in inflicting a serious defeat upon them, had he but been properly supported by his chief.

Unhappily for the revolution, Mieroslawski not alone failed to support his lieutenant in proper time, but he managed to incur himself a crushing defeat at Waghäusel, after which he handed the command of the beaten army over to Sigel, who succeeded in effecting a skilful retreat behind the Murg, and subsequently led his forces in safety to Switzerland.

General Sigel was afterwards one of the most successful unionist leaders in the American secession war. He defeated the Confederates at Carthage, at Pea Ridge, Thoroughfare Gap, Centreville, and other places; also in the first day's fight of the second battle of Bull Run; the second day General Pope commanded, and the Federals suffered a grievous defeat.

After Waghäusel, the pacification of the revolted districts in the south-west of Germany proceeded rapidly, the entire campaign being ended in a few weeks.

The honest, upright conduct of Prince William, and the patent integrity of purpose which characterized all his proceedings in the accomplishment of the difficult task that had been intrusted to his hands, gained him golden opinions from all who happened to come in contact with him, and laid the first foundation for the change which soon after began to take place in the popular view and estimation of his true character.

In October, 1849, Prince William was appointed to the most important office of military Governor of Rhineland-Westphalia, in which capacity he took up his regular residence at Coblenz.

One of the gloomiest and most dismal periods in the history of Prussia and Germany was now drawing near. The revolution of 1848 had developed in all patriotic Germans an ardent longing for the political unity of the great Fatherland. The Frankfort parliament was, indeed, specially elected *ad hoc*. The sensible majority of the unionists felt convinced also that the unity of Germany could only be accomplished under the leadership of Protestant Prussia. Austria was, in fact, in the opinion of most German patriots altogether out of the race in this question.

So it had come to pass that the Frankfort parliament had on the 28th of March, 1849, resolved by 290 votes against 248 abstainers to place the hereditary imperial crown of Germany on the brow of the Prussian king.

Now, among Frederick William's mediæval and romantic notions there figured a spurious sentimental veneration for the imperial Hapsburgs, the foolish man going even to such an extent in his voluntary self-abasement pretence, that he publicly avowed it to be the highest aim of his ambition to be permitted in his capacity of arch-chancellor of the empire, to tender the basin to the Austro-German emperor's sacred majesty.

It was not likely, then, that such a man would consent to accept the imperial crown of Germany " over the Austrian emperor's head." Bunsen, who fully knew how the king felt in this respect, did not even venture to urge the acceptance of the proffered imperial crown upon the king ; in his letter on the subject he simply pointed out to his majesty how the acceptance of the crown would be the end of the beginning, whereas the rejection of it would prove the beginning of the end.

On the 3rd of April, 1849, Frederick William IV., whilst still protesting his ardent desire for the unity of Germany, informed the Frankfort deputation that he could not accept the proffered crown.

Some six weeks after, the Berlin cabinet, always rushing wildly after half-measures, had managed to hatch another notable scheme of effecting the unity of Germany. This was the great "union scheme," based upon the "alliance of the three kings" (Prussia, Saxony, and Hanover), of 26th May, 1849.

This alliance had for its object to effect a closer voluntary union of the several German states under the presidency of Prussia. Beust had signed for Saxony, Bennigsen for Hanover.

Both these great diplomatists took excellent care to inform the court of Munich at once, that the refusal of Bavaria to join would be held by them to free Saxony and Hanover from the engagement just entered into by them with Prussia.

The London cabinet having thought fit to protest against the alliance of the three kings, as tending to compromise certain eventual rights and claims of the English crown (!), Count Bennigsen cynically informed her Britannic Majesty's minister for foreign affairs that Hanover never had any honest and sincere intention in the matter, and that the king, his master, had acceded to the alliance simply with a view to reawaken his subjects' old hatred of Prussia, which had lately gone to sleep somehow. Beust gave similar explanations, and both these great and honest statesman acted up most fully to these open avowals of gross treachery on their part.

So the projected union and the Erfurt parliament in connection with it came of course to naught, although it dragged its miserable existence on till the 15th of November, 1850, when the affair finally came to a formal end, in obedience to the Austrian premier Schwarzenberg's arrogant dictation.

For Austria, thanks to Radetzky, had triumphed in Italy; and, thanks to the incapacity of some of the Hungarian leaders and the treachery of others, she had with the aid of Russia stamped out the great insurrection of Hungary. So Austria was a great power once more, and this power was wielded by the vigorous hands of Prince Felix Schwarzenberg, who had sworn to humble Prussia to the dust first, and then to destroy her. *Il faut avilir la Prusse d'abord, et après la démolir*, were the *ipsissima verba* of this man, who did everything in his power to give due effect to them, and found, unhappily, eager allies in the South German States, and in England, France, and Russia.

There were two questions pending then which afforded fair openings for the projected attacks upon Prussia, to wit, the Hessian question and the Schleswig-Holstein question.

In the electorate of Hesse the gross misrule of the elector and his contemptible minister Hassenpflug had driven one of the most patient and submissive peoples into a very mild passive resistance rising—an insurrection in morning gown and slippers, as it was felicitously defined at the time. Prussia took some interest in this affair as it happened, for a wonder on the side of the poor "rebels."

The Schleswig-Holstein question is too well-known to, and too much dreaded by, English readers to invite more special and detailed reference to it here.

Suffice it to say, that in both these questions, Prussia was most clearly in the right; Austria, with her South-German and other allies and abettors, was absolutely in the wrong. But right or wrong signified not in the matter. Might alone is right on the great political board of the world; and Prussia, though she bore latent within her twice the sap and vigour of Austria, and might have defied even a coalition against her had a Frederick the Great been her ruler then, was now feeble and helpless through the lamentable vacillation of her king, the pro-Austrian leanings of her queen, and the gross incapacity of her pseudo-statesmen.

It would lead us too far here to treat at length of the sad events which culminated finally in the ridicule of Bronnzell, the humiliation of Warsaw, and the capitulation of Olmutz. Suffice it to say that Manteuffel signed at Olmutz, on 29th November, 1850, a capitluation by virtue of which Prussia consented to leave the Hessians and the Schleswig-Holsteiners to their fate, and to renounce every right to invite any other German state to the formation of even a voluntary union with herself.

The Prince of Prussia felt these sad events most acutely; they inflicted cruel stabs upon his patriotic heart. But he saw clearly that he could do nothing at the time to interfere with the course of events.

Moreover, he was even then already convinced in his own mind that the military system of Prussia, originally established by Scharnhorst and Gneisenau, had outlived its own vital principle, and absolutely required a thorough reform. The mobilisations of 1832 and 1849 had shown him the glaring defects of the entire system, and the last mobilisation, ordered on 6th November, 1850, only twenty-three days before the disgrace of Olmutz, had revealed to his acute military understanding the cumbrous structure and the heavy working of the machinery.

So he might well feel apprehensive to tempt the fortune of war with such battered and disjointed harness on his back. He accordingly resolved to treasure up his feelings for some more favourable opportunity in the future.

The weakness and vacillation shown by Frederick

VOL. I. C

William in this formidable crisis had demonstrated to most clear-sighted men in the land the absolute necessity of a military ruler on the military throne of Prussia. Even Varnhagen von Ense, who certainly could not be accused of military predilections, had arrived at this conclusion.

So the eyes of all true patriots in the land began to turn with hope to the heir presumptive. The king even recognized the necessity now of consulting his brother upon all important political questions. He raised him to still higher dignities in the state. In 1854 Prince William was made governor of the confederate fortress of Mayence. The new title and charge of colonel-general of infantry, with field-marshal's rank, was expressly created for him. The high function of Grand Master of all Prussian Lodges of Freemasons was also delegated to him.

As the sterling, honest character of Prince William revealed itself more and more to the Prussian people, it became more and more clear to even the meanest understanding how sadly the man had been misjudged, and that he was a foe to all extreme parties, and certainly no friend to the Feudalists and Clericals, who were then having it all their own way at Court and in the Cabinet, and that he had at heart only the true welfare and greatness of the land and the nation.

The result was, that the Prince of Prussia, once almost the most hated and abused man in the land, soon gained great genuine popularity with almost all classes.

Then came the illness of the king, which terminated in softening of the brain, necessitating in the end a transfer of the powers of government to the hands of the Prince of Prussia. The influence of Queen Elizabeth succeeded at first in restricting the power confided to the prince within very narrow limits. The first delegation was given by the king on October 23rd, 1857, for three months only. It was subsequently renewed from time to time, until at length the queen and her party could no longer resist the imperious necessity of a formal regency, which had to be finally intrusted to Prince William's hands on October 9th, 1858.

So soon as the Prince of Prussia had taken the government of the country into his hands, even with the restrictions imposed at first upon his authority by his brother, the Clerical and Feudalist reaction and opposition against all liberty and progress, which had been in full swing under the fostering care of Queen Elizabeth, received at once a wholesome check.

In 1858 the regent formed a Ministry of so-called Old Liberals, under the leadership of Prince Charles Anton of Hohenzollern Sigmaringen and Baron Rudolph von Auerswald.

The year 1859 offered the Prince Regent of Prussia a fine opportunity of taking revenge for Olmutz, by saving Austria from the dire fate impending over her after her grievous defeat in the Italian campaign. The prince had decided upon this generous course of action; but, unhappily for Austria, Francis Joseph would rather elect to submit to the humiliation of Villafranca than concede the command of the auxiliary forces of the German Confederation to the Prince of Prussia.

The experience of the mobilisation of the Prussian army on this occasion again revealed the irremediable defects of the old system, and proved to the mind of the regent the absolute necessity of that reform of the entire system which one of the best and most highly-accomplished general officers in the Prussian army, General Roon, had shortly before proposed.

On the 2nd January, 1861, King Frederick William IV. died, and the Prince Regent succeeded him on the throne of Prussia as William I.

The hopes of the Liberals and Unionists throughout Germany rose high. But the solemn coronation of the new king, and of his consort, Queen Augusta, at Königsberg, 18th October, 1861, and the attendant circumstances, with the open declarations made and the speeches uttered by William on the occasion, showed but too clearly and unmistakably that the man might be expected to cling with desperate tenacity to the antiquated stiff kingship by the grace-of-God notions in which he had grown grey.

The Prussian Progressists believed, then, that they had not much to hope from him for the cause of Liberal progress in Prussia; and the German Unionists, finding that the Prussian monarch made no immediate sign of an intended change in the policy hitherto pursued in German affairs by the Berlin court, grew at once desponding. Nay, even several months before the coronation, one Oscar Becker, who made an attempt on the life of King William, at Baden-Baden, 14th July, 1861, pleaded his intense German patriotism in excuse for his criminal attempt, averring that King William of Prussia had abundantly shown he was not the man to effect the unification of Germany;—and there were many honest German Liberals and Unionists who sympathized with the would-be regicide, if not in his crime, at least in his conviction of King William's unwillingness or unfitness to undertake the great work they had so much at heart.

These impatient people could not understand the man who had thus disappointed their over-eager expectations. He had the great work as warmly at heart as they; but whilst they were simply striving after the end, and endeavouring to anticipate it, he, in his cooler sense and more practical wisdom, was devising the means and using all his best energies to provide them in due time. And among these means the creation of an effective military force occupied the front rank.

The army reorganization, then, was the object nearest and dearest to his heart. Already, on 5th December, 1859, he had appointed General Roon Minister of War, who brought to bear upon the difficult task intrusted to him all the energy of his mind and all the resources of his brilliant intellect. Yet in spite of this the projected reform of the military system of Prussia made only slow progress, comparatively, owing to the hostility of the Chamber and the feebleness of the Hohenzollern-Auerswald Ministry.

The election of 1861 considerably increased the number of advanced Liberals or Progressists in the Prussian House of Representatives; in fact, it took the lead of the House out of the hands of the Old Liberals, and deprived the very honest, indeed, but not very efficient Hohenzollern-Auerswald administration in a great measure of its *raison d'être*. The Old Liberals had not shone very brilliantly either in the management of the foreign affairs of the land. So the king resolved in the spring of 1862 to thank his ministers for their services and to relieve them from the burthen of office.

He appointed a semi-demi Liberal-Conservative Cabinet in their stead, under the lead of Prince Adolphus of Hohenlohe-Ingelfingen and the Elberfeld plutocrat Von der Heydt; and when he found that this new besom was not likely to sweep the obstacles out of the path of his pet army-reorganization plan, he resolved to avail himself of the known force of will and energy of action of his late ambassador to Paris, Baron Otto von Bismarck - Schönhausen, whom he appointed accordingly Minister-President with the portfolio of Foreign Affairs provisionally on the 23rd September, definitely on the 8th October, 1862.

Of the late administration, Roon, Mühler, and Lippe alone were retained; Bodelschwingh was made Minister of Finance, 1st October, 1862; Itzenplitz, Minister of Commerce, 9th October, 1862; Eulenburg, Minister of the Home Department; and Selchow, Minister of Agriculture, 9th December, 1862.

It would lead us too far here to attempt to trace minutely the progress of the reorganization of the army, and the great parliamentary struggle between the Ministry and the House of Representatives. Moreover, these matters will be discussed in the memoirs of Roon and Bismarck—in their proper place, as we believe since, although the king was the ostensible chief these two great men were the actual doers and achievers of the great work.

The popularity of King William, seriously compromised already by the events more or less immediately following his accession to the crown, suffered nearly total shipwreck in these fierce parliamentary struggles, the more so as the Clericals and Feudalists chose to gather round the throne, proclaiming themselves, with loud clamour, the only true and honest supporters of that ancient divine institution.

In August 1863, poor Francis Joseph of Austria and his advisers devised a notable scheme to resuscitate the old Hapsburg German Empire. The Austrian emperor invited the German princes to meet him at the old Imperial city of Frankfort-on-the-Main, to discuss with him anent the true interests of the great German Fatherland.

They came, with the exception of the only one whose presence could be of the slightest practical use—King William of Prussia. As he was not there, the rest had to go home as they had come; and so had the Emperor Francis Joseph also—a sadder if not a wiser man.

Soon after Bismarck succeeded in forming a seeming temporary alliance between Austria and Prussia against the Danish occupation of Schleswig-Holstein. The event and its results and consequences are universally so well known that we need not further expatiate upon them here. The same remark applies to the great struggle of Prussia against Austria and Germany in 1866. Moreover, the political manœuvres will be found recorded in the memoirs of Bismarck, and the military operations, &c., in the memoirs of Moltke, the Crown Prince, the Red Prince, Vogel von Falckenstein, the present King of Saxony, &c.

It may simply be stated here that King William nobly did his duty as the military chief and leader of his people.

In the earlier stage of the great battle of Chlum and Sadowa (called afterwards the battle of Königgrätz), the king, then stationed on Problus Hill, had an aide-de-camp killed by his side.

On the 20th September, 1866, on the occasion of the triumphal entry of the victorious Prussian army into Berlin, King William gave an involuntary proof of the sensibility of his heart, which deeply affected all beholders.

The king had taken up his stand by the great statuary group of King Frederick II. to witness the marching by of the army. His face was beaming at the time with intensest content and happiness, when he espied Prince Charles Anton of Hohenzollern coming up, who had lost his son Anton in the fierce fight of Sadowa. Instantly the usually cold-looking steel-grey eyes of the king softened marvellously, a shade of deep sorrowing regret fell on his face, and hot tears might be seen coursing down his furrowed cheeks, whilst he pressed the hand of the bereaved father in silence.

The events of 1866 and the large strides forward in the unification of Germany replaced King William on his ancient popularity pedestal, although the newly-annexed province of Hanover and the whilom free city of Frankfort long persisted in bearing the king a bitter grudge, up to the final unification of Germany in 1870–1.

In 1867 King William, in company with his nephew, the Emperor Alexander of Russia, paid a visit to the Emperor Louis Napoleon on the occasion of the great International Exhibition of Paris.

There was a wonderful display of cordiality on both sides, but both sides were quite aware that it was only a hollow show, as the Luxembourg question, which was raised in the spring, and renewed in the fall of the year, abundantly proved.

The smouldering fire was covered up at the time, but only to break out all the more fiercely a few years after. That it did not actually burst forth into flame in 1867 was due simply to Count Andrassy and Francis Deak.

It is no longer a secret now that Louis Napoleon on the occasion of his interview with Francis Joseph at Salzburg, 18–21st August, 1867, placed before the Austrian emperor and Chancellor Beust a thoroughly French project of an anti-Prussian Franco-Austrian offensive and defensive alliance.

In this notable document it was laid down as a chief condition of a continued friendly understanding of the two contracting powers with Prussia, that the latter Power was to renounce then and for ever all alliances with any of the South German States, who were to be invited to form a South German Confederation under the presidency of the Emperor of

Austria, and under the joint protection of Austria and France.

Prussia was to be summoned to evacuate Mayence, and to permit the Grand Duke of Hesse to join the South German Confederation with the whole of his dominions, the portion situate on the northern bank of the Main included. Austria and the South German Confederation were to form a Customs' Union of their own, with full liberty to make commercial treaties with France on the one side, and North Germany on the other.

In the event of Prussia declining to accede to these sweet terms, France and Austria were jointly to declare war against Prussia. After the defeat of Prussia in the field, which was taken as a matter of course by the high contracting parties, Prussia would be summoned to hand over to victorious Austria the southern part of Silesia; to victorious France, Sarrelouis and Sarrebourg, and the great coal-basin of Saarbrücken.

A plebiscite, taken in the newly-annexed Prussian provinces under the superintendence of Austria and France, would then determine the question of the restoration of the dispossessed princes: Prussia was to be summoned also to come to an arrangement with Denmark within three months.

Should any of the South German States be foolish enough to decline joining the proposed South German Confederation, an Austro-French invasion would soon bring that recalcitrant state to reason ; and the victors would afterwards deal with the "conquered territory" as they should mutually agree.

There is very little historic doubt but that this pretty scheme was actually proposed by Louis Napoleon to Francis Joseph at Salzburg in August 1867, and that the Austrian emperor and Chancellor Beust had made up their minds to accept it.

But Count Andrassy, who had got wind of the affair, went to Salzburg for the express purpose of nipping the plot in the bud. He saw Louis Napoleon, and told him that Hungary would never consent to join in a war against Prussia; and that even if the French emperor held in his hands a treaty of alliance with Austria, signed by Francis Joseph, and countersigned by Chancellor Beust, the firm opposition of Hungary would make such a treaty a mere piece of waste paper. So the great scheme came to naught.

In 1869 King William visited the newly-annexed parts of his realm. He was everywhere cordially received. The same cordial reception he met with at Lubeck, Hamburg, and Bremen, and more especially at Wilhelmshafen.

A show of friendly relations at least was also re-established with Austria, the Crown Prince of Prussia and the Archduke Charles Louis interchanging reciprocal visits to Vienna and to Berlin.

On the 8th December, 1869, the Emperor Alexander of Russia, King William's nephew, on the occasion of the Centenary Jubilee of the Russian Military Order of St. George, bestowed the highest class of that order upon King William, who in return made his nephew a Knight of the Order *pour le Mérite.*

It was looked upon at the time as a significant circumstance that both monarchs in their letters patent mutually recalled to memory the great, glorious, and ever-memorable epoch when their united armies had striven hand in hand for a common sacred cause —to wit, the overthrow of the French Empire under the first Napoleon.

In July 1870, began the great Hispano-Hohenzollern imbroglio, which was made by France the pretext of war with Prussia.

The incidents and episodes of that memorable war will be found recorded in the memoirs of the military commanders. Suffice it here to note simply that King William was proclaimed Emperor of Germany at Versailles, 18th January, 1871, and that the preliminaries of peace were signed on the 26th February, 1871.

In his notification of this most gratifying fact to his nephew, the Emperor Alexander of Russia, the Emperor William expressed his deep gratitude to the Russian monarch for his friendly conduct to Prussia throughout the war, adding that Prussia would never forget that it was owing to that noble conduct alone that the war had not assumed the most gigantic dimensions.

On the 11th August, 1871, the Emperor William met his imperial brother Francis Joseph at Ischl. Another friendly meeting took place between the two emperors, attended by Bismarck and Beust, at Salzburg and Gastein, where the foundation was laid of a more frank and cordial understanding between Austria and Germany.

The Crown Prince Humbert of Italy and his wife, Princess Margaret, came to Berlin on the 28th May, 1872, to be witnesses at the baptism of the youngest daughter of the Imperial Royal Crown Prince and the Princess Royal of England.

On the 5th September of the same year the Emperors Alexander of Russia and Francis Joseph of Austria came to Berlin on a visit to the Emperor William.

These imperial meetings, and others that have taken place since, more particularly the late visit of King Victor Emmanuel to Vienna and Berlin, had avowedly for their object the insurance of the peace of Europe; also the concerting of mutual measures of protection against Ultramontane aggression and intrigues.

These matters, however, as well as the giant struggle now waging in Prussia and Germany between the government and the Ultramontane and episcopal conspiracy against the authority of the State, will be found noticed at length in the proper place—in the memoir of Bismarck.

In the last days of the past year (1873) the Emperor William was taken seriously ill, when the tender and anxious solicitude of the whole people, from one end of Germany to the other, showed how deep-rooted and wide-spread is the love and reverence for the noble old monarch.

Quite recently, when the unexpected Army Bill imbroglio had raised high the hopes of the Feudalists and Clericals, and seemed to threaten Prussia and Germany with the advent of a Manteuffel *régime*, the emperor once more gave proof of his moderation and good sense, by consenting, upon the advice of his great minister, to a compromise—an immense concession on his part, considering that in all military matters he is generally as hard and unbending as steel.

The cruelly disappointed feudal and black crew, in their fierce rage at being thus foiled in their vile reactionary plot, insulted both king and chancellor, by proclaiming openly and aloud, that the latter had forced his master's hand by a threat of instant resignation should His Majesty decline to grant the concession demanded. The story was of course a base lie, like most of the productions coming from that mint.

King William has now reached the seventy-eighth year of life, a venerable age, rarely if ever yet before attained by any of his predecessors. He has been painfully affected of late years by successive family bereavements. He has lost a dear brother and a beloved sister; a cousin for whom he entertained the warmest affection; the Princess Augusta of Liegnitz, his father's second wife and widow, whom he esteemed most highly; and, in December last, the Dowager-Queen Elizabeth, his brother's widow, who also occupied a high place in his affectionate regard.

As this lady had exercised, to within a few years before her death, a most powerful influence upon the political and religious affairs of Germany, a brief memoir of her life may not be deemed altogether out of place here, as a corollary to the memoir of the Emperor William, which may serve to place certain sections of it in a clearer light.

THE LATE QUEEN DOWAGER OF PRUSSIA.

AMONG the rather numerous progeny of King Maximilian I. (Joseph of Bavaria), figured two pairs of twin sisters, to wit, Elizabeth and Amalia, born 13th November 1801, and Sophia and Maria, born 27th January 1805. Their mother was King Maximilian Joseph's second wife, Caroline, daughter of Charles Lewis, hereditary Prince of Baden.

Princess Amalia was married to the late King John of Saxony, Princess Maria to the late King Frederick Augustus of Saxony, Princess Sophia to Archduke Francis Charles of Austria, and Princess Elizabeth to the late King Frederick William IV. of Prussia, who left her a widow January 2, 1861.

The Archduchess Sophia died May 28, 1872. The Queen Dowager Elizabeth of Prussia died Sunday midnight, December 14, 1873, at Dresden, where she was staying on a visit to her twin sister Amalia, recently bereft of her husband, the late King John of Saxony.

Princess Elizabeth of Bavaria was married by procuration at Munich, November 16th, 1823, and in person at Berlin on the 29th November, to Frederick William, then Crown Prince, afterwards King of Prussia.

She had been brought up a most devout, nay, it is not going too far to say a bigoted Romanist; and though in 1830, when she had been married some seven years, certain considerations, and chiefly the wish to please her father-in-law, old King Frederick William III., who was a pious Protestant, induced her to embrace ostensibly the Evangelical Confession of Faith, she yet remained at heart to the last hour of her life an uncompromising Romanist.

Again, although she was the wife of a Prussian prince, and during a period of twenty-one years Queen Consort of Prussia, it may truly be averred that she never took frankly and sincerely to the country of her adoption, but that she felt and acted throughout her public career as a Bavarian princess, always preferring, wherever the choice was left open, the petty fancied interests of the House of her origin to even the plainest, most vital, and most urgent requirements of Prussia and Germany.

Unhappily, perhaps even for herself, but certainly most unhappily for poor Prussia—her husband was a man of weak mind, albeit of bright intellect; and, whilst deeply imbued with strange mediæval notions of "Christian kingdomship" and of the absolute supremacy of the grace-of-God monarchic principle, he was of a most uxorious disposition.

His inferior in brightness of intellect, his wife was immeasurably his superior in strength of mind and will; and it is not too much to say, that during the twenty-one years of his nominal reign over Prussia, he was simply the puppet, whilst she pulled the wires. In very truth she held almost absolute sway over his mind and over his resolutions, and all the most strenuous and sustained efforts of men like Humboldt, Bunsen, Tellkampf, and many others to counteract this most pernicious influence were of little avail.

The worst of the matter was, that the strong-minded woman who thus ruled her husband was herself only a half-seeing and most pliant instrument in the hands of the crafty leaders of the great Jesuit and Ultramontane reactionist party bent upon depriving the Prussian people of even the small measure of civil, political, and religious liberty that had been grudgingly granted by narrow-minded Frederick William III., in paltry part acknowledgment of the blood and treasures so nobly and freely shed and spent by the nation in the great liberation war of 1813–15.

In 1807, when the Prussian monarchy had been laid low in the dust, the great Stein, the chief of the regenerators of the fallen State, in his famous "Memoir on the Proper Organization of the Supreme State Departments, and the Provincial, Financial, and Police Departments in the Prussian Monarchy," laid it down as an axiomatic principle, that "Church and School stand in no natural connection with each other, and that the Ecclesiastic Department should only be permitted to co-operate in a subordinate capacity with the Department of Public Instruction in the religious teaching in schools."

The total separation of Church and School demanded by Stein was of course too much for poor Frederick William III.; still the new Ministry of Public Worship, Public Instruction, and Medicinal Affairs, which was formed in 1817, was in a great measure organized upon Stein's notions, and the first Minister of Public Worship, &c., Baron Altenstein, who held the office for twenty-three years, till his death in 1840, kept the scholastic department as independent of clerical influences as circumstances would allow, and up to the time of his death the management of the school system in Prussia was highly commendable.

It was at this juncture, unhappily, that Frederick William IV. succeeded his father on the Prussian throne, and that the pernicious influence of his wife became all powerful.

Elizabeth found a fitting instrument to work her mischievous will in the notorious Eichhorn, whom she made Minister of Public Worship, &c., and who speedily subjected the schools under his control to the deadening influence of the vilest priestcraft, Romish and Pietistic.

This wretched man, who held the office of Minister of Public Worship, &c., up to the days of March, 1848, when the great Berlin rising kicked him out at last, wrought incalculable harm to the cause of education in Prussia. The traces of his misdeeds have not yet been completely obliterated even to the present day. Now, he was a man after the queen's own heart, and he was also of sufficiently small intellect to please the king, who could not brook superior men about him—at least, not in any really influential official capacity.

It was between Eichhorn, the queen, and the Jesuits, aided and abetted by the Pietist and Mucker party, that all the reactionary measures were concocted that marked the period from 1840 to 1848. Under the dire influence of this sad conspiracy against liberty and progress, concession after concession to the Roman Church and Hierarchy was wrung from the feeble king, until at last a separate Catholic section was created in the Ministry of Public Worship and Public Instruction.

To the late Queen Elizabeth, and to her fatal ascendency over her husband's feeble mind, is to be attributed, chiefly at least, the monstrous growth of Romish presumption in Prussia, and the almost incredible arrogance of Romish bishops and priests, which it now taxes all the power of will and all the energy of action of even a Bismarck to contend against, and which may yet force the State to have recourse in the end to repressive measures of a nature but ill reconcilable with the great principle of religious freedom.

Had it not been for the baneful work of this Romanist and Romanizing lady, acting under the inspiration and guidance of the craftiest and astutest enemies to liberty and progress let loose upon the world by Rome, the present age would certainly not have to wrestle with the Melchers, the Krementzes, the Ledochowskis, the Martins, the Försters, and so many more of the same stamp who are setting the State boldly at defiance now, openly avowing the most monstrous doctrine, that they owe obedience to the Pope alone.

In very truth, all liberal-minded men who are striving after and struggling for the ultimate emancipation of the human race from the trammels of priestcraft must feel a glow of satisfaction at the thought that this strong champion of the enslavement of man, the late Queen Dowager of Prussia, has had to witness with her dying eyes the struggle fairly engaged at last, and with the final chances dead against her own priestly pets. But what compensation is there in this for the sufferings so ruthlessly inflicted upon a whole generation of a generous and enlightened people?

Just as Queen Elizabeth of Prussia made the interests of the Church of Rome her chief guiding rule and principle in the internal administration of the kingdom which had the misfortune of being ruled over by her uxorious spouse, so was she swayed in the foreign relations and affairs of the State by the pettiest and narrowest Bavarian particularism.

Even the humiliation which Prussia had to endure at Olmütz in 1850, and which it took all the Austrian blood spilt in the seven days' campaign of 1866 to wash away, was mainly her work.

When poor Frederick William IV. had actually managed to screw his courage up to the point of instructing Count Gröben, the appointed commander of the Prussian forces in Hesse, to act in a manner to do honour to the name and fame of Prussia, this Bavarian princess, justly dreading what might be the fate in store for the Bavarian forces in Hesse that would find themselves opposed to her husband's army, prevailed upon the weak man to recall the general before his final departure from Berlin, and to make the distracted commander personally responsible before God and man for every drop of blood that should be spilled in this "fratricidal" war!

The result was, as a matter of course, the brilliant "battle" of Bronzell, where the only casualty was the premature death from a bullet of a white or grey equine animal—whether a horse or a donkey history would appear to be slightly doubtful. In the eternal fitness of things it ought to have been a mule.

Even after the death of her uxorious spouse, Elizabeth of Bavaria continued to weigh heavily upon poor Prussia. King William also, though a man of vastly superior mind to his unhappy brother, submitted in but too many things to the baneful guidance and counsel of his brother's widow. In 1866, more notoriously, it was the one day's fatal delay granted at her instigation to the Saxons and Hanoverians which added 40,000 excellent troops to the forces of Benedek, and led to the bloodshed of Langensalze.

In his present giant struggle against Ultramontanism, Bismarck has had to contend more than once against the crafty, occult machinations of this pupil and tool of the Jesuits.

Taking the late Queen Dowager of Prussia in her private capacity as a woman, not a breath hath ever dimmed the clear mirror of her fair fame. She was a most excellent daughter and sister, and, her Romanist tendencies and Bavarian predilections apart, a very good wife, who actually loved and admired her feeble husband for his many amiable qualities of heart and mind. Alexander von Humboldt, who struggled in vain against the ascendency she exercised over her husband, always paid her the tribute of his sincerest respect, and maintained that she was a thoroughly well-meaning, though mistaken, woman.

Perhaps, had children blessed her union with Frederick William, her career and his might have been different. It was also certainly her misfortune much more than her fault that she had to do with so weak-minded and soft-hearted a man as was Frederick William IV.

Of that poor king's soft-heartedness and delicate tenderness of feeling, the writer of this brief obituary memoir of the late Queen Dowager Elizabeth is in a position to adduce an instance from his own experience. It is now some twenty years ago that he happened to witness the performance of the *Orphan of Lowood* (Jane Eyre) at the Royal Theatre, Berlin. Their majesties were present on the occasion. The king might be seen leaning against one of the pillars of the royal box, with his pocket-handkerchief in active operation mopping up the tears coursing down his cheeks in copious abundance, excited by the moving nature of the drama. Her majesty's handkerchief was lying perfectly idle meanwhile in her lap, whilst the strong-minded lady was casting looks of wondering pity upon her affected lord and master.

Had the case been the reverse, it might have made the difference of some twenty or thirty years' advance of the Prussian people in the path of progress and political, civil, and religious liberty.

II.

FIELD-MARSHAL VON ROON.

It is a moot question whether the famous saying attributed to Bismarck, that he would cement the unity of Germany with blood and iron, was ever actually uttered by the great minister, or whether it may not be simply referable to a certain passage in one of his diplomatic communications to Baron von Schleinitz, the then Prussian Foreign Secretary, in which the then Ambassador of Prussia to the Court of St. Petersburg gave it as his deliberate opinion, that the political connection and relations of the Prussian monarchy with the German Confederation could only be looked upon as a grievous growing malady of the State, which, if not taken in hand in proper season, would have to be eradicated in the end, *ferro et igni*.

But no matter which of the two versions is the correct one, thus much is certain—that the operation indicated either way by the future Chancellor of the German Empire, whether intending to act as State constructor or as State surgeon, could not possibly be performed by him without the proper instrument made to his hand.

This instrument was a well-organized army, fit to cope with fair chances of success at least singly with either of the three great military powers surrounding Prussia. Such an army Prussia did not possess then; but at the very time Bismarck was penning the above communication to Schleinitz (May, 1859), the man of rare organizatory genius was already hard at work in laying the foundations for its creation. This man was Baron von Roon, who had just then attained the grade of Lieutenant-General in the Prussian army.

Albrecht Theodore Emile von Roon was born on the 30th April, 1803, at Pleushagen, near Colberg, an old estate of the Roon family. In early infancy he was sent to Alt-dabum, near Stettin, where he received his first education in one of those excellent elementary schools which abound nearly everywhere in Prussia.

Here also he was introduced first to the chances and dangers of war. It was in 1813, when he was just about ten, that a Swedish bombshell burst at his feet, one of the splinters inflicting a slight wound upon him. It is narrated that the little boy was so entirely absorbed in watching, with the keenest interest, the course of the projectile, its bursting, and the shattering of the fragments, that it was some time before he realized the fact of one of the splinters having hit him.

Having finished his preparatory course of education at one of the Stettin grammar schools, young Roon was, at the age of sixteen, sent to the Cadet School at Culm, which he left two years after for the Cadet Corps at Berlin. Both at Culm and Berlin his studious habits and his rare facility of apprehension and comprehension attracted the attention of his teachers and of the military authorities.

Soon after his transfer to Berlin, on the 9th of January, 1821, he obtained his first commission, being appointed sub-lieutenant in the 14th Regiment of infantry, then in garrison at Stargard. There he remained three years, learning the routine of military service, and continuing his studies.

His high qualifications having again attracted the attention of the military authorities, he was detached in 1824 to the General War School, that splendid educational establishment for officers which has supplied so many eminent men to the Prussian military service. Here he turned his time and opportunities to such excellent account, that he was appointed in 1827, at the early age of twenty-four, Instructor in the Berlin Cadet Corps, in which he had himself been a cadet only six years before.

His great master, the famous geographer Ritter, was at that time director of studies there. This learned man was so struck with the extensive knowledge of geography possessed by the young lieutenant, that he urged him to write a "Guide" to the study of that science for the use of the cadets. The book was a great success. It was subsequently published, considerably enlarged, in three volumes, in 1832, under the title of "Outlines of Geography, Ethnography, and Statistics." Close upon a hundred thousand copies of this book, and of a smaller extract from it, have since been sold in Germany.

In 1832, Lieutenant Roon was ordered to join his regiment, then in garrison at Minden. Shortly after he was called to the head-quarters of General Müffling, commander of the Prussian corps of observation stationed at the time on the Belgo-Dutch frontier, to watch the siege of Antwerp by the French. After the fall of the citadel, the lieutenant returned to his regimental duties.

In 1833 he was appointed on the staff of the Topographic Bureau, where he distinguished himself greatly by numerous surveys and other scientific labours.

Two years after he was appointed on the general staff of the Prussian army, being named at the same time lecturer on geography and tactics at the General War School.

In 1836 he obtained his captaincy, retaining his position on the staff, and being appointed also a member of the military Board of Examination.

In 1837 he published another valuable work—a military description of the countries of Europe. A monograph on the "Iberian Peninsula from the Military Standpoint," followed in 1839.

In 1841, when on a tour of military inspection, he was taken seriously ill. For several days his case was considered hopeless, and he recovered only slowly. It would certainly be a subject for curious speculation to consider how many of the great events that have mainly contributed to the establishment of the new German Empire might not have happened at all, or might have resulted very differently, had this master-mind succumbed to this critical illness. He recovered, however, and the year after he was promoted to the rank of major, and appointed on the staff of the 7th Corps of the Prussian army.

In 1843 he returned to Berlin to resume his lectures.

Here Prince Charles of Prussia had more than once occasion to admire his singularly clear and lucid exposition. The prince's son, Frederick Charles, was then in his sixteenth year, and it was intended to send him to the University of Bonn. The brilliant major was named instructor in geography and tactics to the young prince, whom he attended to Bonn as military attaché, and subsequently on a series of voyages through Switzerland, Italy, France, and Belgium.

A warm friendship sprang up between Mentor

and Telemachus, which continues undiminished up to the present day. After the prince's return from his tour, Major Roon resumed his practical duties as a high staff officer.

In May 1848, he was made chief of the staff of the 8th Corps, stationed in Rhineland. These were troublesome times, when the reflex action of the French February revolution was deeply agitating Rhineland-Westphalia. The position of the new chief of the staff was most difficult and delicate; but he showed himself fully up to the mark.

Equal good fortune attended him the year after in the Baden campaign, when he acted as General Hirschfeld's chief of the staff. His services were rewarded by a lieutenant-colonelcy. In 1850 he was made commander of the 33rd Regiment of Infantry. Six years later he was promoted to the grade of major-general, and to the command of the 20th Infantry Brigade. In 1858 he obtained the command of the 14th Division.

From the commencement of his military career, Roon had made the organization of the army in its several branches his special study. He had reflected deeply upon the causes that had led to the lamentable downfall of the military system bequeathed by the Great Frederick to his successors, and equally upon the causes that had made Scharnhorst and Gneisenau's new organization a success in the War of Liberation.

He had arrived at the conclusion that that success was attributable mainly to the burning patriotism and the deep hatred of the foreign foe that had pervaded the great citizen host through the campaign of 1813–15; and that the system as such, however admirably it had answered at the time of its creation, had survived itself, and had grown more and more defective in the course of years. Since Roon had entered the service, there had been three several occasions to order the mobilization of the Prussian army—in 1832, 1849, and 1850; and on each of these occasions he had detected graver and graver defects in the system.

He knew that the Prince Regent (the present Emperor of Germany) shared these views, and had more than once expressed his resolution to remedy these defects. There is even some reason to believe that the prince had actually invited him to elaborate a plan for the reorganization of the army.

Be this as it may, General Roon drew up an exhaustive memoir on the subject, with special reference to the infantry branch of the service, and submitted it to the regent, who found it so thoroughly consonant with his own views, and was so much struck with the clearness of the general's exposition and the soundness of his practical conclusions, that he adopted the whole plan *en bloc*, and invited General Roon to come to Berlin to discuss the question in detail with General Bonin, the Minister of War.

Meanwhile the Franco-Italian war of 1859 had necessitated another mobilization of the Prussian army, on which occasion the old defects of the system had appeared still more glaring. When Roon came to Berlin he found the new organization plan ready cut and dried, based entirely and in every respect, even to the minutest details, upon his own memoir. No wonder, then, that he should express his fullest concurrence with the views of the minister.

But a plan on paper, however admirable in conception, may turn out of very little use indeed where tardiness is shown, or want of energy in carrying out its provisions.

Now, this particular plan of military reorganization had provoked the most determined hostility of the majority of the Second Chamber; and the Ministry —Hohenzollern-Auerswald—hardly dared to submit it to the hostile Commons.

Roon, who had set his heart upon it, on the other hand, and who was determined to carry it against all and every opposition, went to Baden-Baden, where the Prince Regent was staying at the time, and conferred earnestly and warmly with his Royal Highness upon the subject, equally dear to both of them. On his return to Berlin, he joined energetically in the discussions of the commission named by the Prince Regent to draw up the bill on the subject. As General Bonin showed some backwardness in coming forward in the matter, the Prince Regent prevailed upon him to resign his place as Minister of War, and appointed Lieutenant-General Roon his successor (5th December, 1859: the grade of lieutenant-general had been conferred upon Roon in May of the same year).

This high position the general retained under the successive administrations of Hohenzollern-Auerswald, Hohenlohe-Heydt, and Bismarck, and up to the end of the year 1872, when the still higher, but to him most uncongenial and unsuited, place of Prime Minister was thrust upon him.

The new Minister of War set at once to work with all the ardour of his temperament, all the energy of his character, and all the unyielding firmness of his mind.

He knew full well how arduous, how well-nigh impossible, was the task he had set himself to accomplish. It was not a simple reconstruction, it was a new creation which he had to call into life, and the materials he had to work with were alarmingly slender and most insufficient. He had to fight against the openly-proclaimed hostility of the great majority of the representatives of the Prussian people, and he had to fight the battle almost single-handed, as his colleagues in the two successive administrations of Hohenzollern-Auerswald and Hohenlohe-Heydt were but faint-hearted in the cause, and gave him only a lukewarm support.

But, steadfast and unswerving, he pursued his

purpose, and worked out his great plan even to its minutest details. He lavished upon his darling project all the resources of his brilliant intellect and of his profound organizatory genius. Nothing ever discouraged him; he quietly disregarded all hostile votes, and undismayed he tranquilly pursued the path he had traced out for himself.

Meanwhile King Frederick William IV.'s death had placed the crown on the Prince Regent's brow (2nd January, 1861), and the new king had more openly and uncompromisingly than before proclaimed his firmest resolve to stand by the Minister of War and the reorganization of the army, which he emphatically declared to be the great idea and purpose of his reign.

At the end of the summer, 1862, Otto von Bismarck-Schönhausen returned from France, where he had been ambassador since spring.

That great statesman saw that the time had come for more energetic action in forcing on the forging of the instrument indispensable to the execution of his own gigantic plans and projects, and the realization of his most towering aspirations. So it was speedily settled between himself, the king, and Roon to send the latter's weak and vacillating colleagues adrift and form a new, strong, and energetic government, resolved to let nothing stand in their way.

With the exception of Roon, Lippe, and Muhler,

the Ministry resigned, and Bismarck was named Premier of the new Cabinet, provisionally on the 23rd September, definitively on the 9th October, 1862.

All vacillation and hesitation was now at an end. The reorganization of the army progressed rapidly, all the hostile votes of the majority of the Second Chamber notwithstanding.

Strange to say, the name of the man whose labours were destined to contribute so materially in changing the political state of Europe was even then barely known beyond the confines of Prussia. It may almost be said that the first time the people of England ever heard the name of Roon was in connection with the famous hat episode in the constitutional history of Prussia.

It was only in 1866, when the brilliant success of his patient labours was made so brightly apparent by the overwhelming results of the "Seven days' campaign," that his name and fame may be said to have burst for the first time upon the surprised attention of Europe.

How the same exquisitely-tempered weapon, with which Bismarck and King William had wrested supremacy in Germany from the strong and tenacious grasp of Austria, served some four years after to wrest supremacy in Europe from the proud grasp of France, is still too recent and lives too vividly in the recollection of all to need aught here but this passing allusion; nor need we dwell upon the brilliant rewards which the great army organizer and war administrator has received at the hands of his grateful king and country. But we may mention that the reward most grateful to his stubborn heart was, in his own words, that his stanchest and most stubborn opponents in the fierce seven years' Parliamentary war fully admitted, after Sadowa, the justness of his views throughout, and the integrity of his purpose.

We may pass over also with indulgent silence the attempt—almost forced upon him, moreover—to travel beyond his legitimate province in taking the place of the giant Bismarck as Prime Minister of the kingdom. Our purpose here has simply been to show the man in connection with his stupendous work, and as one of the architects of the new German empire.

Broken in health, and sadly afflicted by the loss of some nearest and dearest to him, Field-Marshal Count von Roon has now retired from the political stage. Epaminondas, when struck to death at Mantinea, hearing some one near him lament that the great man should die without leaving issue, could, with his last breath, point with conscious pride, to his two immortal daughters—Leuctra and Mantinea. With equal pride Roon may justly trust to the German army, his own creation, to perpetuate his memory for evermore.

III.

FIELD-MARSHAL GENERAL MOLTKE.

The instrument, then, was made to the aspiring statesman's hand. The army created by Roon might be compared, if a somewhat imperfect and perhaps not altogether appropriate simile may be allowed to pass muster here, to a splendid set of chessmen, solidly wrought, from king to pawn, without flaw or blemish, out of the hardest, toughest, and most enduring material.

But something besides was required—to wit, the genius to breathe the true spirit of life and strife into the set, and to prove its excellence against any other set on the world's great chequer.

Bismarck's perilous game had to be played simultaneously on two distinct boards or fields—the diplomatic and the battle field; and the moves on either must necessarily be co-ordinate and mutually dependent.

"*Non omnes omnia*" is a saying equally trite as true. History records but a few doubtful instances of the requisite qualities of the consummate politician being united in one and the same man with those of the all-conquering war-chief. Rosni was a great minister, but he made only a very indifferent general in the field; and the great Armand Duplessis would certainly have saved France a vast expenditure of blood and treasure had he been less eager to emu: to the fame of the destroyer of strong cities, Demetrius, the captor of Salamis and the besieger of Rhodus, and had he confided the siege of La Rochelle to professional hands.

Bismarck is not a general, though he now holds high nominal rank in the Prussian army. He is perfectly aware of his deficiencies in that line; and even if his own strong common-sense were not proof against the temptation to which Richelieu yielded, the Prussian state and military system would never permit command in the field being intrusted to the Chief of the Cabinet.

A consummate general was indispensable, then, to lead the army in the field—a general who, to cope successfully with the immense task before him, would have to display the rarest combination of the highest strategic genius with the highest tactical ability.

The powers on high, propitious to Prussia and Germany, had ordained it so that when the hour came the man should reveal himself.

Helmuth Charles Bernard von Moltke was born on

the 26th of October, 1800, at Parchim, in the Grand Duchy of Mecklenburg-Schwerin.

From his boyhood he showed uncommon powers of thought and reflection, and a marvellous capacity for acquiring knowledge.

At an early age he entered the Danish army, but he soon felt that this could never afford him sufficient scope for the realization of his own high aspirations. So at the age of twenty-two he exchanged the Danish for the Prussian service, where his extensive and solid acquirements, his singularly simple and modest character, and his affectionate disposition, soon gained him the love of his comrades, and the regard and esteem of his superiors.

He ardently and assiduously pursued his military and other studies, more particularly geography, strategy, tactics, and fortification, in which he soon attained such high proficiency that he was jocularly nicknamed the "Compendium of military science."

The same ardour and assiduity he brought to bear upon his linguistic studies, which have through life remained a favourite pursuit with him — rather a curious feature in a man so infinitely more given to thought than to talk as Moltke is; a man whom the late Burgomaster Sydow, of Berlin, characterized so felicitously as "eloquently silent in seven languages." Although not a philologist perhaps in the strictest sense of the term, Moltke may at present justly claim to rank with the most distinguished linguists of

Europe. He is a thorough proficient in the languages which he professes to know, not a mere cultivator of linguistic smattering.

The learned young officer attracted the attention of the high military authorities, so that he was appointed on the general staff of the Prussian army at the comparatively early age of thirty-two.

Three years after, when Sultan Mahmud asked the Prussian Government to lend him a few officers to aid in the reorganization of the Turkish army, Moltke was one of the Prussian staff officers detached on this special service. Moltke made a most favourable impression upon the Sultan, who, not without considerable difficulty, obtained permission for him to stay in Turkey.

The young Prussian staff officer accompanied the Sultan on a tour of inspection to Bulgaria, where he visited the fortifications of Rustschuk, Silistria, Varna, and Schumla, ordering everywhere improvements and additions to be made in the same, which some nineteen years after gave the Russians occasion to complain bitterly, in the words of General Lüders, that "somebody had passed through these places who knew what he was about."

The Dardanelles, too, had the benefit of Moltke's careful inspection and practical suggestions.

He subsequently proceeded to Asia Minor, where he remained for two years with the Turkish army, witnessing the campaigns against the Curds and against the Egyptians. The death of Sultan Mahmud (July, 1839) having released Moltke from his Turkish engagement, he returned to Berlin, where he was immediately re-appointed on the staff.

His "Letters on the Condition of Turkey, and on the Events and Occurrences in that Country in the years 1835-1839," published in Berlin in 1841, form one of the most valuable contributions to our knowledge of Turkey. His and some other Prussian officers' itineraries through Natolia have most materially altered our maps of Asia Minor. His map of Constantinople and the Bosphorus (on the scale of 25,000-1) is a marvel of clearness and correctness. In 1842 he was raised to the rank of major.

In 1846 he was made adjutant of Prince Henry of Prussia, who was then residing in Rome.

After the death of the prince, in the following year the major returned to his duties on the staff. An excellent map of the environs of Rome was one of the fruits of his stay in the Eternal City.

In 1848 he was appointed chief of division in the great general staff of the army. The year after he became head of the staff of the 4th Corps, which position he retained till the end of 1855.

Having from 1856 to 1858 acted as adjutant of Prince Frederick William of Prussia, now Prince Imperial of Germany, General Moltke attained the highest position on the staff of the Prussian army, and a year after he was raised to the rank of lieutenant-general.

In 1859 Moltke had occasion to draw up his first plan of campaign. The war which Austria was then waging against France and Italy gave the cause for this. The Prince Regent of Prussia had determined to intervene between the belligerents in favour of Austria, and the Prussian army had been mobilized for the purpose.

But as the Austrian emperor had an insuperable objection to concede the Prussian Prince Regent's demand of having the auxiliary army of the German Confederation, which would in that case have taken the field, placed under Prussian command, and actually preferred the humiliation of Villafranca to this to him far harder alternative, there was no opportunity afforded to test the merit of the new chief of the Prussian staff, and his name and fame accordingly continued almost unknown in Europe.

It was very different in Prussia, where Moltke's renown spread far and wide as the genial master who, by his admirable system and mode of instruction, and by his marvellously clear and lucid lectures, was enriching the army with a host of brilliant staff officers, such as Voigts-Rhetz, Blumenthal, Steible, Stosch, Podbielski, Sperling, and many more of the same high stamp.

In the Danish war of 1864, General Moltke assisted in drawing up the plan of the campaign. After the retirement of Wrangel from the supreme command at the end of April, he joined the new Commander-in-

Chief, Prince Frederick Charles of Prussia, as Chief of the Staff. After the conclusion of peace he returned to his former position and functions.

In the beginning of 1866, when it became more and more apparent that war with Austria was a contingency that had to be seriously contemplated, General Moltke was specially invited by the king to assist in the deliberations *ad hoc* of the highest officers of the Prussian army. In these deliberations the Chief of the Staff soon took the lead, and the conception and elaboration of the plan of the probable campaign was left to him. He submitted his plan to the king, who thoroughly approved of it, leaving the executive arrangements unconditionally to him.

Moltke's motto is, "*Erst wägen, dann wagen*," which may be freely translated, "Ponder and Dare," (first to ponder, then to dare; literally, first weigh, then wage). His brilliant plan of the campaign of 1866 gave the world a first proof of how thoroughly he understands how to act upon that motto. Every detail of that plan had been maturely pondered in all its bearings and contingencies; and the bold daring that followed was the deliberate consequence and result of such pondering.

Moltke's great war maxim is, "*Getrennt marschiren, vereint schlagen*," which may be freely rendered, "To separate for the march, to unite for the battle."

Upon this maxim the invasion of Bohemia was conceived and planned. Two large armies and a smaller corps, commanded severally by the Crown Prince, Prince Frederick Charles, and General Herwarth von Bittenfeld, were to enter Bohemia through five different passes, to drive the Austrian corps before them that might be sent by Benedek to oppose their advance, to concentrate finally near Königgrätz, and there to crush the Austrian host between them.

The surprising results of the fierce "seven days'" campaign are too well known by all to need recapitulation here. Moreover, they will be found reported in the memoirs of the military commanders. But what is not so universally known, is the fact that the great Prussian chief would seem to have originally contemplated a still more astounding issue of the struggle —a Bohemian Sedan, in fact; and that the bold plan would appear to have failed only because one of the sub-commanders, to whom the execution of the several parts and details of the complex manœuvre had necessarily to be intrusted, failed in achieving his share of the work.

The army of the Crown Prince, ordered to enter Bohemia from the Silesian side, consisted of four corps —to wit, the Guards, under the command of Prince Augustus von Würtemberg, instructed to enter through the Braunau Pass; the 1st Corps, under the command of General Bonin, instructed to enter through the Trautenau Pass; the 5th Corps, under the command of General Steinmetz, instructed to ente through the Nachod Pass; and the 6th Corps, under the command of General Mutius, originally instructed to watch the 2nd Austrian Corps, under the command of Count Thun, which was threatening Glatz, but, after the withdrawal of that corps, intended, it would appear, to enter over Habelschwert, Mittelwalde, and Grulich, seize upon the Wildenschwert line, thence march rapidly on to Pardubitz, and, by seizing the important line there, cut off the Austrian army under Benedek from its communications and from its retreat into Moravia.

Generals Bonin and Steinmetz were to overcome severally the resistance of the Austrian corps detached from Benedek's army to oppose their advance into Bohemia, whilst the Guards at Braunau were to be kept in readiness to support either the one or the other corps, or both, as circumstances might require.

On the 27th of June the combined operations designed by Moltke commenced. General Steinmetz succeeded in defeating the Austrian corps opposed to him, and General Bonin might have succeeded equally in the accomplishment of his part of the task, had he not been over-anxiously intent upon making war with rosewater-scented, kid-gloved hands.

The position of Trautenau is commanded by a small eminence, called the Capellenberg, or Chapelmount, on account of the small Chapel of St. John erected on the brow of it. This Chapelmount, held only feebly by the Austrians, and completely under the command of Prussian artillery, might have been carried by Bonin at an early period of the day, when the Austrian general, Gablentz, had not yet been able to bring up all his forces. But General Bonin lost two precious hours through his reluctance to shock the religious feelings of the Bohemians by directing the fire of artillery upon the chapel!

He had also so little notion of the formidable force which Gablentz would later in the day be able to bring up against his own corps, that when Prince Augustus of Würtemberg informed him of the arrival of the Guards at Braunau, and offered to detach 15,000 men to his aid, he politely declined the offer, assuring the prince that he had ample forces to cope successfully with the Austrians opposed to him.

The result of Bonin's folly was, that he was driven back in the afternoon upon Goldenöls, and that it required the aid of the whole corps of the Guards next morning to make good the position of Trautenau and Old and New Rognitz, and render possible the advance upon Königinhof.

Meanwhile Steinmetz, though victorious in the battle of Nachod on the 27th, found himself, with his corps considerably reduced, opposed to a fresh Austrian army vastly superior in numbers to his own.

Moltke was still in Berlin at the time. Upon receiving the telegraphic news of the unexpected complication which Bonin's failure had wrought, he unhesitatingly resolved, it would appear, to sacrifice the pet part of his plan, and ordered General Mutius to advance at once to the support of General Steinmetz, whom he joined at Gradlitz on the 30th of June.

It is also said that Moltke at once took counsel with the king to guard against the chance of Bonin committing another blunder in the course of the campaign. But the mischief already done could not be repaired, and so it came to pass that the Pardubitz road was left open for Benedek's retreat from Sadowa's fatal field.

Bonin tried hard to attribute the chief cause of his disaster to an act of gross treachery on the part of the citizens of Trautenau, and a most circumstantial romance was concocted, which obtained almost universal credence at the time, how, the city having duly and fairly surrendered to Bonin, an Austrian force treacherously concealed in the houses had fallen suddenly upon the unsuspecting Prussians, and how the vile citizens—male and female—had poured boiling pitch and boiling water and sulphuric acid, and Heaven knows what else besides, upon the devoted heads of Bonin's poor soldiers.

To give a colouring of reality to the romance, the Burgomaster of Trautenau, Dr. Roth, was laid by the heels, and sent a prisoner into Prussia, to be tried there for his horrid misdeeds. The writer of this sketch happened to see the poor man on his dolorous trip; so did his Majesty the king, who indignantly turned his back upon the reputed miscreant.

King David is reported to have said in his haste, that all men are liars. If the Psalmist had visited Trautenau about this time, as the writer did, he would certainly have found ample grounds there—anent this treachery romance—to repeat his hasty remark at his fullest leisure. The poor Burgomaster was afterwards honourably acquitted of the charge so foully brought against him.

The writer is bound, however, to admit, that in the Prussian army the existence of this brilliant plan was not at the time generally believed in. It was held by many, that General Mutius had been instructed from the commencement to join General Steinmetz so soon as he should be fully convinced of the withdrawal of the second Austrian corps from the Silesian frontier. Be this as it may, Moltke's brilliant strategy was thoroughly successful in all other respects. Indeed, Benedek's retreat was gravely imperilled, and the entire Austrian army would have run the most imminent risk of being compelled to surrender after Sadowa, had General Herwarth von Bittenfeld been as successful in his operations as the Crown Prince.

General Moltke was personally present at Sadowa. After the great battle he continued to direct the onward march of the Prussian army upon Olmütz and Vienna. It was he to whom was intrusted the negotiation of the five days' suspension of arms, beginning on the 22nd of July, and followed after by the armistice and peace preliminaries of Nikolsburg.

After the conclusion of peace, General Moltke, who had already in June been raised to the rank of general of infantry, received from his grateful king the high distinction of the Order of the Black Eagle, together with the chiefship of the 2nd Pomeranian Grenadiers. He shared also largely in the dotations subsequently voted by the Chambers.

The attempt made by France to intervene in the peace negotiations between Prussia and Austria, and the curious demand advanced by Benedetti—that Mayence should be ceded to France, could not but have directed the most serious attention of Bismarck, Roon, and Moltke to the possibility of grave complications presenting themselves sooner or later on the Rhine.

There can be no doubt but that this contingency had been duly pondered by each of the three leaders in his own special department. The writer knows for a fact that Roon had taken provident steps to increase the Prussian force in the field by an addition of some three hundred and fifty thousand to four hundred thousand men if needed.

Notice had in fact already been served upon all men of military age who had never yet been summoned to serve their time. The number of such men of the several classes within the limits of the age of service was said to amount in the city of Berlin alone to some 50,000! In the hotel in which the writer was staying at the time, the landlord, the porter, the boots, the head waiter, and two other waiters came all of them within the category of this call to arms.

It is quite clear that Moltke also must have been ready with his cut-and-dried plan for the contingent campaign. Perhaps one of these days that plan will see the light. It will certainly afford a curious study.

In 1867, when the Luxemburg complication threatened to lead to hostilities between France and the North German Confederation, Moltke designed a fresh plan of campaign, suited to the somewhat altered circumstances of the case. This plan he subsequently modified, and then submitted it to the king in 1868, or early in 1869, who fully adopted it for the foreseen contingency of the *inevitable* war with France.

It was upon this identical plan that the campaign of 1870-71 was subsequently conducted—that campaign which has raised the fame of Moltke as a strategist to the highest pinnacle of glory. The space at our command precludes the possibility of aught beyond this passing allusion to the late Franco-German war, which besides amply satisfies the requirements of the object which we have in view here in connection with this slight sketch of the character and career of one of the chief architects of the new German Empire.

On the 26th of October, 1870, General Moltke celebrated his seventieth birthday at Versailles. The day after, the telegraph brought him a glorious birthday gift, in the shape of the news of the capitulation of Metz, to which the king added next day the title of Count. On the 22nd March, 1871, Count Moltke was named Grand Cross of the Order of the Iron Cross; and on the 16th June, 1871, the highest military rank, that of Field-Marshal General, was bestowed upon him.

In 1871 he accepted an eager invitation of the Emperor Alexander to pay a visit to St. Petersburg and Moscow. He was received with singular honour by the emperor, the imperial family, and the chiefs of the Russian army. The commander's Cross of St. George was bestowed upon him by the emperor on this occasion. The St. Andrew's Cross had been given to him before.

In 1872 the Emperor William made Count Moltke a life member of the Prussian House of Lords. The Count also again shared largely in the ample dotations voted by the Prussian parliament in 1871. The city of his birth, Parchim, presented him with the diploma of honorary citizenship in 1867, and Colberg, Magdeburg, Berlin, Hamburg, Bremen, Lubec, Leipzig, Worms, Schweidnitz, Görlitz, Dresden, and other municipalities have since followed the example.

Rarely indeed have so many honours of all kinds and from all quarters been accumulated upon the head of any one man; and still more rarely have they been borne so meekly. It may in truth be said, that unpretending simplicity and unassuming modesty constitute the cardinal features of Moltke's character.

Were it not for the antique head and the fine features, cast in a true classic mould, few might notice the tall, lean officer in plain military undress, with simple cap on head, who may be seen every day walking along the Linden, or some part of Berlin, gently waving to the sentinels of the numerous guards he is passing his desire to dispense with the customary military honours. Yet no one can look a minute upon his face and into his eyes without being struck by the unconscious consciousness of power, if an expressive paradox may be permitted, engraven on that tranquil brow, and beaming from those steady orbs. He is a spare man like Cassius, whom two Cæsars have already had ample reason to wish fatter.

The most salient mental and intellectual feature in him is his marvellous clearness of conception and apprehension, and the limpid lucidity with which he places before others the things that are clear to him, so as to make them equally clear to them. In his orders to the generals under his guidance he confines himself strictly to the great outline of the general plan of campaign conceived by him, leaving to them individually the fullest and freest initiation of filling in the details, each according to his own best notion and understanding.

Is the military career of this greatest strategist of all ages ended now? Who can say? He bears his seventy-three winters wondrous well. Germany had to dread three military powers, and only two of them have as yet been overthrown. Three is a sacred number—"*Aller guten Dinge sind Drei,*" is a time-honoured German saying.

If the writer of this brief sketch remembers aright, Moltke's first literary essay was a history of the last Russo-Turkish campaign in European Turkey, published in 1835; and this much is certain, that the young staff officer lent by Prussia to the Sultan in the very same year, turned the first fruits of his arduous military studies to the best account in devising and advising ways and means to strengthen the Turkish empire against Russian aggression. It would be a most glorious ending indeed for the most trusty and most trusted military counsellor of Sultan Mahmud in 1835–39, if for a last achievement he should place the integrity of the Turkish empire beyond the chance of peril, by inflicting a lasting blow upon its mortal foe.

It has been stated in this memoir that the great strategist has been felicitously characterized as being "eloquently silent in seven languages." Yet, though actually not much given to indulgence in speech, he can speak remarkably well, and more to the point and purpose than most great orators. Quite recently he has given the world brilliant proof of this by his two marvellous speeches on the Army Bill.

The subjoined report of the negotiations which terminated in the capitulation of Sedan, and in which Moltke acted as chief negotiator on the part of

Germany, may not be deemed out of place here, as it will serve to throw considerable light upon the character of the general as well as upon that of the great German Minister. The writer has every reason to believe this report authentic.

THE "VÆ VICTIS!" OF DONCHERY.

(AN EPISODE OF THE LATE FRANCO-GERMAN WAR.)

It was on the night of the 1st of September, 1870 Sedan had been desperately fought, and hopelessly and irretrievably lost by M'Mahon and his unlucky successor, Wimpffen. The infernal din of nigh upon a thousand pieces of artillery was hushed for a time, the victorious Germans having granted a brief suspension of arms for discussing the terms of capitulation to be imposed upon the crushed and shattered host of France.

King William had finally dismissed for the night Count Bismarck and General Moltke, and had gone from the field of battle to his quarters at Vendresse. The statesman and the general had wended their way to the small township of Donchery, about three English miles from the walls of Sedan, where a large hall on the ground floor of a mansion had been prepared and arranged for the reception of the French and German negotiators.

At about eleven o'clock the French generals, Wimpffen, Faure, and Castelnau, attended by a number of French officers, entered the hall, in which they found a crowd of German officers assembled. Some ten minutes after, Count Bismarck and General Moltke, accompanied by Generals Blumenthal and Podbielski, Lieut.-Colonel Verdy, of the German staff, and other officers, made their appearance.

After a brief exchange of salutations, General Moltke asked General Wimpffen for his powers. Having verified these, he courteously inquired of General Wimpffen in what capacity Generals Faure and Castelnau, who had just been duly presented to him, were attending the conference. General Faure, whilst waiving all claim to an official character in the matter, asserted nevertheless his right to be present in his capacity of chief of the staff of Marshal M'Mahon, and accordingly now attending General Wimpffen in the same capacity. General Castelnau simply pleaded that he was the bearer of an oral and official communication on the part of the Emperor Napoleon, which communication he was, however, empowered to impart to General Moltke only at the end of the conference. He admitted that he had no official character in the matter, and that he could claim no right to be present in an official capacity.

The negotiators on both sides then took their seats at a square table, with a red cover on it, placed in the centre of the hall. General Moltke, with Count Bismarck on his left and General Blumenthal on his right, occupied one side of the table. On the opposite side sat General Wimpffen quite alone, Generals Faure and Castelnau, and several other French officers, taking their places a little in the rear. Lieut.-Colonel Verdy took up his position by the mantelpiece, to act as secretary to the conference. About half a dozen German officers also remained in the hall, in obedience to General Blumenthal's invitation to stay. The other officers had of course left the apartment almost immediately after the entrance of General Moltke and his companions.

After the negotiators had taken their seats, several minutes passed before poor General Wimpffen could muster sufficient resolution to begin the discussion. He might have been waiting for some slight sign of benevolent encouragement on the part of General Moltke. In vain: the great strategist kept his seat and his face alike as immovable as a statue.

"I wish to know," said Wimpffen at last, "what terms of capitulation His Majesty the King of Prussia intends to offer us?"

GENERAL MOLTKE: "Our conditions are very simple. We demand the surrender of the whole French army in Sedan, now surrounded by our forces, with arms and baggage, all officers and men alike as prisoners of war. As a mark of our esteem for the bravery displayed, we will allow the officers to retain their swords." (Even this trifling concession was subsequently withdrawn.)

WIMPFFEN: "These are hard terms; very hard

terms indeed. I think the valour shown by our troops should entitle them to somewhat more generous conditions than these. Might it not be feasible that you should content yourselves with the surrender of the fortress, with all its artillery and other armaments, allowing the army to march off with arms, banners, and baggage, on the solemn stipulation that it shall not fight again during the present war against Prussia? The emperor and his generals to take this engagement for the army, and the officers for their own persons in writing; the army to be led to any part of France that may be chosen by Prussia for the purpose, or to Algeria, and to remain there until the conclusion of peace?"

After a brief pause Wimpffen continued—"It is only two days since I came here from Africa, from the outermost borders of the desert. Up to this no stain ever soiled my military reputation. In the very midst of a battle I have supreme command thrust upon me, and find myself fatally compelled to put my name to a disastrous capitulation, having all the responsibility thrown upon my shoulders—I, who had nothing whatever to do with the initiative of the battle which alone is the cause of this capitulation. You, General Moltke, who are a general the same as I am—you cannot but conceive and feel the bitter painfulness of my position. You have it in your power to make my unhappy task less bitter, less acutely painful to me. Grant us more honourable terms. Why should you not consent to what I have just proposed? Should you, however, persist in imposing upon us the harsh conditions stated by you, I must declare that I cannot subscribe to them. I shall in that case appeal to the valour of my army, either to force our way through your lines, or to defend ourselves to the last in Sedan."

MOLTKE: "I entertain, indeed, the highest esteem for you, general, and feel deeply for your position; but I can only express my sincere regret that I am unable to comply with your wishes. I have to observe to you, that the defence of Sedan, which you would seem to contemplate, is just as absolute an impossibility as the forcing of our lines would be sure to prove were you to attempt it.

"You have indeed some excellent troops. Part of your infantry (Zouaves, Turcos, Rifles, and Marines) I acknowledge to be first-rate fighting material. Your cavalry is bold and brave to temerity; whilst for your artillery, it is truly admirable, and has inflicted great losses upon us. On the other hand, you should not forget, however, that the larger portion of your infantry is in a state of demoralization, in proof of which I need only call your attention to the fact that we have in this day's battle captured from you some 20,000 unwounded prisoners. You have only 80,000 men left, and you must know that I have thrown a girdle of 240,000 men round your army, with five hundred pieces of artillery, three hundred of which are already in position to bombard Sedan, and the remaining two hundred will be in position by to-morrow's dawn.

"If you wish to assure yourself of the truth of my words, I am willing to allow one of your officers to inspect the several positions occupied by my forces. I am sure he will confirm the correctness of my statement. The defence of Sedan, of which you have also spoken, is the purest matter of impossibility. Why, you have not provisions enough to last you for forty-eight hours, and you are also short of ammunition."

WIMPFFEN: "I think it would be to your own interest, looking at the matter from the political standpoint, to grant us honourable terms, to which the army I have the honour to command is surely entitled in consideration of the bravery shown by it in these disastrous battles.

"It is your wish to make peace, and to make it soon. The French people are magnanimous and chivalrous beyond any other nation. France will know how to appreciate the generosity shown her. She has always been grateful to those who have treated her with forbearance in the days of her misfortune. If you consent to grant us terms that will not hurt the feelings of the troops, but will rather gratify their self-esteem, the people will feel equally flattered. Your generous conduct will tend to assuage the natural grief of the people at the defeat of all their cherished notions and hopes.

"A peace concluded under such auspices would alone afford reasonable chances of proving lasting; for your noble conduct would lead to a return of those feelings of mutual friendliness that ought to exist between two great neighbouring nations, and which you yourselves can only wish to see restored once more between the Germans and the French.

"If, on the other hand, you persist in those harsh conditions you would impose upon us, you will surely kindle anger and hatred in the heart of our soldiers, and deeply offend the self-love of the whole nation. All the evil and brutal instincts of man, barely lulled to slumber by the progress of civilization, would then be re-awakened, and you would risk kindling an endless war between France and Prussia."

After this passionate pleading of General Wimpffen, Count Bismarck, who up to this had taken no active part in the conference, went in for his innings in his habitual ruthless way, his usual incisive manner, and with his customary sledge-hammer logic.

"General," said the Count, "your argument would seem at first glance to rest upon sound premises and principles; but, looked at more closely, it turns out to be merely specious—it will not hold water, nor will it bear discussion.

"Gratitude generally is a feeling no wise man would much trust to, but specially and least of all the gratitude of a people. A prince may, under certain circumstances, prove grateful for acts of generosity to him and his. One may to some extent trust in his and his family's feelings and professions of gratefulness; but, I repeat it, the case is very different with a nation. Still, if the French people were like other peoples, if they had firmly-established, lasting institutions, and due reverence and affection for them, and also a sovereign firmly seated on the throne, we might, trusting in the emperor and his son's gratefulness, shape our conditions accordingly.

"But for the last eighty years past France has seen a most strange variety of governments succeed one another with bewildering rapidity, beyond all prevision and calculation. There is no reliance to be placed in any way upon your nation. If a neighbouring people were to build hopes upon the gratitude of a French sovereign, it would be an act of madness simply—something like attempting to build in the air. It would be the merest folly to imagine that France would ever forgive us our successes. You are an excitable, envious, jealous people, arrogant to excess.

"In the course of the last two centuries, France has made war thirty times upon Prussia and Germany, and now once more has your envy and jealousy led you to make war upon us, because, forsooth, you could not forgive us the victory of Sadowa, which yet had cost you nothing, and could not dim your glory. But you clung to the notion that victory should be held your own especial and exclusive privilege, and military renown your proud monopoly. You could not endure another equally powerful nation at your side.

"You could not forgive us Sadowa, which yet did not touch your interests nor your *gloire;* and would you make us believe that you could ever forgive us Sedan? Never! If we were to conclude peace now, you would be safe to begin again in five or ten years; in fact, as soon as you should consider the chances promising. Such would be all the gratitude we might expect at your hands.

"We, on the contrary, are an honest, peaceful people, that have never run after conquests beyond the legitimate limits of our own land; and we now ardently desire peace; only that your contentious, grasping, and conquest-gluttonous disposition will not permit us to enjoy it. There must be an end to this. France must be punished in her pride and in her ambitious aspirations. We will at last, for once, take guarantees for the safety of our descendants, and to this end we must build up a fence between us and France, by securing the possession of a territory, with fortresses and other solid boundaries, that shall place us for evermore beyond the danger of another aggression from your side."

WIMPFFEN: "Your pardon, Excellency. You are deceived and misled in your judgment of the French as they are to-day. They are no longer the people of 1815. Do not judge the French nation of the present day by the verses of a few poets, the writings of a few authors, and the articles of a few journalists. The French of to-day are quite different from the French of the past. Thanks to the prosperity of the empire, the minds and aspirations of the people have turned to speculation, to business, to the arts, &c. Every individual in the land is bent upon increasing his wealth and adding to the sum of his enjoyments, and certainly thinks much more of his own personal interests than of national glory. We are quite ready in France to proclaim the universal fraternity of all nations. Just cast your glances upon England. What has become of the ancient hatred and enmity between the two peoples? Are not the English our best friends now? It will be the same with Germany, Excellency, if you are generous now, and do not insist upon such harsh conditions."

BISMARCK: "I must interrupt you, General. No! France has not changed. France would have this war which the Emperor Napoleon has made upon us, merely to flatter the mad hankering of the French people after glory. We know very well that the sound and rational portion of the French did not urge on this war, although they over-eagerly fell in with the notion when once started. We also know that it is not the French army now that is the most hostile to Germany, but the same old restless section of the nation which has always driven France into war, and which makes and unmakes governments with you.

"With you it is the mob and the journalists who

do these things, and whom we intend to punish. Therefore we must march upon Paris. Who knows what may happen meanwhile? Perhaps some government may suddenly spring up that will pay heed to naught that has passed before, and will refuse to ratify the capitulation made by you, absolving the officers from the obligations contracted with us. We know full well that soldiers are easily improvised in France; but young soldiers have not the worth of old soldiers, and an efficient body of officers and under-officers is not to be created on the spur of the moment.

"We wish for peace; but we would have a lasting peace, and to obtain this it seems indispensable that we should place France in the impossibility of resisting us. The fate of battles has placed in our hands the best soldiers and officers of the French army. It would be madness to be generous and let them go again, with the almost certainty staring us in the face finding them once more opposing us in the field. Such an act would simply mean the prolongation of the war, which is so much against the best interests of our people. No, General, deeply though we feel for your position, and however flattering the opinion we entertain of the excellence of your army, we cannot comply with your request; we cannot modify our conditions."

WIMPFFEN: "I could not think of signing such a capitulation. The fight will have to begin again."

CASTELNAU: "I believe the moment has now arrived to give you the emperor's message. The emperor has charged me to inform his Majesty the King of Prussia that he has unconditionally sent him his sword, and that he places his person entirely in his power. He has done so, however, purely in the hope that such an act of absolute devotion would move the heart of the king, and that he would, in appreciation thereof, grant the French army a more honourable capitulation—in short, such a capitulation as that army may justly claim in consideration of its bravery."

BISMARCK: "Is that all you have to say to us?"

CASTELNAU: "Yes—all."

BISMARCK: "To whom does the sword belong which the Emperor Napoleon III. thus surrenders to the king? Is it the sword of France, or is it simply his Majesty's sword? If the former, we may feel disposed to considerably modify our terms, and your mission would in that case assume a more serious character."

CASTELNAU: "This sword is simply the emperor's alone."

MOLTKE (hastily and almost joyfully): "In which case we can concede no modification of our terms. The emperor will obtain for his own person all he may please to demand."

WIMPFFEN: "We shall have to renew the battle then."

MOLTKE: "To-morrow morning at four o'clock the armistice expires. With the stroke of four I shall resume firing."

Then all parties rose from their seats, and the French officers called for their horses. There was a painful silence in the hall for several minutes, when Count Bismarck addressed himself once more to Wimpffen. "General," he said, impressively, "you have indeed brave and heroic soldiers, and I doubt not but that they would do wonders of valour to-morrow, and would inflict grievous losses upon us if the fight were renewed. But what can be the use of all this? To-morrow night you would find yourself no farther advanced than to-night, and you would only have burdened your conscience with the blood of our soldiers and of yours, which you would have caused to be shed in vain. This conference must not be permitted to come to naught owing to a moment of passion. I trust General Moltke may yet succeed in demonstrating to you the hopelessness of any attempt at further resistance on your part."

The parties sat down again.

MOLTKE: "I affirm once more to you that you cannot break through our lines, even if your troops were in the best possible condition. Not to dwell unduly upon the great numerical superiority of my army, more particularly in artillery, I hold positions from which Sedan can be set on fire by our guns in a couple of hours. These positions command all outlets from which an attempt might be made upon our lines; and they are so strong as to defy all attempts at capturing them."

WIMPFFEN: "These positions are not so strong as you assert."

MOLTKE: "You do not know the topography of the country round Sedan; and this curious fact most strongly marks and characterises your vain-glorious and frivolous nation. At the opening of the campaign, you supplied all your officers with maps of Germany, whilst you lacked the means of studying the topography of your own country, as you had no maps of France. Well, I tell you once more that my positions are not simply strong, but that they are formidable, and cannot possibly be taken by you."

WIMPFFEN: "I will accept, then, the offer which you kindly made at the beginning of the conference, and I will send an officer to inspect your formidable positions, that I may be guided in my resolutions by his report."

MOLTKE: "You will send no one now to inspect my positions. You may give credence to my assurance that it is so. There is no longer time now. It is just upon midnight, and the armistice expires at four o'clock in the morning. I will not grant you even one minute's extension of the time."

WIMPFFEN: "But, General, you must know that I cannot by myself take such a momentous step. I must consult my fellow generals; and as I do not know where to find them in Sedan, it is impossible for me to give you a reply by four o'clock in the morning. It is absolutely indispensable that you should consent to grant me an extension of time."

MOLTKE: "I regret my inability to consent to your wishes even in this."

Here Count Bismarck whispered to Moltke that they would under all circumstances have to await the arrival of the king, who could not well be expected before nine o'clock. Moltke then turned again to Wimpffen, and briefly informed him that the time of the armistice would be extended to nine o'clock in the morning, which was the utmost limit of concession he could go to.

The French general uttered a few brief words of thanks even for this very small concession. It was clearly apparent to every one present that he had as good as accepted the capitulation, despite the harshness of its terms, and that all he was striving for now was to have his own awful responsibility in the matter covered and lightened, to some extent at least, by the sanction of the other commanders of the army.

The French officers then took their leave with aching hearts and clouded brows.

The great statesman and the great strategist felt naturally much elated at the immense results achieved, but they were also deeply moved. "Væ victis!" said Bismarck, turning to Moltke. "Heaven grant we may never again have to exchange positions with these irreconcilable foes; they would surely blot us out from the map of Europe." "True," replied Moltke; "and for this very reason we must utterly crush them ere we can afford to grant them peace even on our own terms, and these terms must absolutely include the cession to us of their strategic frontier. With the Vosges for our boundary line, and Metz-Diedenhofen in our hands, we need never fear them again."

IV.

PRINCE BISMARCK.

On the 2nd of September, 1871, the first anniversary of the *dies mirabilis* of Sedan, the writer happened to be at Elberfeld-Barmen, the great manufacturing twin city, the Manchester-Salford of Germany. The people of the Wupperdale are, as a rule, a sober-minded, hard-working set, devout votaries of the great god of money-making, and but little given to cultivate or celebrate the pride and pomp of glorious war. But on this special occasion, on the first anniversary of the "crowning mercy," the twin-sisters had made up their minds to go in for a grand celebration, and they had accordingly doffed their grimy every-day garb of industry, and donned instead their gayest gala dress.

The woods and forests all round had been stripped bare of their leafy covering. The streets had literally burst into an eruption of oak, from tall young trees, through every size and variety of branches down to crowns, wreaths, and garlands, and monstrous boa-constrictor ropes of immense length. Numerous triumphal arches, some of them of surpassing magnitude and corresponding beauty and splendour, spanned the principal thoroughfares. Hundreds upon hundreds of banners fluttered gaily in the breeze; thousands upon thousands of smaller paper flags, of all colours and combinations of colours, were hung out from roofs and windows to heighten the effect of the bigger bunting. The fronts of nearly every house were covered with strings of paper balloons and Chinese lanterns, whose bright, gay colours looked brighter still in the glorious sunshine; for not even the slightest cloud dimmed the serenity of the sky on that festival day. There was not a nation in the world whose flag had not a representative hoisted somewhere in the streets and lanes—even Otaheite and the Sandwich Isles were there!

The Wupper, that soiled mountain-stream, allowed freedom for this one day from the defiling embraces of the Giant Industry, seemed to join in the general rejoicings, and actually began to look less dirty as the day advanced.

At about eight P.M. the illuminations began on the grandest scale, throwing into shade the happiest efforts in that line in the palmiest days of old Vauxhall. Some were extremely tasteful, others very gorgeous, and others, again, pleasingly simple. The Townhouse and many other buildings seemed actually floating in a sea of light. Chinese and Bengal fires threw their bright green and red glare far and wide around them, charmingly clothing the white gaslight streaks in the vicinity with their complementary colours. Electric, magnesium, and lime lights strove successfully to turn night into day.

Transparencies and illuminated inscriptions—tasteful or ingenious, or both—were to be seen by the dozen in nearly every street.

In the course of his nocturnal perambulation the writer was particularly struck with one transparency rather out of the common run. This was in the Auerstrasse, at the shop of a M. Langensiepen, stationer and bookbinder.

This patriotic citizen exhibited a gigantic illuminated poster, all done in writing, executed in a variety of styles of most graceful and elegant penmanship. The literary composition was equal to the penmanship. It was all anent the "noblest structure of the world's history" (*der Prachtbau der Weltgeschichte*), to wit, the new German empire, and the men who had been chiefly instrumental in the raising of it, marked with appropriate designations indicating the nature of their respective shares in the great work. Among these figured, first and foremost, the architect—the projector and planner of the whole, the presiding genius over all—Bismarck.

"Der Mann, der hohen Geist's den grossen Plan gemacht,
Mit mächt'ger Willenskraft das Herrliche vollbracht."

Which may be rendered into English somewhat freely—

> "The man whose mighty will, with giant power combined,
> The noble fabric reared his genius had designed."

Many other names came after Bismarck's. King William, here surnamed "the Upright" (*der Biedere*), who was designated as "head-master of the works;" Moltke, Roon, Blumenthal, Stosch, Sperling, Stiehle, Podbielski, &c., who were designated as "conductors of the technical department;" the Crown Prince, Prince Frederick Charles, Prince Albert (now King) of Saxony, Vogel von Falkenstein, Voigts-Rhetz, Göben, Werder, Steinmetz, &c., who were designated as "foremen in the executive branches," &c.

The only name omitted from the list of leading chiefs in the field was that of poor Manteuffel, whom his Majesty the Emperor-King has since raised to the supreme military rank of Field-Marshal General, but to whose merits in the field, if not in the Cabinet, the German people, and to a very considerable extent the German army, always will persist in remaining obstinately blind.

But the enthusiastic crowd gathered round the poster seemed to have eyes only for the leading name—Bismarck. Hurrah after hurrah, and *Lebehoch* after *Lebehoch* were shouted forth from a hundred stentorian lungs in connection with the name of the popular Chancellor, who was acclaimed as the "Pride of Prussia," the "Genius of Germany," the "Glorious Creator of the Glorious new Empire," &c.

By way of finish, the crowd burst out spontaneously into singing the distich, "Der Mann," to an improvised air, something of an impracticable cross between "God save the Queen" and "Froggy would a wooing go."

The Germans are a musical people, but somehow the singing induced the writer and his companions, two of the fathers of the city of Elberfeld, to take discretion to be the better part of valour, and "move on" at the double quick. It might be that the profuse libations that had been universally poured all day at the shrine of King Gambrinus had somehow got between the vocal chords of the chanters and rendered the sounds passing through less agreeable to the ear.

To one who, like the writer, has had many opportunities in former years to feel the pulse of public opinion in Germany anent one Bismarck-Schönhausen, who was, up to as late as 1865 and the first half of 1866, held up to almost universal execration as the bane and curse of poor Prussia, and as the anti-German demon, it might have seemed almost incredible that this hero of the *aura popularis* of the hour, whom all the people around were heard talking of so affectionately as "our own Bismarck," could possibly be the same man.

The explanation of this phenomenal popularity of

the man, which not alone has remained unabated up to the present day, but may be said to have grown into actual *love* bordering on idolatry, may in a measure be found in the fact that Bismarck has always honestly striven, not to *court* popularity, but to *deserve* it. And the secret of his marvellous success may be found in the two lines cited above. A mighty genius, a mighty will, a mighty power combined in one man—a man puissant alike to conceive, to will, and to do.

The origin of the family Bismarck, or Bismark, as some of the branches write the name, is lost in the grey antiquity of the earlier middle-age centuries. Some genealogists would trace it to Gottschalk,[1] the famous prince and ruler of the great Wendean or Vindish confederation of the Slavic tribes settled from the fourth to the eleventh century in North Germany, from the Fichtel Mountains to Holstein.

This "glorious" origin (Slava means "glory") finds not much favour, however, with the Bismarcks, who pride themselves rather upon their pure German descent, and feel accordingly much more inclined to adopt another genealogical account, which makes a certain German Athaling, or Baron, rejoicing in the name of Bismarck, come from Bohemia to the so-

---

[1] He was the contemporary of the German emperors from Conrad II. to Henry IV. In the time of the former he had apostatized from the Christian faith, which Archbishop Adelbert of Bremen induced him subsequently to re-embrace. He was finally slain by his own people.

called Altmark, or Old March, in the governmental district of Magdeburg, some time about the twelfth century. He and his immediate successors founded here the town of Bismarck, near Stendal (this Bismarck is now a petty township with close upon 2,000 inhabitants), and the village of Burgstall. Several members of the family figure on the civil registers of the cities of Stendal and Prenzlow, as having filled certain important municipal positions.

In the year 1494 the town of Bismarck was handed over to the family of Alvensleben, and in 1562 the Elector Joachim II., of Brandenburg, acquired the village of Burgstall from the then possessor, Friedrich von Bismarck, governor of the Altmark, in exchange for the manors of Schönhausen, Fischbeck, Crevese, Briest, and others, which remain still in the possession of the several branches of the family.

Frederick von Bismarck, surnamed the Permutator, on account of this exchange of estates, had two sons, from whom the present two lines of the family spring—the Schönhausen line and the Crevese line.

Both lines have furnished to the state several leading men in the field and in the cabinet. Christopher Frederick von Bismarck-Schönhausen was a distinguished soldier in the times of the great Elector and of the first King of Prussia. He was a general in the army, and governor of the fortress of Cüstrin. Levin Frederick von Bismarck was for eighteen years

(1746-64) Minister of State and of Justice in Prussia under Frederick II., and first President of the Exchequer Court. His son, Augustus William, was Minister of State and of War, and Minister-President; also Chief of the Customs and Excise Department, and President of the Board of Trade, Commerce, and Manufactures. He died in 1783.

The head of the Rhenan branch of the Schönhausen line, William von Bismarck, general in the Würtemberg service, was in 1816 made a count by the King of Würtemberg, with succession to the descendants of his elder brother, Baron Ludwig.

Another of the Schönhausens, Theodor, married, in the year 1817, the daughter and heiress of Frederick Lewis, Count of Bohlen, the last male member of an ancient Pomeranian family. This Theodor was made a count by the King of Prussia, and took the name of Bohlen in addition to his own. His son, Frederick Alexander von Bismarck-Bohlen (born the 15th of June, 1818), late governor of Alsace-Lorraine, is a cousin of the great German Chancellor.

Otto Edward Leopold von Bismarck was born on the 1st of April, 1815, at Schönhausen, in the Altmark. His father, Charles William Ferdinand, was born on the 13th of November, 1771. He was the head of the Altmark-Pomeranian branch of the Schönhausen line, and proprietor of the manors of Schönhausen in the Altmark; also of the manors of Kniepholz, and Külz, and Jarchelin, in the Naugard district, in

Pomerania. He had been captain in the Carabineer regiment of the Prussian Horse Guards.

His wife, Louisa Wilhelmina, born in 1790, was the daughter of Privy Councillor Menken, a distinguished high official in the Prussian service.

There were six children born of the marriage, of whom the two eldest and the youngest died early in life. The three other children survive. The eldest of these, Bernhard, born in 1810, is now lord of the manors of Külz and Jarchelin, Chamberlain and Privy Councillor, and Landrath, or Prefect, of the Naugard district. The only surviving daughter, Malvina, born in 1827, is married to Chamberlain von Arnin-Kröchlendorf.

The mother was a very superior woman. Brought up in the old-fashioned school of female training in Germany, she combined a rare proficiency in the accomplishments and refinements of the highest society, with an equally rare proficiency in every branch of domestic economy; and more than this, she was a Christian woman and Christian mother in the highest sense of the term, free from the least taint of religious zealotry or bigotry. The father, it would appear, was by no means a man of vigorous mind: he was slightly indolent, and given much to the pursuit of pleasure. The mother exercised a most powerful influence upon the formation of the mind and principles of Otto in the earliest and most plastic period of the boy's life. The great Chancellor may indeed be said to afford a most striking example of the vital importance and the glorious results of a mother's early training and teaching.

Otto had not yet completed his seventh year when his parents placed him with Professor Plamann of Berlin, a gentleman who at the time enjoyed a high and well-deserved reputation as a successful instructor and educator of youth. Five years later the boy was transferred to the Frederick William Gymnasium, and in 1830 to the Grey Conventual School, where his preparatory education received the finishing touch.

At Easter 1832, when he had just completed his seventeenth year, the young lad was sent to the University of Göttingen to study law and political economy in all its branches. The year after, 1833, he exchanged Göttingen for Berlin, where he completed his studies.

At Easter 1835, he passed a most brilliant examination, and was appointed soon after Auscultator [1] at the city court of Berlin. A year after, he exchanged the law for the administrative branch, and was appointed referendarius, or reporter, at Aix-la-Chapelle.

In Prussia high and low are bound alike to serve the country in a military capacity, the only distinction in this matter being made in favour of young men of proved superior education and knowledge, who, besides

[1] Auscultator, a listener, hearkener, or hearer; the lowest step on the Prussian law ladder—a kind of sucking barrister.

being only called upon to serve one year in times of peace, are permitted, within certain necessary limits, to choose the branch of the service which they prefer, and the city or place where they would like to pass their year of voluntary military duty. Young Bismarck selected the Rifles of the Guard, stationed at Potsdam, and was accordingly transferred from Aix-la-Chapelle to the latter city.

Meanwhile his mother's health had given way, and the administration of the paternal estates in Pomerania began to show lamentable signs of lack of the former skill and vigour, which induced young Bismarck to turn his attention to the study of agriculture.

There was at the time a famous agricultural institute at Eldena, near Greifswalde. To enable him to pursue his studies there, he asked for and obtained his transfer to the Pomeranian Rifles, stationed at Greifswalde (in 1838).

After the death of his mother (on the 1st January, 1839), and the expiration of his time of military service, in the spring of 1839 he, with the free consent of his father, conducted, in conjunction with his elder brother Bernhard, the administration of the paternal estates. In 1841, when the elder brother was appointed landrath, or prefect, of the Naugard district, the brothers divided the administration of the estates between them, the elder taking Külz, the younger Kniephausen and Jarchelin.

After the death of the father, in 1845, Otto handed Jarchelin, vastly improved, over to the elder brother, receiving in exchange the old family seat of Schönhausen, where he took up his residence. He was appointed by the government deichhauptmann, or warden of the dikes.

He was soon after sent by the knights and squires of the second riding of the Jerichow district as their representative to the Provincial Diet of the Province of Saxony, in which capacity he attended the sittings of the first United Prussian Diet at Berlin in the summer of 1847.

These were critical times for Prussia. The ardent aspirations of the Prussian people after greater political and social liberty than the nation had been permitted to enjoy under narrow-minded old Frederick William III., had been persistently thwarted for the last seven years by his successor Frederick William IV., who had just then, however, at last reluctantly and grudgingly consented to grant his people something like an imitation constitutional charter, with a Brummagem system of representation. This was the famous Royal Patent of the 3rd of February, 1847.

The then leaders of the Liberal and Progressist party in Prussia were men of high intellectual culture and great attainments, but perhaps somewhat idealistic, slightly deficient in practical sense, and wanting in directness and clearness of purpose.

With his clear head and vigorous intellect, Bismarck saw and comprehended this fact, and the consequences to which it tended. He understood also how the power and greatness of Prussia had rested up to this time, and still continued to rest, in a great measure upon the intact monarchic principle, supported by the landed aristocracy and squireocracy. He saw, in brief, that the times had not yet come, and that the people were not yet ripe, for the rapid onward march in the path of political freedom which the leaders of the Liberal and Progressist party would urge.

In the same way then as our own Sir Robert Peel, at the beginning of his career, threw in his lot with the old Tory party, Bismarck made his first appearance on the great political stage of the country as an uncompromising Royalist and Feudalist. He soon made his way to the foremost ranks of the champions of the Royal and Conservative cause.

With the whole energy of his powerful mind he combated the axiom propounded by the Progressists, that the people had an inherent right to constitutional liberty and representative institutions. The king alone, he boldly maintained, had the right to judge what amount of freedom might be bestowed upon the people out of his own generous bounty. He would not hear of discussing the February Patent, which he declared to be simply a royal act of grace that ought to be gratefully accepted without discussion or cavilling.

The February revolution in France was speedily followed by the events of the 18th March in Berlin, when the Crown was for the time prostrated to the dust.

On the 2nd of April, 1848, the second session of the United Diet was opened at Berlin, to discuss and vote the electoral law for the convocation of the first Prussian National Assembly. Bismarck took barely any share or part in the discussion.

He made no attempt to obtain his nomination to the New National Assembly. He, with his clear understanding, saw how hollow and unreal the entire affair was. He withdrew accordingly for a time altogether from the political stage, devoting his leisure to the improvement of his Schönhausen estate, where he took up his residence, and to the consideration and study of the great political and social questions and problems of the times.

He attended, however, in the summer of 1848 the great meeting of landed proprietors and squires and Conservative statesmen at Berlin (the so-called Junker Parliament, or Cavalier Parliament), and remained in the capital to watch the course of events. He soon witnessed the easy overthrow of the revolution.

Under the new constitution granted by the king he was elected a member of the Second Chamber, where he again took up exactly the same line of politics he had pursued at the session of the United Diet in 1847. He showed himself a most vigorous and eloquent antagonist of the modern representative system, and maintained that the lasting welfare of Prussia and of Germany imperatively demanded a strong royal power in Prussia, and the cordial co-operation of Prussia with Austria in the regulation of the affairs of Germany.

He absolutely condemned the ill-advised and ill-directed efforts of the National Parliament in Frankfort-on-the-Main to create a German Empire and an imperial constitution, and figured among the strongest and most eloquent opponents of the foolish attempt to place the imperial crown of the new-fangled parliamentary empire upon the head of Prussia's king. He equally combated the project of the so-called union, which he declared to be simply a scheme to weaken the power of Prussia. The same position he maintained in the Erfurt Parliament in 1850.

In the great debate of the 3rd of December, 1850, in the Second Prussian Chamber, Bismarck openly declared his fullest concurrence with Manteuffel's pro-Austrian policy.

Here ends the first stage of Bismarck's political career.

The future truth-seeking and painstaking historian of the life and times of Bismarck, will find it a knotty point to decide whether the ostentatiously exuberant professions of ultra-loyalty and absolute royalist tendencies and pro-Austrian proclivities so profusely and intensely indulged in by Bismarck at this, the initiatory period of his political career, ought to be held the true echo of the man's inner promptings, the faithful mirror of his mind's convictions at the time, or whether they were not perchance simply the outcomings of a *ruse de guerre*, resorted to by the future great statesman that he might storm the difficult outworks defending the citadel of high office in the state, which it clearly was from his earliest manhood the object of his ambition to enter.

Now it has already been said that the then leaders of the Liberal and Progressist party in Prussia were men of high intellectual culture and great attainments, but certainly somewhat idealistic and slightly deficient in practical sense, and wanting in directness and clearness of purpose.

Bismarck had witnessed the great upheaving of 1848. He had seen the glorious chances afforded these said Liberal leaders to carry out their own professed views, and to reconstruct the somewhat shaken social edifice upon a brand-new plan of their own. He had seen the "professors" at work, or, more correctly speaking, at talk, in the Frankfort Parliament; he had watched that mountain in labour, and had seen the ridiculous, tailless mouse to which it had given birth. He had watched the boiling and bubbling of the revolutionary caldron in South-Western Germany, and he had not been very favourably impressed certainly with the scum that had arisen to the surface there, and had been skimmed off speedily and without much trouble by the old *régime*.

There were, indeed, some honest, well-meaning patriots among the leaders of the revolution in the south-west of Germany; but, unhappily, most of these lacked all the qualities essential to success in the arduous task of pulling down the worn-out and putting up something better in its stead.

There were also, it is true, some really sensible and practical men among them, such as Joseph Fickler (of Constance), Karl Blind, Franz Sigel, and a few more. But these were somehow soon got rid of by their companions in the rising, or placed in impracticable or even impossible positions, where they could not possibly be of much use to the cause which they had espoused.

Karl Blind, for instance, had been uselessly expended at the very beginning by an idle mission to Paris; and Joseph Fickler, it was strongly suspected at the time in revolutionary circles, had simply been betrayed by "some one" of his colleagues into the hands of the Würtemberg police. Brentano's name was openly mentioned in connection with the dirty transaction.

Franz Sigel, who afterwards showed in the American secession war that he had the real stuff in him, was completely overlaid and effaced by the Pole, Mieroslawski. Still he fought gallantly and with some slight success at Wiesenthal, and made a skilful retreat behind the Murg, and thence into Switzerland, after the defeat at Waghäusel had destroyed the last hope of the revolution.

With the experience of the last ten years before the world, there can be barely a doubt left on the mind of a sagacious observer of men and events but that Otto von Bismarck-Schönhausen had from the commencement of his public career made the unity of Germany the aim of his political strategy. With his cool head and vigorous intellect, however, he had clearly discerned the formidable, nay, the apparently insuperable, obstacles in the path of the ultimate achievement of that unity. He had seen that the German people were not yet ripe for it.

The popular mind in Germany had not realized then the primary and most indispensable condition of that unity, to wit, the political and military lead of Prussia.

Bismarck saw that the Liberal leaders were not the men to make the people throughout the great Fatherland understand this first necessity. He could not cast in his lot then with these unpractical and impracticable men, who could not or would not see the immense elements of force, the unlimited promise of success in a great national movement, which lay in the strength of the monarchical principle in Prussia, in the landed aristocracy and squireocracy, and in the Prussian military system.

So he was led to offer his services to the other side—to which he belonged, moreover, naturally by birth and position. His ultra-royalist utterances at this period of his career may simply be taken for bids to secure an opening for himself, a first introduction to the charmed circle of official life and action; and the somewhat exaggerated volume of these utterances and professions may in a measure be looked upon as appearing to him the most promising means to attract the attention of the king and his advisers.

His league with Gerlach and Stahl, and his vigorous contributions to the columns of the great feudal and royalist organ, the *Kreuz Zeitung*, may be considered to have been intended to work in the same direction.

Be this as it may, this much is certain, that Frederick William had his attention drawn to this stalwart Junker—this doughty champion of the most absolute royal prerogative. The very exuberance of his professions of loyalty tended perhaps to gain him the royal favour, as the king might well fancy he had before him one of those second-rate mediocrities whom he loved so much, as they could not offend him with a display of mental or intellectual superiority over himself.

In May 1851, Baron Bismarck was accordingly named Privy Councillor of Legation, and appointed First Secretary to the Prussian Embassy to the German Confederation at Frankfort-on-the-Main. General von Rochow was the Prussian Ambassador at the time.

The new First Secretary was soon perfectly *au fait* in every detail of his difficult and delicate diplomatic duties. Three brief months after his first appointment, in August 1851, he was named Ambassador to the Confederation in the place of General von Rochow, recalled.

Count Thun was at the time the Austrian Ambassador to the Confederation, and, as such, President of the august body.

Bismarck, in the first three months of his probation as First Secretary, had had abundant opportunities of witnessing the haughty arrogance of the Austrian President's conduct to his colleagues, more particularly to the Prussian Ambassador. The sturdy Junker was resolved not to stand any nonsense in this respect, such as his predecessor had submitted to. *Principiis obsta* is the principle upon which it may be said he has always acted in his public career, even from his earliest day up to the present time; and the noble Count Thun, unfortunately for himself and his own dignity, chose to put him at once upon his mettle.

Thinking, most likely, what a good thing it would be to make the new Prussian representative, at the very outset of his ambassadorial career, feel his relative inferiority, he ventured to receive Bismarck upon his first visit of ceremony in his shirt-sleeves. The Saxo-Pomeranian Junker had hardly caught sight of the Ambassador-President in his coatless costume when he called out to the amazed and confused Count, "You are quite right, Excellency; it is awfully hot here!" and coolly proceeded to pull his own coat off. Thun was completely taken aback. He jumped up, flung himself into his uniform, and apologized to the Prussian for his mistake.

Bismarck took the matter in good part; but he had checked for evermore Thun's inclination to take liberties with his Prussian colleague, who from that time forward held his own in Frankfort upon a becoming footing of perfect equality with the Austrian. If Bismarck ever really had had the pro-Austrian proclivities which he had so loudly professed in the Prussian Chambers, he got certainly very soon cured of them in Frankfort, and speedily inaugurated a new thinly-veiled anti-Austrian policy.

After a time Count Thun was recalled, Baron Prokesch-Osten succeeding him, who was again succeeded in his turn by Count Rechberg. They all found the grim Prussian a tough party to deal with, who would never give way to them to the extent even of a line. And strange enough he communicated his anti-Austrian feelings in a measure to the king and cabinet whom he represented.

One of the Austrian Archdukes visited Frankfort during the time Bismarck represented Prussia in the Confederation. Bismarck was then still a simple lieutenant in the Prussian Landwehr Cavalry. Still, several orders had been bestowed upon him by his grateful king even at that time. At length a review was held in honour of the visit of the Austrian Archduke. The Prussian Ambassador attended on horseback in his Landwehr-lieutenant's uniform, with his orders on his breast. His Imperial Highness rode up to him and asked him, with polished irony and a courteous sneer, whether he had gained his orders before the enemy. "Yes," replied Bismarck, without an instant's hesitation, "Yes, Imperial Highness, I have gained them all before the enemy—here, in Frankfort."

Then came the Regency of Prince William, which gave Bismarck still freer scope for the open manifestation of his anti-Austrian convictions and feelings.

In 1859, when the war between Austria and France and Italy broke out, Bismarck openly opposed the notion that Germany, and more especially Prussia, had the least interest in aiding Austria against her foes. He used to go ostentatiously about in Frankfort arm-in-arm with Count Barral, the then Sub-Alpine Ambassador to the Confederation. As the Prince Regent, however, took a different view of the matter, it was thought expedient to bring Bismarck's official career at Frankfort to a close. He was raised to the rank of major in the Landwehr Cavalry, and appointed Ambassador to the Court of St. Petersburg—put by in the cold, like champagne, till wanted, as he humorously expressed his transplantation from the city on the Main to the city on the Neva.

It may be subject for speculation what influence Bismarck's bold anti-Austrian demonstration at the time may have exercised in 1866 upon Louis Napoleon's demeanour at the commencement of the Germano-Prussian war.

The new Prussian Ambassador to the Court of St. Petersburg handed in his credentials on his own forty-fourth birthday, April 1, 1859.

During his stay in St. Petersburg he exerted himself to the utmost of his ability to cement a good understanding and friendship between Russia and Prussia. He felt that a cordial understanding with Russia was indispensable to the execution of the mighty plans and projects he was then no doubt already revolving in his mind. It is even a moot question whether his ostentatious display of anti-Austrian feeling at the threatened outbreak of the Austro-Franco-Italian war, in the face of the Prussian Regent's professed benevolent intentions towards Austria, was not a clever comedy got up between the ambassador and the ruler of the state represented by him, to mask the true motive of his promotion to the St. Petersburg embassy.

However this may be, Bismarck succeeded most fully in his object, which was not quite so easy a task as it might at first sight appear. The Russian court and the Russian statesmen could not but be aware of the bitter feeling created in the heart of every Prussian patriot by the brutal arrogance with which that Asiatic despot, the late Emperor Nicholas, had dared to treat Prussia and Germany in the sad days of Warsaw and Olmütz; and people so sharp-sighted as Russian statesmen are would not easily be led to believe that the deadly insult and injury had been absolutely forgiven and forgotten. Who knows but that the wound may even now still keep rankling and festering in secret, despite all that the son has done since to atone for the father's offence?

Count Brandenburg (an illegitimate scion of the royal house of Hohenzollern) had been sent to Warsaw in the last days of October, 1850, to endeavour to gain the support of the Russian Emperor Nicholas in the questions of Hesse, Schleswig-Holstein, and the Union. The Prussian Minister had not only failed altogether in the object of his mission, but Nicholas had treated him with revolting brutality. When the Count ventured to plead in favour of the unhappy Hessians, so grievously oppressed by their wretched ruler and his still viler tool, Hassenpflug, the Russian despot rudely cut him short. "What!" he exclaimed, "you prate to me about the rights of man and of the people, and about national and international rights and law! Learn, Count, that I acknowledge only one right and one law in this world—the Will of the Ruler. Subjects have to submit and obey without murmuring. If they dare rebel, like these vile Hessians, they must be put down by the strong hand, and by G— they shall be so long as I wield power. My poor, chicken-hearted brother-in-law has a set of bandits for Ministers: the sooner he sends this Radowitz and his consorts to the right-about-face the safer it will be for him. I will stand no nonsense, Count, I can tell you. You will have to give way on every point—Hesse, Schleswig-Holstein, and your ridiculous Union. Tell your master from me, Count, that I will have it so." The unhappy Count, who felt but too acutely how the fatal weakness and vacillation of his king had paralyzed the power of Prussia, and how the only proper answer this gross insolence merited, alas! could not be given then, went back to Berlin struck to death. On the 1st of November he reported to the Council the result of his mission; then body and mind gave way, delirium seized upon the unhappy man's brain. "My helmet, quick! my sword —my horse!" he raved. "Woe, woe! too late! the enemy is in Breslau! Oh, my fine corps—my gallant band, my unhappy fatherland!" A few days after, the broken body and crushed mind found rest in the tomb. But these are moments in the life of a nation which are never forgotten. It took all the blood spilled at Sadowa to wash away the recollection of Olmütz. Will it take less to wash away the remembrance of Warsaw? Who shall tell?

It was from St. Petersburg that Bismarck despatched his famous letter of the 12th of May, 1859, to Baron Schleinitz, then Prussian Foreign Secretary, which saw the light of publicity some seven years after, when the leading idea pervading it had been fully carried into effect by the great statesman who penned it. In this letter, which was written in special reference to the debates and negotiations then in course of progress respecting the proposed participation of the German Confederation in the Italo-Franco-Austrian war, there occurs, *inter alia*, the following pregnant passage:—

" My eight years' experience in Frankfort has led me to the conviction, that the present constitution of the German Confederation simply weighs like a heavy chain upon Prussia, threatening to stifle her in critical times without affording us Prussians the same compensations in return which Austria derives from it, who is left so much freer to move and act as she pleases.

" The princes and governments of the middle and smaller states will not fairly apply the same measure to the one as to the other of the two leading powers in Germany. We find that the purport of the Confederation and the laws of its constitution are read and interpreted differently, as the interests of the policy of Austria may require. Prussia has always and in all questions found herself face to face in the Confederation with the same compact majority against her wishes and interests ; she has always been invited to give way to the demands of her co-confederates.

"The chief aim and object of the policy of the German princes and their ministers is to work the Confederation under the lead of Austria at the cost of Prussia, who is expected to perform the useful part of insuring the lesser states of the Confederation against the chances of an overwhelming preponderance of Austria, and to bear, with uncomplaining resignation and quiet submission to the wishes of the majority, the monstrous disproportion in which the duties put upon her by the Confederation stand to the rights graciously conceded to her share by that body.

"When we find that states which could not even exist without our protection presume to direct our political movements, basing such presumption upon pretended rights derived from the constitution of the Confederation—rights which, were we to admit them, would put an end to all autonomy of Prussian policy— it is high time indeed for us to mind that these would-be leaders who so coolly invite us to follow them, pursue other than Prussian interests, and that the cause of Germany, which they profess to have at heart, means with them something quite different from the cause of Prussia, unless the latter power should be willing to commit self-effacement.

"I see in our political connections and relations with the German Confederation a grievous, growing malady of Prussia, which, if not taken resolutely in hand in proper season, will have to be eradicated in the end, *ferro et igni*. It is my firm opinion that, were the confederation to be broken up to-day, without supplying a substitute for it, even this negative gain would soon place the relations of Prussia with her neighbours upon a much more satisfactory footing than can be said to be the case at present."

The death of King Frederick William IV. (2nd of January, 1861), and the accession of the Prince Regent William to the Prussian throne made no alteration in Bismarck's political position and prospects. There was the most perfect understanding between the ambassador and the new king, whom he continued about a twelvemonth longer to represent at St. Petersburg.

In the spring of 1862, it was thought in the council of King William that the time had come for another indispensable preliminary move in the difficult game that would have to be played sooner or later. There was another power whose benevolent abstention from interference in certain contingencies it was of the utmost importance to secure—France, to wit. Bismarck was the man selected to gain this most desirable end.

He was accordingly recalled from St. Petersburg, and named ambassador to the Tuileries.

His openly-declared friendship for France and Italy in 1859 had made him certainly a *persona grata* in the eyes of the Emperor Napoleon, and had thus in a measure prepared the way for a successful opening of his mission. The seductive charms of his manner and his wondrous power of suasion succeeded speedily in moulding the ruler of France to his will and wishes.

But the new ambassador did more than this: he looked with his sharp eyes at the wheel-work of the French state-machine, and he saw how thoroughly rotten the whole imperial system was, even at that time. He formed a correct estimate of the strength and weakness of that army which the lucky chances of the Crimean and Italian campaigns had raised so high in its own estimation, and in that of the French nation, so much given to self-glorification.

He knew that Roon and the king were hard at work upon the creation of a new war machine that promised to be of harder and tougher material, and of better and more enduring temper than the French army of the period could boast of.

He also saw and appreciated the great wealth and the immense material resources of France, and took them duly into account in his estimation of the future chances of success in the carrying out of his gigantic plans and projects.

Meanwhile the king and Roon had got tired of the

weak vacillation shown in the great army reorganization question by the Hohenlohe-Heydt administration, which had succeeded the Hohenzollern-Auerswald ministry. The king thought the time had come to turn the energy and ability of Ambassador Bismarck to proper account nearer home. So he made him Minister-President and Foreign Secretary—provisionally the 23rd of September, definitely the 9th of October, 1862.

Here begins the third stage of Bismarck's political career.

Three of the old ministers—Roon, Lippe, and Mühler (War, Justice, and Public Worship, &c.)—retained their offices in the new Bismarck ministry. Another, Itzenplitz, was transferred from the Agricultural Department to the Board of Trade, where he replaced Holzbrink. To the other offices new men were appointed, to wit—Bodelschwingh to the Exchequer, Selchow to the Agricultural Department, and Eulenburg to the Home Office, where he replaced Jagow. The last two were named only two months after—December the 9th, 1862.

This was a queer team for a man like Bismarck to have to work with. All his colleagues, without exception, were Ultras. Roon, indeed, was a man of brilliant attainments; but he was a stanch Junker of strongly pronounced Absolutist and Feudalist opinions and tendencies. Still, being a man of kindred mind, he was to some extent open to

Bismarck's influence, and would, on important occasions, throw the weight of his vote into the president's scale. As Roon personally represented in the cabinet the king's dominant idea, the reorganization of the army, his support on such occasions was of the utmost value to the premier, the lesser members of the ministry following Roon as their leader.

Eulenburg and Itzenplitz were capable men and good administrators, but there was nothing very brilliant about them. Eulenburg, moreover, was a rank Mucker, with a mind almost hermetically sealed against the admission of larger and more liberal views.

Selchow was a respectable mediocrity, who conscientiously deemed it his duty to his king and his party to resist all attempts to leave the beaten track of routine and red-tapeism.

Mühler, doubled by his wife, the redoubtable Adelheid of anti-nude-in-art fame, was simply objectionable in every respect, without a single redeeming point in or about him.

Bodelschwingh, a *homo novus*, who had taken to the starkest and stiffest antediluvian Prussian Toryism, and Lippe, a scion of the noble house of that name, every member of which deems himself something like an *avatar* of Brahma, were thoroughly impracticable Absolutists, who hung as a dead weight upon every generous effort made by Bismarck to enter, however cautiously, upon the path of progress which he had clearly traced out for himself from the very commencement of his political career.

It was with this set that Baron Bismarck-Schönhausen had to work out his great political problems of the future. It was really something like Pegasus yoked with a thorough-bred racer, a couple of stout carriage-horses, a decent cart-horse, a vile screw, and a couple of unqualified mules.

It is generally, though most erroneously, assumed in this country that the president of the Prussian ministry is also the actual leader of the cabinet, who necessarily imposes his own policy upon his colleagues. This is not so. The president of the Prussian ministry is simply *primus inter pares*, with no preponderance whatever, except, of course, such as the natural ascendant of a powerful mind must always exercise over men of lesser stamp. In fact, the actual position of the Prussian Prime Minister—at the time, at least, when Bismarck took office—might not inaptly be illustrated by a slightly altered adaptation addressed to him by his colleagues of the old formula of the oath sworn by the Aragonese nobles to their king: " Nosotros, que cada uno por si somos tanto como os, y que juntos podemos mas que os, os hacemos nuestro Rey, contanto que guardareis nuestros fueros; si no, no!"—something to the following effect:— "We, each of us, severally your equals in power and attributes, jointly your master, will follow your lead so long as you will be guided by us—but no longer."

It may, under the circumstances, be almost deemed a lucky conjuncture for Bismarck and the ultimate success of his policy, that the fierce contest the ministry had to wage for years against the Progressist majority of the Second Chamber necessarily precluded all premature attempts on his part to introduce reforms into the inner administration of the kingdom. This parliamentary conflict compelled him in a measure to go along hand in hand with his colleagues, whilst it obliged the latter also in a measure to submit to his guidance, as they felt that he was the only chief who could lead them and the crown represented by them to victory in the desperate struggle.

The Progressist majority of the Second Chamber, who had already succeeded in killing two administrations, and in seriously retarding and impeding the progress of the king's darling plan of army reorganization, thought they would find it an easy task to settle the pretensions of the Saxo-Pomeranian Junker, who had presumed to accept office with the deliberate purpose of carrying the army reorganization through, in the teeth of even the most determined and sustained opposition on their part, and although the country had emphatically pronounced against the project.

On the 23rd of September, 1862, Bismarck made his first appearance in the house of representatives in his new capacity as premier. He informed the house briefly that, considering how the adverse vote of the house on the military expenditure for 1862 left no expectation that that for 1863 would meet with a more favourable reception by the house, the proposed budget for 1863 would be withdrawn. On the 11th of October the House of Lords rejected all the amendments made by the Second Chamber in the budget for 1862, and adopted the original government proposal.

As there was no prospect of settling the dispute with the Lower House, the session of the Diet was closed on the 13th of October, with a declaration made by the premier that the government, seeing no chance of an arrangement with the house on the important budget question, found itself compelled to conduct the administration of the state even without having obtained the parliamentary sanction of the budget demanded by the constitution.

This was the first step which showed the Progressist majority of the house that they had no longer to deal with the vacillating and feeble Hohenzollern-Auerswald and Hohenlohe-Heydt administrations.

Bismarck was looked upon by them, and by all the Liberals in the land, as the very incarnation of ultra-royalism and Junkerdom, and was most cordially hated accordingly by all partisans of liberty and progress; and this hatred of him grew the more and more intense, the more clearly it became apparent to his opponents how much they had to dread the energetic will, the vigorous mind, and the powerful intellect of the statesman who had undertaken to see the crown safe through the parliamentary struggle, and who was evidently determined to break down all opposing barriers to the royal will, at least in the army reorganization question.

In his own special department, the Foreign Office, Bismarck found himself placed in a most difficult position.

There were then three principal knotty questions pending, to wit, the Hessian question, the Holstein question, and the great German question.

The first of these three—the Hessian question—had been pending long years before the Confederation, without the remotest chance, apparently, of a satisfactory settlement. The Elector did meanwhile exactly as he listed, and the unhappy states of the electorate had to submit in silence to all the whims and vagaries of their wretched ruler.

Bismarck initiated his foreign policy by an earnest invitation addressed to the Elector of Hesse to grant the just demands of the states; and the Elector and his advisers, who happened to know Bismarck's nature, through their former Frankfort experience of him, deemed it the wiser course to give way at once, and entered without further delay upon the settlement of the long-pending question.

Prussia had just then concluded a treaty of commerce with France, both for herself and for the Customs Union, and Austria had of course at once set about exciting the opposition of the smaller states of the Customs Union against this proceeding on Prussia's part. Austria had also, without consulting Prussia, proposed to the Confederation the creation of a species of representative assembly at Frankfort, consisting of delegates from the several diets in Germany. The success of this project, it was expected, would enable Austria to ride roughshod over Prussia.

Now, Bismarck's first great purpose was, as we have seen from his letter to Schleinitz, to free Prussia completely from the trammels put upon her by her connection and relations with the German Confederation. He was determined to effect a reform in the constitution of the bund which would give to each individual state exactly the amount of influence to which its actual importance might entitle it,—and no more.

The anti-Prussian Austrian intrigues led to a sharp remonstrance on the part of Prussia. With his habitual frankness and directness of purpose, Bismarck invited the Austrian ambassador, Count Károlyi, to discuss the several questions in dispute in confidential conference with him. Several conferences of this nature took place between the two statesmen at Berlin in December, 1862.

Bismarck declared at the outset, that it was absolutely impossible the relations between Austria and Prussia could be permitted to remain on the present unsatisfactory footing. Either they must grow more friendly, he said, or the reverse. It was Prussia's ardent wish, he added, that Austria should elect the former alternative. Austria might choose either to continue her present anti-Prussian policy, leaning upon a coalition of the lesser German kings and princes, or to form a sincere and honest alliance with Prussia.

If she chose the latter, it was of course expected that she would renounce henceforth her anti-Prussian intrigues and agitations at the German courts. It was also indispensable that she should admit Prussia to an equal share in the conduct of the affairs of the German Confederation.

It was on this occasion that Bismarck pointed out to Count Károlyi how much better it would be for Austria were she to transfer her centre of gravity to Pesth, instead of seeking to plant it in the German Confederation, to the exclusion of all legitimate Prussian influence.

Bismarck told the count also, in the plainest terms, that any attempt to stretch the competence of the Confederation by majority resolutions, such as were clearly contemplated in the Austrian project of a representative assembly at Frankfort of delegates from the several diets in Germany, would be held by Prussia to be a breach of the federal compact, and would be treated accordingly. The Prussian premier warned Austria also not to indulge in vain illusions of the certainty of Prussian aid in any war she might deem fit to engage in.

These leading points of Bismarck's confidential conference with Count Károlyi were brought to public notice in the Prussian premier's circular despatch of January 24, 1863.

It will be seen that, from the very commencement, Bismarck placed thus before Austria the alternative of a fair and honourable understanding with Prussia, or a war sooner or later with that power.

The confidential conferences with Count Károlyi had no result. The Austrian emperor and his advisers could not make up their minds to treat with Prussia on a footing of perfect equality. The easy victory of Olmütz had apparently dazzled them to such an extent as to blind them to the actual power and resources of Prussia. All that Bismarck obtained in this first attempt to come to an amicable understanding with Austria was that the delegates project was thrown out at the sitting of the Confederation of the 22nd of January, 1863. The Austrian cabinet, however, though a consenting party at the time to the defeat of the project, reserved for itself the right to renew the proposal at a more fitting time.

It was about this time that the Polish insurrection afforded Bismarck a fine opportunity of giving Russia proof of Prussia's friendly feelings towards that power. This drawing nearer to Russia was Bismarck's reply to Austria's continued anti-Prussian proceedings.

On the 14th of January, 1863, the new session of the Diet was opened. The budget for 1863 was again placed before the house, together with a law supplying a legal foundation to the reorganization of the army effected by the king and his government.

The majority of the house voted an address to the king, in which it was set forth how ministers had grossly violated the constitution in the budget question. In the debates upon this address Bismarck urged the majority, in the common interest of all parties, to consent to an amicable compromise. He said both parties believed themselves to be in the right—the government as well as the majority of the house. If that majority, then, should persist in its unyielding opposition to the government, the final result would be, that the factor who possessed the power would solve the question in his sense. This, which truly was a simple statement of a plain fact, was tortured afterwards into the famous profession of political faith imputed to Bismarck, that might is right.

The parliamentary conflict continued to rage fiercely. It reached its climax on the 22nd of May, 1863, when the hat for the second time played an important part in the modern history of Prussia. In 1848, King Frederick William IV. had been compelled by the victorious people to take off his hat. On the 22nd of May, 1863, Bockum-Dolffs, one of the vice-presidents of the house, who occupied the speaker's chair on that day, put on his hat with a vague view to bring Roon to obedience thereby, who denied the speaker's disciplinary authority over ministers.

The lamentable failure of the attempt led to a second address of the majority of the house to the king. The majority declared in this address, that the house must decline all further co-operation in the policy of the ministers, and must demand a thorough change of persons and of the entire system hitherto pursued by the king and government.

The king's answer to this demand was the closing of the session of the Diet on the 27th of May, 1863, when the discussion on the budget had not yet come to an end.

This proceeding created intense agitation in all liberal circles throughout the land, and curses both loud and deep greeted every mention of Bismarck's name. The royal ordinance on the press of the 1st of June, 1863, was intended to deprive the agitation of the free use of one of its most formidable weapons.

Meanwhile Austria had not been idle. She had, on the contrary, cleverly taken advantage of the internal complications in Prussia to secure for herself absolute preponderance in Germany. Having come to a friendly understanding with the western powers upon the Polish question, the Emperor Francis Joseph invited the princes of Germany to meet him at Frankfort-on-the-Main on the 16th of August, 1863, to discuss a project of reform of the Confederation proposed by Austria.

This project of reform had not been submitted previously to Prussia. The Austrian scheme simply was, to subject Prussia to the sway of the German Confederation, which was merely an instrument in the hands of Austria. Acting under the advice of Bismarck, King William firmly declined to go to Frankfort, and his absence made the meeting of German princes there look very much like the cast of "Hamlet" with the principal character left out. The famous Austrian reform project was, indeed, adopted in the main by the other princes, but it was never after mentioned again.

The relations between Austria and Prussia were becoming more and more difficult every day, when an important political event suddenly altered the face of affairs, for a time at least.

On the 15th of November, 1863, King Frederick VII. of Denmark died. As his successor on the Danish throne, King Christian IX., stubbornly refused to obey the high behests of the mighty German Confederation in the affair of the Duchy of Holstein, the Confederation resolved to occupy the duchy militarily, to enforce obedience to its commands.

Hanover and Saxony were charged with the execution of the decree: Saxon and Hanoverian troops accordingly took possession of Holstein. As King Christian persisted in his recalcitrance, Bismarck, with admirable diplomatic skill, actually succeeded in inducing Austria to join Prussia in a war against Denmark, thus dealing at the same time a heavy blow to the pride of the lesser kings and princes of the German Confederation, who were simply invited after to join in the war if they so listed. They, however, sulkily declined.

On the 1st of February, 1864, the combined Austrian and Prussian forces crossed the Eider. The two great powers having embarked in the war unaided by the Confederation, declared their resolution to exclude that body from all participation in the final settlement, whilst the Confederation, under the leadership principally of Beust, presumed to dictate to both great powers the policy they were to pursue in the duchies, and to claim the fruit of the victory for the Confederation, insisting that the two duchies (Schleswig and Holstein) should be erected into an independent confederate state under the rule of the hereditary Prince Frederick of Augustenburg.

These ludicrous attempts at interference troubled Bismarck very little indeed. He continued to pursue the even tenor of his way both at home and abroad. He had particularly at heart the politico-economical and commercial interests of Prussia and Germany. With wondrous skill he succeeded in 1864, in the teeth of the strongest and most persistent opposition, in concluding a new treaty of union of customs with the states that had belonged to the old union, and in following this up the year after by a new treaty of commerce with Austria.

The Danish war had meanwhile been brought to a successful issue, the peace of Vienna, concluded on the 30th of October, 1864, having handed over the duchies of Schleswig-Holstein and Lauenburg to Austria and Prussia jointly.

The struggle between crown and parliament in Prussia had continued meanwhile with unabated acerbity. Several sessions of the Diet had passed without bringing about a satisfactory arrangement of the burning military and budget question. At every fresh session Bismarck met with the same determined opposition on the part of the Lower House.

The new parliament, which had been opened on November 9, 1863, opposed the government policy in the Danish question, and even refused, January 23, 1864, a war loan of about 2,000,000*l.*, besides rejecting, as usual, the military reorganization law and the military expenditure in the budget. However, the then sheet-anchor of Bismarck's hopes, the Upper House, cheerfully voted all the ministry demanded, and so the session of the Diet was closed with a stinging speech most stingingly delivered by the prime minister, which certainly did not serve to lessen the intense hatred of the Liberals against him.

He, however, continued his work undismayed. He soon found himself again face to face with a new difficulty with Prussia's "faithful" ally, Austria. Bismarck naturally endeavoured to turn the great Danish victory and conquest to the best account for Prussia, more especially in the way of providing that country with a war fleet. Austria, on her part as naturally perhaps, could not see the desirableness of this, and opposed the Prussian plan tooth and nail. She was even mean enough to join the lesser kings and princes of the Confederation in their support of the pretensions of Prince Frederick of Augustenburg, who was then holding his court at Kiel.

Bismarck, with rapid decision, made a move forward to bring the matter to a speedy issue. In a despatch sent on the 22nd of February, 1865, to Baron Werther, the Prussian ambassador to the Austrian court at Vienna, he laid down categorically the conditions on which Prussia would consent to admit the Augustenburg candidature to the projected new Schleswig-Holstein throne. The principal of these conditions was, the closest connection of the new duchy with Prussia. Of course neither Austria nor the similar confederate states could stomach this; so they did their best to encourage Augustenburg in his refusal to submit to the Prussian conditions.

By this time the reorganization of the Prussian army was completed, and the Danish war had afforded the men who had carried it out, in the teeth of every obstacle which the most formidable opposition could possibly raise against its success, a first opportunity of showing how brilliantly it had succeeded. Bismarck had then no longer the least hesitation to enforce his will, even by the strong hand if it must be so. As Augustenburg, in his foolish conceit and futile reliance upon Austrian and German support, persisted in his refusal to consent to the Prussian demands, Bismarck quietly dropped the pretender altogether, and shaped his course of policy towards securing the direct and absolute incorporation of the duchies in the Prussian kingdom.

As early as December, 1864, he succeeded in inducing the Confederation to admit that the peace of Vienna had removed the motive of the occupation of Holstein by German troops, and to order accordingly the withdrawal of the Saxons and Hanoverians from the duchy.

Austria, however, continued to intrigue might and main against Prussia, more particularly at the Augustenburg pretender's little court at Kiel. Bismarck protested sharply and energetically, and for a time matters assumed a most threatening aspect. However, Austria did not see her way clear yet to an open breach with Prussia, and she wanted a little money very badly, so Bismarck succeeded in settling the affair for the nonce amicably by the Convention of Gastein of the 14th of August, 1865, by which Lauenburg was ceded absolutely to Prussia for a certain sum in hard cash, whilst Holstein was left in the exclusive occupation of Austria, and Schleswig in the exclusive occupation of Prussia.

The great services rendered by Bismarck to his king and his country received the king's grateful recognition. The order of the Black Eagle was bestowed upon the premier, and on the 28th of September, 1865, the day of taking possession of Lauenburg, Baron Bismarck was made a count, and appointed at the same time minister of the duchy of Lauenburg.

The new session of the Prussian Diet had opened on the 14th of January, and been closed again on the 17th of June, 1865. It had passed away, like its predecessors, without leading to the least approach of an arrangement of the army question. The commercial policy of the government alone had received its warmest approbation.

The ink had barely dried on the Gastein Convention, when the Austrian government renewed its anti-Prussian intrigues and machinations in the duchies and at the Frankfort Diet with redoubled vigour. The Austrian governor in Holstein, more particularly, acting of course upon the instructions of the Vienna cabinet, favoured more and more openly the pretensions of Prince Frederick of Augustenburg and the most hostile demonstrations of the democratic party against Prussia. He went even so far as to afford his high protection to a great popular meeting held at Altona on the 23rd of January, 1866, which all but proclaimed the Augustenburg pretender Duke of Schleswig-Holstein, and indulged in the grossest insults to Prussia.

This led to a formidable paper war between the two great powers. In his despatch of the 26th of January, 1866, three days after the Altona meeting, Bismarck complained bitterly of the conduct of the imperial government. He accused the Vienna cabinet of wittingly permitting Holstein to be made the centre of the anti-Prussian intrigues and agitations of the South German democrats, and of fomenting the old hatred and ill-feeling against Prussia; and he demanded that the Austrian governor in Holstein should at once be instructed to put an end to the aggressive manifestations of the Augustenburg party, and to the gross insults heaped upon Prussia by the aiders and abettors of the pretender. He hinted, in the plainest terms, that a denial on the part of the Vienna cabinet to do Prussia full justice in the matter would be regarded by the Berlin cabinet as an avowal that Austria wished to drop all friendly co-operation with Prussia.

Instead of disavowing the Austrian governor in Holstein, as Prussia demanded, the Vienna cabinet coolly declared that Prussia had no business to interfere in any way with a "measure of internal administration" in Holstein (note of February 7, 1866). Considering that in the very terms of the Gastein Convention Prussia retained just as much right in both duchies as Austria, this was certainly cool on the part of the Vienna statesmen. Bismarck did not reply to this note.

The Austrian government took this silence for a sign that the Berlin cabinet had given up all hope of obtaining redress by diplomatic means, and began accordingly to initiate measures of warlike preparations. A council of war was held at Vienna, which was attended by the commanders of the several army corps, and a great number of other distinguished Austrian officers, including Benedek, the Archduke Albrecht, Ramming, Clam-Gallas, Festetics, Edelsheim, Legeditsch, and others.

Meanwhile the Austrian governor of Holstein had made another step forward in his anti-Prussian manifestations. Seventeen members of the Holstein nobility had signed an address to the King of Prussia in favour of the annexation of the Elbe duchies to Prussia: the Austrian governor threatened to have them prosecuted for this "most illegal proceeding" on their part, which of course could only tend to envenom the quarrel. Indeed, by the end of March, 1866, there remained very little rational hope of a peaceful solution of the difficulty.

It must be conceded, as a tribute to justice, that Austria was not wholly to blame in the matter. She was placed in a very peculiar position. To her it could not be a matter of indifference that Prussia should acquire a large accession of territory, with all the finest opportunities attached of a considerable naval development, whilst she herself should come empty-handed out of the struggle in which she had taken an important share. It is very true that Bismarck had done his best to devise an equivalent compensation for Austria; he had, in fact, cast his eyes upon the Danubian principalities, which would have answered the purpose excellently well.

Unfortunately, Austria dreaded serious European complications, which might lead to a gigantic war, were she to try to annex Moldavia and Wallachia to her dominions. It may well be questioned now whether she would not have done better after all to trust to the formidable power which she, united with Germany and Prussia, could have opposed to even a hostile European coalition, and to seek and take her compensation for her share in Schleswig-Holstein on the Danube.

There can be no doubt that, with the Danubian principalities in the hands of a first-rate military power like Austria, there would be an end, for a very long time to come at least, of Russia's ambitious dream of the conquest of Turkey in Europe—a consideration certainly of some weight with the western powers. Nay, it may even be taken for granted, that Louis Napoleon at the time would gladly have consented to the incorporation of the Danubian principalities in the Austrian empire, in exchange for the cession of Venice to Italy; and the majority of sensible

Austrian statesmen had even then already arrived at the full conviction that the retention of Venice by Austria had become an object of rather doubtful utility.

The Danubian principalities would have afforded more than ample compensation to Austria both for the loss of Venetia and for her share in the Elbe duchies. England would certainly have offered no opposition to the scheme, and Russia alone would hardly have ventured to face a European coalition, but would have quietly submitted to the inevitable.

But the Vienna cabinet could not be induced to see the matter in this light; so the Danubian compensation project came to naught; and Bismarck, who had prepared everything in the principalities in anticipation of Austria's acceptance, had to fall back upon Prince Charles of Hohenzollern, whom he got subsequently elected Prince of Roumania, by *plébiscite* of the 20th of April, 1866.

As the cession to Austria of the principality of Glatz and some other portions of Silesia, which had been remotely hinted at by the Vienna cabinet, was utterly repudiated by Bismarck and King William, and as the mediatization of some of the middle and lesser states of Germany—the only other feasible project of territorial compensation—seemed to present then peculiar difficulties which Austria would not like to face, there remained only the project of a repetition of the Lauenburg transaction of the year before. This, however, found an insurmountable barrier in the Austrian people, who indignantly declared their disgust with the notion of a great empire trafficking away land and souls for money.

By the end of March, then, it had become clearly apparent to all people with proper discernment in them, that the Gordian knot would have to be cut by the sword, and both powers prepared seriously for the final appeal to the great arbitrament of war.

It was of course of the utmost importance for Prussia to know which of the other German powers would stand by her in the quarrel, and which by Austria. Bismarck was quite aware that the four kings—Saxony, Hanover, Bavaria, and Würtemberg—the two Hesses, and Nassau, would throw their weight into the Austrian scale. Baden, with the friendliest disposition towards Prussia, would be forced by her geographical position to join the Anti-Prussian League. The two Mecklenburgs, Oldenburg, the Anhaltine and the Thuringian duchies, and the Hanse towns and Brunswick, perhaps, might be counted on the Prussian side.

Bismarck wanted certainty on this important point; so he addressed, on the 24th of March, 1866, a circular despatch to the several governments of the German Confederation, asking them bluntly which side they intended to espouse in the event of a war between Austria and Prussia.

The same despatch contained also an intimation that Prussia had resolved to moot the great question of confederative reform. Accordingly, on the 9th of April, the Prussian ambassador to the Frankfort Diet presented to that august body a Prussian proposal to abandon the vain pursuit of an unattainable agreement between the confederate governments, which had always lacked the compensating and impelling force of the national spirit and will, and to substitute instead the co-operation in the great and indispensable work of reform of a general German assembly of men elected *ad hoc* by the German people.

This liberal proposal brought matters nearly to a crisis. A commission was indeed named to examine the proposal, but the representatives of the lesser governments declared the time to be inopportune for the proposed reform. A frank reply to Bismarck's question, which side the other German powers were likely to espouse in the event of a war between Austria and Prussia, was cleverly evaded by referring the Prussian minister to Article 11 of the Federal Pact, prohibiting war between members of the Confederation.

Austria now began to arm in earnest. Vast masses of Austrian troops were collected on the Bohemia-Silesian frontier, and also about Leitmeritz, and all along the Bohemia-Saxon frontier, securing thus for Austria the possession of the south side of the Erzgebirge, a most important strategical position in the event of war between the two powers.

Bismarck had meanwhile been much hampered in all his steps and measures by the rancorous hostility of the Second Chamber of the Prussian Diet. The new session had been opened on the 15th of January, 1866. The majority showed from the very first day of the new session that they were fully determined to thwart the ministry systematically in all its proposed and projected measures. The leaders of the majority felt fully convinced in their own minds that, in the face of the determined opposition of the house, Bismarck would find himself absolutely unable to carry out the programme of his foreign policy, and would thus be ultimately driven from power. This was certainly neither patriotic nor rational; but then parties will but too often sacrifice reason, sense, patriotism, and even common honesty to their party prejudices.

As there was no chance of arriving at an amicable agreement with this systematic opposition, the Prussian ministry, who felt the absolute necessity of freedom of action, closed the session on the 23rd of February, continuing thus to govern without a legally and constitutionally voted budget. The quarrel between the government and the hostile majority of the house was still more envenomed by a decision of the Supreme Tribunal, which made members of parliament responsible and amenable to the law for speeches delivered by them in parliament, in clear and open contravention of Article 84 of the constitution.

But although the exasperation of the men of the parliamentary majority against Bismarck rose now to the highest pitch, a great many Liberals in the country were beginning to reflect seriously upon the wisdom or otherwise of the parliamentary tactics hitherto pursued. They felt compelled to admit that Bismarck had achieved great and patriotic measures. His foreign policy had raised the country out of the hopeless slough of despond and utter prostration into which the incompetence, pusillanimity, and vacillation of former governments had plunged it. His successful commercial policy had raised the land to a high state of material prosperity. His proceedings in the great German reform question were conceived upon the most liberal principles. Altogether the man had not shown himself in his ministerial career the rank absolutist and feudalist he had been believed to be, and there had been many indications of decided anti-clerical and anti-orthodox leanings.

The Danish war and its results had also opened the eyes of many sensible Liberals to the real meaning and purport of the king's army re-organization plan: they began to perceive that, but for this re-organization of the army, so virulently opposed by the Liberal party in parliament, there would have been but scant chance of the Danish successes, and there would be now but little hope of a successful resistance to Austrian arrogance and dictation.

These opinions made their way slowly but surely

in many Liberal circles, and Bismarck and his king began to be looked upon with much less blind prejudice than formerly.

Prussia had not yet taken even the preliminary steps to a mobilisation of her army. She had a right, then, to remonstrate with Austria upon the massing of troops on her frontiers. Bismarck sent a note to this effect to the Vienna cabinet, which replied on the 26th of April by demanding the installation of Prince Frederick of Augustenburg as Duke of Schleswig-Holstein, without offering Prussia the least tangible concession or compensation in return. She ordered, however, the withdrawal of her forces from the Bohemia-Silesian frontier. Under these circumstances Prussia could no longer delay the mobilisation of her army.

Now, although, as just now stated, many Liberals were beginning to have faith in Bismarck and in his policy, yet the vast majority continued hostile, and took every imaginable step to impede the warlike measures and preparations of government. The city of Berlin sent a deputation to the king, to urge the strongest possible protest on their part against a war with Austria. Many other cities and corporations followed the example set them by the capital.

But it was not only with the hostility of the Liberal party that Bismarck had to struggle in his efforts to carry out his truly patriotic policy. He met also with determined opposition in the bosom of his own cabinet; the finance minister, Bodelschwingh, more especially deprecating war with the great Austrian empire.

Queen Elizabeth also worked her hardest against the great minister, whom she had instinctively disliked from the beginning. It was through her and her sister, the Queen of Saxony, that Beust was led to take up an uncompromisingly hostile position against Prussia in the Frankfort Diet, and that Austria was encouraged to refuse to make the least concession to Prussia. Austria was, indeed, misled by the unpatriotic ultra-orthodox and feudalist clique in Berlin to believe in the possibility of a second Olmütz. Bismarck cared little for this multitudinous host of foes; he was prepared for all of them.

In the beginning of May, Austria proposed to refer the question of the duchies to the arbitration of the German Confederation. This cool proposal was firmly declined by Bismarck, who declared that the peace of Vienna had given the duchies absolutely and unconditionally to Austria and Prussia, and that no other German power, singly or jointly, could claim the slightest competence in the matter. If Austria would consent, Prussia was ready and willing to treat with her, but with her alone, honestly and seriously, about the best way of settling the question between them. On the 1st of June, Austria, disregarding Prussia's solemn protest against the proceeding, referred the decision of the affair to the Frankfort Diet.

On the 7th of May, Ferdinand Cohen, a young political enthusiast, who honestly believed Bismarck the greatest foe to freedom, and the most formidable obstacle to the ultimate union of the great Fatherland, made an unsuccessful attempt upon the great minister's life at Berlin. This attempt absolutely served to convert many stanch antagonists of Bismarck into friends and supporters of the minister. These men felt how indispensable Bismarck was to the state and to the nation in these critical times.

Public opinion veered round more than half, and the number of Liberal sympathisers with the man who had been so long the bugbear of the Liberal and Unionist party in Germany, henceforth went on increasing with astonishing rapidity. Indeed, many thoughtful men had, as early as 1863, perceived the real tendency of Bismarck's mind, and had comprehended his true political faith.

A little anecdote anent this subject may be permitted to find a place here. In the year 1864 there was a large society, principally of Roumanians, assembled in one of the leading saloons of Jassy. Prince George Sturdza, one of the Roumanian aristocracy present, was fiercely denouncing Bismarck and his policy, and predicting his downfall before the end of the year, when the Russian Prince Obolenski replied to him very quietly, "I'll lay you 200 ducats that Bismarck will in ten years from this, if he lives, be the most popular man in Germany and the greatest statesman in Europe." The bet was taken and booked. On the 25th of November, 1871, when it wanted still three years to the date of the decision, Prince Obolenski passed through Jassy. He had barely taken up his quarters at the Hôtel Gerbel, when a servant of Prince Sturdza presented himself to him with a purse of 200 ducats, and the following short note:—" Prince, you have won your wager. Bismarck is indeed not only Germany's, but Europe's greatest statesman. Please receive the amount of our wager." Prince Obolenski forwarded the 200 ducats to Bismarck for distribution among necessitous widows and orphans.

On the 9th of May the Prussian Diet was dissolved; the primary elections of the electors were ordered to take place on the 28th of June, the actual election of the members of the new chamber on the 3rd of July.

On the 14th of June, 1866, the German Diet at Frankfort resolved, upon Austria's motion, by the barest majority, constituted, moreover, by an unauthorized vote (that of the Schaumburg-Lippe representative, Victor von Strauss), and in gross violation of all proper forms of proceeding prescribed by the federal pact, to put an army into the field against Prussia. The Prussian ambassador thereupon declared at once that Prussia considered this resolution as a breach of the federal pact, and looked upon the pact as dissolved and at an end *ipso facto*. He added, that the King of Prussia, though thus declaring the federal pact to be at an end, did not mean to include at the same time the national foundations of the federal constitution, but would, on the contrary, firmly adhere to those foundations, and to the unity of the nation, which stood high above all mere perishable forms. He would, accordingly, at once place before the representatives of the several states the outlines of a new project of union. This important document, which bore date the 10th of June, 1866, was simply an amplification of the Prussian proposal of the 9th of April, with this most important modification, however, that it contemplated the formation of a new federal union of the German states, *with the exclusion of Austria.*

The nearer the time was drawing for the final decision of the momentous question of peace or war, the fiercer and the more factious grew the opposition of the great majority of the Liberal party in Prussia to the king's government, and more specifically to the man at the head of it—Bismarck.

But it was not alone the bitter hostility of the Liberals that the Prussian premier had to encounter at this most critical juncture: he found also arrayed against him and his policy the occult influence of the Dowager Queen Elizabeth, supported by a powerful party at court and by a large section of the feudalists and pietists. Nay, in his own cabinet some of his colleagues pronounced openly against a war with

Austria, whilst others gave him only a hesitating, half-hearted, lukewarm support. Bodelschwingh, who held the important portfolio of the finances, went so far in his blind enmity to his chief, and to the policy represented by the latter, as to declare that there was not a thaler in the state treasury to provide for war expenses, though he knew full well at the time that there was a little nest-egg lying there of something like three million pounds sterling immediately available for the purpose, and that the state could freely dispose, moreover, of the large resources that would accrue to it from the sale of the Cologne and Minden Railway line.

The Crown Prince of Prussia also, who, though a born commander in the field, and a second Frederick, has always shrunk from the horrors of war, exerted his influence warmly in favour of the preservation of peace. Moreover, his royal highness, a man strongly imbued with the liberal and progressist spirit of the times, and of much broader and larger views, political, social, and religious, than his father, felt disposed at the time to look upon Bismarck as the champion of obsolete, absolutist, and feudalist ideas. The great minister had not then had time and opportunity given him to reveal to the world his true nature.

A war with the coalesced forces of Austria and Germany seemed also to his royal highness a rash undertaking at the time, and the prince dreaded the result of a miscalculation of chances. So it came to pass that the relations between his royal highness and the premier were somewhat strained.

Now, upon the slender substratum of this slight fact the sensation-mongers raised a stupendous superstructure of violent scenes between Bismarck and the prince in presence of the monarch. It was said the prince had roundly declared that he would never be a party to a war with Austria, and would oppose its outbreak to the utmost extent of his power and ability; and that he had taunted Bismarck with wanting to "ape Richelieu," whereupon the minister, stung to the quick, had advised the king to send his son to the fortress of Spandau to teach him better manners and proper submission to the will of his father and king!—a pretty little story which only lacked the trifling element of truth to make it really interesting, but which at the time was religiously believed for all that. The name even of the Crown Princess, our own Princess Royal, was dragged in, the august lady, it was averred, having been "brutally threatened" by Bismarck.

Even to the present day this fiction is kept alive by certain professional purveyors of news for an eager public. For instance, the Berlin correspondent of a leading London paper, who clearly cannot forgive Bismarck his anti-Ultramontane proceedings, and who some time ago coolly imputed to the chancellor of the German empire such revolting brutality of manner that every one of his colleagues in the cabinet with a spark of self-respect in him had been compelled to resign his office and position in the ministry, took advantage of the funeral of the late Queen Dowager Elizabeth to tell the readers of his paper that "when the Crown Prince passed out of the church, leading the mourners, Prince Bismarck bowed low and gravely, and, *as it appeared to me, not without a degree of irony*"—(whatever that may mean)—"which they who understand the relation of the chancellor to his royal highness and family will easily comprehend." Of course "family" can here only refer to the Crown Princess.

The same veracious chronicler of events informs us also, that "the Crown Prince conducted himself with dignity, as he always does on state occasions," which looks almost like a covert insinuation that on other than state occasions his imperial and royal highness does not invariably conduct himself with becoming dignity. Now, as this sharp-sighted gentleman who can detect "a degree of irony" in a bow, is so deep in the intimacy of these august and high personages as to know all about the private relations of friendship or otherwise existing between them, one would imagine that he should at least be equally well informed on the subject of their public relations. When, then, we find him, in the same letter, talking of the Grand Duke of Baden as "brother-in-law of the emperor," and of "burly King George of Saxony," we may well be excused if we venture to doubt the general accuracy of the information vouchsafed to us.

Being on this theme, it may not be deemed altogether out of place here to call to mind the startling announcement of Bismarck's impending death, which the special correspondent of another London paper wired to his employers from Berlin on the 18th of September, 1866. When the Prussian premier was found, two days after this announcement, to take his part in the triumphal entry of the army into Berlin, looking certainly as stalwart as ever on his magnificent charger, albeit a little pale and fatigued, the same correspondent marvelled much at the almost superhuman power of will which alone could have enabled the "dying man" to be present at the ceremony on horseback, and gave a most graphic description of how poor Bismarck had looked the very image of death on the occasion.

A short time after, when the obstinate minister still persisted in living on, in the very teeth of the "well-informed" correspondent's confident prediction of his imminent death, the special got so angry that he actually deftly managed to look inside Bismarck's head, where he found the veins most dangerously congested. If this were not actually a fact, it would certainly read like a very absurd invention.

The present Berlin correspondent of the same great journal has treated us of late to special and exclusive bulletins of the German emperor's health, in which the aged monarch has been kindly presented with an apoplectic stroke, and with unremitting pains in his feet, which have induced his medical advisers to prescribe absolute solitude—a new discovery, certainly, in therapeutics, as a remedial agent in catarrhal and rheumatic affections. That the official organ of the Prussian government should all the time have ventured to reduce the emperor's illness to a common catarrh which, albeit more than usually severe, was running its usual course, and that it should have sent ministers and generals galore into the emperor's sick-room at the very time when his majesty was kept in perfect solitude by order of his physicians, of course simply shows the bold mendacity of the said official organ.

The Crown Prince has long since learnt to appreciate the great minister at his true value. It may safely be averred that, since the meeting between the two high personages at Miliutin, or Miletin, in Bohemia, on the night of July 1-2, 1866, there has been very little difference of opinion between them. The asserted dissatisfaction of the Crown Prince and Crown Princess with the new ecclesiastical laws, and with the German unionist policy of the emperor and his chancellor, is the merest figment of a Romish fiction. Both the Crown Prince and Crown Princess are sound Protestants; and the future emperor and empress of Germany are as ardent and loyal in the cause of the great United

Fatherland as the Emperor William and his great chancellor themselves can possibly be.

To return to the state of affairs at the end of May and beginning of June, 1866: What with the actual stern opposition to his policy and projects which the Prussian premier had to encounter at this most critical juncture, and what with the hostile shadows the lively imagination of his foes would thus throw across his path, Bismarck's position was by no means enviable at the time; and he had certainly to strain every nerve to overcome first the home foes of his policy before he could think of devoting his energies duly to meet the foreign enemies of his country and king.

But the worst of the matter for the great minister was, that even his royal master seemed at least to hesitate much and vacillate not a little in taking his final supreme decision—so much, indeed, that Queen Elizabeth was actually encouraged thereby to write to her sister Sophia to be of good cheer, as Prussia would certainly not fight, but submit again, as she had done before in 1850.

To account rightly for this apparent hesitation even on the part of the king, and for the dread with which the impending war was contemplated by many even who were not necessarily hostile to Bismarck, the state of affairs at the time must be taken into due consideration. Prussia, it was clear, would, in the event of a war with Austria, find arrayed against her, Bavaria, Würtemberg, Saxony, Hanover, the two Hesses, and Nassau, and most likely Baden also, compelled thereto by its geographical position; whilst the most she might reckon on in the shape of allies on her side was confined to Mecklenburg, Oldenburg, the Hanse towns, the Anhaltine duchies, and the Thuringian duchies and principalities, and perhaps Brunswick. How true this anticipation was could be seen afterwards at the outbreak of the war, when Prussia was for a time left standing alone almost, that is to say, with only Lippe-Detmold and stanch Ernest of Saxe-Coburg-Gotha to support her in the desperate struggle.

It was calculated at the time that her foes could lead into the field against her a million and a half of men! whilst only about half a million of defenders were generously awarded to her. Besides, her strategic position was most critical. The Austrians held the south side of the Erzgebirge, and were threatening the important provinces of Saxony and Silesia with an apparently overwhelming invasion, whilst the hosts of the German Confederation might force themselves as a wedge between the eastern and the western parts of the kingdom. Then Prussia was exposed, moreover, to threatening demonstrations by Russia on her eastern frontier, by France on her south-western frontier, and she must be prepared also for a Dano-Scandinavian attack on the very Elbe duchies which formed the ostensible bone of contention between her and the Kaiser.

The look-out was not cheerful, it must be confessed, for the mere superficial Prussian observer. Italy, it was considered, would prove but an indifferent help in so far as the war in Germany was concerned; and it was held by many true Prussian patriots even that Bismarck was overbold in bidding defiance to the combined powers of Austria and the German Confederation, and in hurrying his king and his country into a worse than doubtful struggle without having duly reckoned the cost and the peril of the hazardous venture.

But Bismarck had closely calculated every chance and contingency in the impending game.

He knew full well that Austria could at the most bring 650,000 men into the field, of which one-third at least must necessarily consist of very indifferent soldiering material, and that from the remaining two-thirds some 30,000 men might safely be struck off, composing the Venetian contingent, who would surely feel tempted, should the occasion offer, to do as the Saxons did at Leipzig—go over to the enemy; that 150,000 men at least would have to be placed in Venetia, with some 20,000 more to guard the Tyrolese passes, &c.; that large bodies of troops would have to be massed in Transylvania and in Galicia, and some other parts that would require to be carefully looked after; that she could at the most dispose of an effective force of some 250,000 men for aggressive warfare against Prussia.

He knew also the material of which the Prussian army was made, and he had the fullest confidence in Roon and in Moltke, and in the officers of Moltke's school. He also knew the Red Prince, and with the clear-sightedness of genius he discerned the great commander in the Crown Prince.

The history of the past was there also to show him that a Wallenstein or an Archduke Charles might fairly be looked upon as a rare exception from a very ordinary rule of mediocre capacity in the general run of Austrian commanders; and that for one Kheven-hüller, Daun, or Laudon, there were always to be found ten generals of the calibre of a Neipperg, Grüne, or Duke Charles of Lorraine; for one Clerfait, Wurmser, Kray, or Melas, ten Beaulieus, Alvinzis, and Maoks; for one Radetzky, ten Giulays.

He knew also that the anti-Prussian states of the German Confederation, although making a most formidable show of military forces—on paper (Bavaria pretended to number some 260,000 men for her own self alone in the enumeration of these forces)—would find it an impossible task almost to put more than some 200,000 to 220,000 effectives into the field against Prussia; and that, though the 40,000 Saxons reckoned in this grand total might find an easy way of joining the Austrian forces in Bohemia, the 30,000 Hanoverians would find it rather difficult to swell the south German host. He knew that the strategical position of south Germany was bad, and that the land lay invitingly open to an invasion. He knew that he had fully secured the benevolent neutrality of Russia, and that Prussia had nothing to dread from France—for a time, at least. As for a Dano-Scandinavian attack, Russia, he was sure, would look to it that nothing of the kind should take place—for some time to come, at all events.

The calculation of chances made by himself and his chief coadjutors—Roon, Moltke, and Prince Frederick Charles—was perfectly accurate. He could from the very outset of the coming campaign oppose an adequate force to the Austrian host, and check by anticipation the intended great wedge movement of the forces of the German Confederation. Provision had also been made to draw the utmost benefit from the alliance with Italy. Moltke had drawn up a plan of campaign for the Italian army, to be submitted to the Italian cabinet by the Prussian ambassador at Florence. That La Marmora, instead of acting upon this plan, would simply send a copy of it to Louis Napoleon—*that* the great Prussian minister could not possibly have foreseen.

Then there was still another important element in the calculation of the chances of success—to wit, the state of the finances in Austria and in Prussia. The latter country was in a flourishing condition in this respect, the former well-nigh in a state of bankruptcy.

All these considerations Bismarck urged upon the king. He was ably supported by Roon, Moltke,

Prince Frederick Charles, Herwarth von Bittenfeld, and other leaders of the army, and the apparent hesitation of the monarch was finally overcome. That this hesitation had been only apparent was proved by the fact, that the preparations for war had from the commencement of the " difficulty " between the two powers been pushed on most vigorously.

Bodelschwingh's almost summary dismissal from the ministry of finance towards the end of May, convinced the other anti-Bismarckians in the cabinet that the king was at one with the minister in the matter of the impending war. They accordingly submitted cheerfully to the law of necessity.

All went on smoothly now. Three armies were formed against Austria and Saxony, commanded respectively by the Crown Prince, Prince Frederick Charles, and General Herwarth von Bittenfeld. General Manteuffel was ordered to hold himself in readiness to march with his division from Schleswig through Holstein into Hanover. Vogel von Falkenstein, who was stationed at Minden, in command of a division of the seventh corps, received orders also to march into Hanover.

This general, unquestionably one of the ablest, if not positively the ablest, of all Prussian commanders, was appointed to the command-in-chief of the forces that would have to act against the hosts of the German Confederation.

General Beyer, another most able chieftain, received

instructions, in the event of a hostile anti-Prussian declaration on the part of the German Confederation, to gather the Prussian garrisons of Mayence and Rastatt, and lead them into the electorate of Hesse.

Now, had everything been done as pre-arranged, there can scarcely be a doubt that, after the German Diet at Frankfort had once thrown down its gauntlet of battle to Prussia, on the 14th of June, 1866, the immediate invasion of Saxony and Hanover on the 15th of June would have prevented the 40,000 Saxons joining Benedek in Bohemia, and the Hanoverians compelling General Flies to fight them one against two at Langensalze, on the 27th of June, to prevent their escape to south Germany. The proof of this lies in the fact that they were compelled the next day to capitulate to Vogel von Falkenstein, notwithstanding their victory over Flies on the day before.

The king and Bismarck remained in Berlin. On the 18th of June the minister drew up the king's proclamation to the Prussian people, which made a powerful impression upon the nation, even upon those who had up to this been most strenuously opposed to the war.

The patriotism and the warlike feelings of the people were aroused; the smouldering fire was fanned into a fierce blaze by a foolish order of the day by Benedek, in which the Austrian commander spoke slightingly of the "Prussian citizen army," who would certainly never dare face his Austrian veterans, grown grey on so many fields of battle, and by a still more stupid address to the inhabitants of Silesia, in which Benedek, counting his chickens long before the eggs were laid, promised the Silesians indulgent treatment by the invading Austrians if they would only abstain from all anti-Austrian demonstrations.

When the news of the first Prussian successes in Bohemia reached Berlin, the ever-fickle people, who so shortly before fiercely denounced Bismarck and his policy, and had all but hooted the king, went mad with enthusiasm, making an idol of the monarch and a still greater idol of the minister. Bismarck used to drive up to the palace in a modest "one-horse shay." When the people of Berlin so suddenly took to adore him, it took all his powers of persuasion to prevent them taking out the horse and drawing him along themselves instead.

On the 30th of June the king left Berlin for Bohemia, attended by Bismarck, Moltke, and others.

As the description of the Bohemian campaign and of the German campaign will come in its proper place in the memoirs of the Crown Prince, Prince Frederick Charles, Herwarth von Bittenfeld, Steinmetz, Vogel von Falkenstein, Voigts-Rhetz, and others, it may be passed over here; nor need we dwell upon the results, which are sufficiently well known.

Benedetti's attempts to claim a share in the spoils of the victory for France were met with such firmness by Bismarck, and France was then, as the great Prussian minister well knew, so very little prepared for war with the formidable "needle-gun power" which had so suddenly burst upon a surprised world, that Louis Napoleon deemed discretion the better part of valour, and abandoned for the time all claim to compensation.

Austria, humbled and exhausted, and seeing the enemy at the gates of Vienna, consented readily enough to Bismarck's conditions of peace; so the preliminaries were settled at Nikolsburg on the 26th of July. General Moltke represented Prussia at the negotiation, and peace was definitively concluded at Prague on the 23rd of August.

Weeks before this, Bismarck had enjoyed the sweet satisfaction of receiving one of his greatest enemies, the Bavarian minister, Von der Pfordten, as a suppliant for tolerable terms of peace, and to win him over completely by the grant of terms generous beyond his most sanguine anticipations. Through Von der Pfordten, Bismarck offered equally favourable terms to Würtemberg and the Grand Duchy of Hesse. There was no question about Baden, as it was patent to all concerned that she had only joined the Anti-Prussian League under the pressure of irresistible compulsion.

Bismarck took care, however, to make a considerable step forward in the direction of the future unification of Germany, by concluding a secret treaty with

Würtemberg on the 13th of August, and with Bavaria and Baden on the 22nd of August, 1866. These treaties gave Prussia the disposal and command of the military force of south Germany, thus preparing and paving the way for the universal German rising against the intended French aggression in 1870.

It was at this period also that Bismarck rendered the greatest service of all to Prussia and to Germany, by annexing to Prussia Hesse-Cassel, Nassau, and the free city of Frankfort, and even overcoming the king's very strong reluctance to consent to the absorption of Hanover in the Prussian dominions. For the first time in her history Prussia formed now a compact mass, with her former strategic weakness turned into actual strength, which was still further increased by the accession of the kingdom of Saxony to the North German Confederation formed by all the German states north of the Main. Bismarck was made Chancellor of the Confederation, retaining also his offices of Prime Minister of Prussia and Prussian Foreign Secretary.

On the 25th of June the primary elections of Electors had taken place throughout Prussia, under the influence of the patriotic feelings aroused by the war. The results foreshadowed a considerable accession to the government party in the house, and a corresponding weakening of the Progressists and Radicals. The final elections, made on the 3rd of July, the great day of Sadowa, under the impression of the victories of

Nachod, Rognitz, Skalitz, Königinhof, Hühnerwasser, Podol, Gitschin, &c., more than fully confirmed these anticipations.

When, on the 5th of August, the first session of the new Diet was opened at Berlin, the government found itself, for the first time for years, no longer face to face with an irreconcilable hostile majority. This was the time selected by Bismarck to step back to constitutional usages, and to show that if he had violated them in former sessions, it had not been done wantonly, but in the true interests of the country alone, which a hostile majority had been unwilling or unable at the time to discern and understand rightly. The great minister made his colleagues and the stiff old king understand that the constitution had been violated by the king's government, and that it behoved that government, in returning now to the constitutional path, to ask the representatives of the people to grant a bill of indemnity for the past.

This was certainly a most signal service rendered by Bismarck to the cause of constitutional liberty in Prussia. It extinguished the lamentable conflict of years, which, as it were, had divided the government and the land into two hostile camps. With any other minister at the head of affairs that conflict might have been perpetuated.

New honours and dignities were showered upon the great statesman. A large dotation was voted by the house, which was divided between Bismarck and his two chief coadjutors, Moltke and Roon. It was much talked of in Berlin at the time how Bismarck, who is too great a man, and of too high aspirations to care for money for the mere sake of money, had long declined accepting his share of the dotation, and had only yielded at last to the king's express commands; his majesty having, moreover, called his attention to the fact that, though he and Moltke might be in a position (pecuniarily) to decline the proffered dotation, the case was different with Roon, who yet would be compelled to decline also if Bismarck persisted in his refusal.

It was related at the time, that when Bismarck's *fidus Achates*, Kendell, urged him to give way to the royal demand, the great minister said, among other things, that he would like posterity to read upon his tombstone, "Here lies Otto von Bismarck-Schönhausen, who lived for his country, and died poor."

After the glorious achievements and the brilliant acquisitions of 1866, the great statesman might well feel firmer and more secure in his seat, and he might well think that he could now venture to assume greater freedom of action in exhibiting the more liberal side of his character. It may, indeed, be said that he aspired henceforth to be a truly constitutional minister. This was no easy task, however, and required caution and wariness.

With the single exception of Von der Heydt, the new Minister of Finance, who had replaced Bodelschwingh (the 2nd of June, 1866), the cabinet over which Bismarck presided consisted of thoroughly reactionary materials—even Roon, with all his genius, being too strongly imbued with the old ultra-Conservative " Junker " spirit to be easily accessible to larger and more liberal views—whilst the king, the most important factor with whom the minister had to deal, albeit an honest, sterling man, was yet a true Hohenzollern, with a very considerable drop of the arbitrary blood of his race in him. He was, moreover, stubborn to a degree. He had grown grey in his antiquated " unlimited monarchy " notions. As Waldeck used to say, Constitutionalism did not suit his temper; and when he would graciously condescend to don the constitutional shoe in lieu of the absolutist boot, it was on condition only that it should never pinch him. His majesty was also much given to periodical fits of " concrete piety," as poor Kalisch used to have it, in which the Grace-of-God and Divine-Mission notion would wax unconquerably strong within him.

The minister knew full well that he should have to meet all these adverse influences in his proposed constitutional campaign. He knew that he would, in the first place, have to fight hard with his colleagues in the cabinet for the success of every liberal measure attempted by him; that he would then, in the second place, have to overcome the reluctance of the king to what his majesty might deem " a dangerous precipitancy of progress;" and that he should then, in the third and last place, have to reckon with his old

Junker friends and supporters, the Gerlachs, the Kleist-Retzows, the Stolbergs, the Senfft-Pilsachs, and other charming petrifactions of the ante-constitutional period. That he actually invited the battle under these thorny circumstances and most unpromising conditions speaks volumes in favour of the view which claims Bismarck as a liberal statesman from the very outset of his career.

His first success in this great venture was, as has already been stated, the acknowledgment by king and cabinet that the conduct of the government in the budget and military expenditure questions had been anti-constitutional, and that this violation of the constitution could properly be purged only by a bill of indemnity granted by the representatives of the people.

From this time forward Bismarck broke gradually away from the trammels of his old party associations. He worked hard and unremittingly to indoctrinate the king with sound constitutional maxims, and to make him, among other things, clearly comprehend and realize this great fact, that he was ruling over a free people in the best sense of the term; and that such a nation, so cheerfully bearing the heavy burden of universal compulsory military service, was not only entitled to representative institutions, but had the most indisputable right also to the fullest local self-government, free from the wretched trammels of feudal privileges claimed and exercised by a comparatively infinitesimally small caste—privileges dating from the worst and darkest days of the Middle Ages. The difficulty of the task which the great minister had set himself in this direction may be measured by the fact, that it took him six years to mould the royal mind to the acceptance of the Communal Self-Government Bill.

Bismarck tried also his hardest to liberalize his colleagues, but with indifferent success only; though Roon, Itzenplitz, Eulenburg, and even Selchow, would mostly, after a tenacious struggle, in the end submit more or less reluctantly to the powerful ascendant of the great man over their minds. Lippe and Mühler remained always obstinately impracticable, and all Bismarck's efforts to rid his cabinet of these two intractable obstructives broke for a long time against the king's stubborn reluctance to part with what his majesty would persist in designating "faithful old servants of the crown."

It was only in December, 1867, that Lippe had to give way at last to the universal indignation and hatred felt against him, and more or less openly proclaimed by all the judges of the land and the whole legal profession; and Mühler managed for some four long years more to thwart Bismarck's strenuous efforts to rid his cabinet pudding of this most noxious ingredient.

To return again to the foreign branch of Bismarck's action, it may not be altogether out of place here to specify the extraordinary compensation claims put forward by France within a week from the ratification of the Nikolsburg preliminaries. Louis Napoleon coolly demanded that the German territory of the Netherlands should be excluded in future from all connection with any of the German powers, and that Prussia should withdraw her troops from the fortress of Luxemburg; that the territories lost by France in 1815 should be restored to her, and that the Bavarian and Hessian possessions on the left bank of the Rhine should be ceded to her. Such were the French pretensions which, as already stated, were so firmly rejected by Bismarck.

The Indemnity Bill was passed on the 3rd of September, 1868, by a majority of 230 to 75. The annexation of Hanover, Electoral Hesse, Nassau, and Frankfort was sanctioned by the Lower House on the 7th of September, by a majority of 273 to 14; by the Upper House almost unanimously on the 10th of September. The petty squabbles with Saxe-Meiningen and Reuss-Greiz, who had in their ineffable conceit declined to join the proposed new North German Confederation, were of course speedily brought to a satisfactory termination.

On the 15th of October the new electoral law for the North German parliament was published. The principal provisions of this new electoral law were— 1, Direct and secret voting; 2, a member to be elected for every 100,000 inhabitants; 3, every free and irreproachable citizen of any of the states belonging to the confederation to be entitled to vote; and, 4, every elector of three years' residence in any of the states of the confederation to be eligible. No one, surely, would venture to contest the liberality of these provisions.

On the 27th of September, 1866, Bismarck concluded an agreement with the Grand Duke of Oldenburg, by virtue of which the House of Gottorp, in consideration of 150,000*l.* cash and a small territorial cession, consented to drop all eventual claims to the duchies of Schleswig and Holstein. The last obstacle to the union of the Elbe duchies with Prussia being thus removed, the decree of incorporation was published on the 24th of December, 1866. About a week before, on the 16th of December, the lower chamber had adopted the budget for 1867— the first budget legally and constitutionally voted since 1862.

In the early part of 1867 Bismarck concluded a military convention with Saxony, by which the supreme command of the Saxon army was vested in the King of Prussia as commander-in-chief of the forces of the confederation.

It was about this time that negotiations began between France and Holland, contemplating the cession of the Grand Duchy of Luxemburg to France.

About the middle of March a discussion took place

in the corps législatif of France upon the policy pursued by the French government in regard to the events of 1866 in Germany. This discussion showing, *inter alia*, that the French were imperfectly and incorrectly informed upon the actual relation between the North German Confederation and the south German states, Bismarck published the secret treaties concluded in August 1866, between Prussia and Bavaria, Würtemberg, and Baden.

The publication of these important state papers had, however, probably also for its object to calm down the eagerness of the French government to obtain the cession of Luxemburg. The discussion on this latter subject, which took place on the 1st of April in the North German parliament, and terminated in a universal expression of opinion that Germany would never permit the severance of a German province from the Fatherland, and the adhesion of the Bavarian deputies to this declaration, both instigated by Bismarck, were clearly meant by the Prussian premier to act in the same sense.

On his subsequent visit to Paris (5–14th of June), Bismarck did everything to make the French government understand that Germany could not and would not permit the execution of the Luxemburg bargain plot. Louis Napoleon persisted, however, in his purpose, and it was only through the intervention of the good offices of England that Europe was indebted at the time for the temporary postponement at least of the threatening danger of war between Germany and France.

In the summer of 1867 Bismarck achieved another great political and commercial triumph, in effecting a thorough reorganization of the Customs Union, embracing all the states of Germany.

In December, 1867, the prime minister's position in the cabinet was materially strengthened by the dismissal of Count Lippe from the ministry of justice, and the appointment instead of Dr. Leonhardt, a Hanoverian, whose views were much more in harmony with Bismarck's than those of his most impracticable and intractable ultra-feudal predecessor could ever have grown, even under the most favourable circumstances.

All through 1868 and 1869 Bismarck steadily continued to pursue his liberalization policy. He fought many a hard battle in the cabinet and with the king, and there were times when he retired to Varzin (an estate of his in Pomerania) in absolute disgust.

This Varzin estate of his is said to have profited vastly by such temporary fits of discouragement. It is even averred that he has nearly doubled its value in the brief space of a few years, by the establishment on it of breweries, distilleries, and manufactories of every kind and description. Whatever degree of truth there may be in this statement, this much is certain, that Bismarck is universally looked upon by his fellow-landowners in Prussia as the most practical and the most successful cultivator of every species of industry connected with the improvement of the soil and the most profitable utilization of its produce.

With this brief allusion to the premier's doings in 1868 and 1869, we may pass on at once to the *annus mirabilis* 1870. Still, it may not be amiss to mention a certain little episode of the autumn of 1868, which gave rise to the first note of the anti-Papist and anti-Ultramontane policy so ardently and earnestly pursued since by the present chancellor of the German empire.

Pius IX., in his almost incredible arrogance, had dared to invite the Protestant clergy of Germany to his pretended Œcumenical Council, just as if Luther and the Reformation had never been. Bismarck, one of the sincerest and stanchest of Protestants, could not brook this. So he insisted with Mühler until that most dubious Mucker-Jesuit was actually driven, much against the grain no doubt, to instruct the supreme consistory of the land to declare this papal presumption an inexcusably gross trespass upon Protestant ground, and to warn all Prussian Protestants, and more especially the clergy, against paying the slightest heed to the insolently presumptuous papal summons.

It is a moot question whether Bismarck ever really instigated Prim's extraordinary choice of a prince of Hohenzollern for the throne of Spain. True, the

Prussian premier had placed another scion of the same family upon the Roumanian throne. However, to this he had been moved by his earnest desire to diminish or postpone, at least for a time, the burning chances of Eastern complications which were then threatening the peace of Europe; whereas the candidature of a Hohenzollern for the throne of Spain could only tend to rouse to the highest pitch the susceptibilities of the French government and the French people, and to invite, as it were, the outbreak of a fierce war; and Bismarck certainly has always proved himself too clear-sighted and far-seeing a statesman not to have been quite alive to this patent fact, and not to have realized to the fullest extent the probable, nay, the almost inevitable consequences of a decided policy of provocation on his part.

There can be very little doubt, indeed, that Prim apprised the Prussian statesman of his intention, but that Bismarck should actually have been Prim's prompter in the matter is more than doubtful. Had Bismarck really been so eager for the fight with France as it is generally believed, it may reasonably be asked, would he have lent himself so willingly to the ready renunciation of Prince Leopold's candidature? It seems certainly not quite justified by the facts of the case to wish to impute to Bismarck that he not only went cheerfully into the war, but that he had actually himself concocted the *casus belli.*

Be this as it may, however, thus much is certain,

that it was only when the French demands grew absolutely insulting to the dignity of the Prussian king and nation, that Bismarck, supported most ably and energetically at this critical juncture by Count Eulenburg, the Prussian home secretary, counselled his royal master to prefer war to humiliation.

A brief narrative of the events and incidents of the Franco-German war of 1870-71 will find its proper place in the memoirs of the German military commanders.

The surprising results of that campaign have lent a certain colouring of reality to the notion that the war was altogether Bismarck's own work, conceived and executed upon a long-premeditated plan. This notion, however, shows only a very shallow knowledge of the real facts of the case. It is hardly ever sound and safe to judge by the event.

Moltke's genius and the decision and rapidity of the German movements in the field disconcerted a great many intended moves on the great political chess-board of Europe. There is excellent reason to believe that Louis Napoleon did not rush quite so madly into war as has been imputed to him. He had, unquestionably, been grossly misled by his agents in the south of Germany as to the true feelings of the people there, the said agents having themselves been deceived in more than one instance by the ill-disguised or undisguised French sympathies of the governing powers in those parts. But there is ample cause to suspect that the French emperor was not altogether unjustified in his hopes of Austrian aid in the struggle against Prussia.

One single severe reverse suffered by the German forces would have brought the Austrians into the field, and revealed most probably also the hollowness of the lip-professions of patriotic German feelings of certain south German rulers; it might have sufficed also to bring the Francophile Piedmontese statesmen of the La Marmora school to the fore in Italy.

In 1866 Bismarck had, indeed, secured the benevolent neutrality of Russia and the expectant neutrality of France before he ventured to take up Austria's gage of battle. In 1870 he could only be sure of Russia's neutrality, and had to contemplate even the not very remote possibility of finding in Italy a foe instead of an ally. It is not a very extraordinary stretch of the imagination, then, to take it that Bismarck, whilst fully prepared of course to accept the war which he well knew France had been bent upon ever since 1866, had certainly no deliberate intention of forcing on the outbreak of hostilities, and that he would gladly have maintained peace had it only been compatible with the dignity of his country.

Bismarck attended the king throughout the campaign. He took a leading part in the famous capitulation negotiations at Donchéry, near Sedan, on the night of the 1st of September, an authentic report of which will be found appended to Moltke's memoir. The great strategist was the other negotiator on the side of Germany; Wimpffen, attended by Generals Faure and Castelnau, representing the defeated French army.

It was here where Bismarck demolished in his habitual honest, ruthless way, and with his customary sledge-hammer logic, the passionate special and specious pleading of Wimpffen for "generous" terms to the French army. It was here where he bluntly asked General Castelnau, who tendered the sword of the French emperor, whether the sword thus tendered was the sword of France, or simply Louis Napoleon's sword, intimating that, in the latter case, it could make no difference in the terms of capitulation offered. It was here also where he poured oil upon the troubled waters, when Wimpffen and Moltke, in a moment of passion, were on the point of breaking off the negotiations, and threatening a renewal of hostilities in the morning.

In the subsequent peace negotiations with both Jules Favre and Thiers, but more especially with the former, Bismarck has been accused of needless harshness, not to say cruelty, to a vanquished foe. This is certainly a most unjust charge to bring against the great German statesman. Bismarck is a practical man, and naturally likes to act as a practical man of business in the serious transactions of life.

When, then, he met a negotiator who counted

tears and sobs among his diplomatic stock in trade, and professed to look upon the notion of a demand of territorial sacrifice from vanquished France as a species of crime of *lèse humanité*, conveniently forgetting how often and how ruthlessly France had exacted such sacrifices from other nations under similar circumstances, he thought it high time to put the matter in a clear light before the French plenipotentiary, who was shutting his eyes wilfully to the true state of affairs.

Compare the plain frankness of Bismarck at Ferrières and Versailles with the insolent brutality of Bonaparte at Campo Formio, where the French "negotiator" frightened poor Cobenzl, certainly every whit as good an Austrian patriot as Jules Favre could justly claim to be a French one, by smashing a costly china vase (which, by the by, was not his own property) on the floor, threatening to serve the Austrian state the same in the event of any further refusal to consent to the conditions of peace irrevocably laid down by himself in the name of the great and glorious French republic; or with the Emperor Napoleon's cruel declaration at Tilsit, in reply to certain humble remonstrances advanced by the Prussian negotiator against the fearful harshness of the conditions of peace proffered by France, "*Le vaincu n'a pas le droit de discuter ; il n'a qu'à subir la loi du vainqueur. La discussion a eu lieu sur le champ de bataille ;*" or with the same urbane emperor's courteous conduct to the unhappy queen Louise of Prussia, who, when she ventured at a great state ball to plead for the retention of the fortress of Magdeburg in Prussian hands, was coarsely told by the polite Corsican that "he had not come there to discuss politics with a woman."

Indeed, the "*væ victis*" had been a stern truth long ages before Brennus added the weight of his heavy sword to the scale against Rome's ransom, and it is likely to remain so to the end of all days. So there would really seem to be very little call to find special fault with Bismarck's rough frankness to Jules Favre and M. Thiers; nor with the conditions of peace exacted by him, considering how Alsace and Lorraine had been filched from Germany by the vilest frauds in the history of nations, and what heavy war contributions had ever been exacted by France from Germany whenever German dissension had permitted the former country to snatch an advantage over the latter.

On the 18th of January, 1871, Bismarck enjoyed the proud satisfaction of witnessing the keystone let into the arch of German unity, which he had so patiently and valiantly striven for years to erect. On that ever-memorable day the princes and free towns of Germany agreed unanimously to revive the glories of the old German empire, and to place the imperial crown on the brow of the noble old head of the house of Hohenzollern.

Six weeks after this, the preliminaries of peace between Germany and France had been duly ratified at Bordeaux and Versailles. Considering the very peculiar relations which have been gradually developing since 1871 between the now Emperor of Germany and His Holiness Pope Pius IX., progressing in friendship from warmth to coldness, and in enmity up to white heat, it may not be altogether deemed out of place here to reprint a letter which the Pope wrote to the Emperor on the 6th of March, 1871, congratulating the Prussian monarch, with the greatest apparent cordiality, upon his majesty's accession to the imperial throne of Germany. This important historical document runs as follows:—

"Pope Pius IX. to the Most Illustrious, Most High, and Most Mighty Emperor, Greeting,—By your majesty's kind letter we have received information of a nature to call forth our congratulations, not only that the highest imperial dignity has been conferred upon your majesty, but that the princes and free towns of Germany have conferred it upon your majesty by unanimous consent. We have therefore with great joy received the communication of this auspicious event, which we trust will, the Lord God graciously aiding your majesty's solicitous endeavours for the universal weal, conduce to the happiness, not alone of Germany, but of all Europe. We tender your majesty, also, our very special thanks for the expression of your friendship for us, and we venture to hope that this will contribute not a little to the protection of the liberty and rights of the Catholic religion. In return, we beg your majesty to believe, that nothing shall be wanting on our part to serve the interests of your majesty whenever occasion may offer. Meanwhile, we pray to the Almighty Dispenser of all good, that He may abundantly bestow all true happiness upon your imperial and royal majesty, and may unite you with us in the bonds of perfect love.

"Given at St. Peter's (Vatican) at Rome, on the 6th of March, 1871, in the 25th year of our pontificate.

(Signed) "Pius P.P. IX."

There is reason to believe that Bismarck was also favoured by his holiness at the same time with a similarly affectionate epistle.

What a marvellous difference between the papal correspondence with the emperor and Bismarck then and now! The emperor had not yet been turned into "Antichrist," nor Bismarck into a "Demon Minister!"

Mindful of how it was chiefly to Bismarck that he owed his elevation to the imperial throne of Germany, the grateful monarch made his minister, some three months after his own accession, a prince of the new empire. But he also bethought him how to bestow upon him a more substantial reward than mere high rank and title, so he addressed himself to the Estates of the Duchy of Lauenburg, where the crown happened to be possessed of considerable domains. He proposed to the Estates that they should hand over to him, in free personal possession, the great Schwarzenbeck domain, in exchange for which grant he offered to cede to the Estates, in free possession, for the benefit of the country and the people, the whole remainder of the crown domains in Lauenburg. Of course, the Estates gladly consented. King William then bestowed the Schwarzenbeck lordship upon Prince Bismarck.

It would appear that Bismarck's views upon the propriety of dotations bestowed upon successful statesmen and generals had changed since 1866. It is not unlikely that political considerations had come to exercise their influence upon the minister in favour of the system. It is certainly not a very violent stretch of the imagination to suppose that the time may come when Germany will really be one, and when her present knights, grand dukes, dukes, and princes will simply constitute her highest aristocracy and her House of Lords; and a prudent statesman may deem it wise to provide in time, by the creation of a new class of peers taken from the military and civil service of the state, an efficient counterpoise to the weight and influence of the bench of mediatised princes, which might otherwise prove overwhelming and endanger liberty and progress.

When his majesty first intimated to Bismarck his gracious intention to raise him to the rank of prince, the minister, like the thoroughly practical man he is, stipulated that the succession to the rank and title should be limited to the eldest surviving son: he did not wish to people the empire with a race of needy princes. So the younger children of the Bismarck family will always remain simple counts and countesses.

The lordship of Schwarzenbeck was valued at the time it was bestowed upon Bismarck at about £230,000. With prudent foresight the prince at once purchased the adjoining estate of Friedrichsruhe, with the well-known Frascati Hotel. When the late proprietor, M. Specht, expressed to the prince his regret that the good Hamburgers would now no longer be able to enjoy the pleasant walks of Friedrichsruhe, Bismarck replied, in that captivating way of which he is such a thorough master, "Why should not the good Hamburgers continue to visit me just the same as they have been so long in the habit of visiting you? Am I not also a citizen of the brave old Hanse town?"

Anent this citizenship, it would indeed be difficult to find any township, in Prussia at least, of any importance, or of no importance, which has not bestowed upon Bismarck the title of "honorary citizen."

In May, 1871, definitive peace between France and

Germany was at last concluded at Frankfort-on-the-Main. The German empire was represented in these final negotiations by Chancellor Bismarck, the French Republic by Jules Favre and Pouyer-Quertier. The latter had to attend more specially to the interests of his country in the important financial part of the arrangement, Jules Favre having very little notion of international monetary matters, whereas Bismarck might well have afforded to give lessons in finance to the great M. Magne himself; for, indeed, nothing seems to come amiss to this extraordinary man, who would appear to shine equally in all branches of the great science of life.

In the negotiations at Versailles, indeed, Bismarck had been advised on financial matters by M. Bleichröder, one of the leading Berlin bankers. Anent this a little anecdote is told, which may well be permitted to find a place here.

When Bismarck first mentioned the sum of five milliards as the war indemnity exacted from France, poor Jules Favre protested that this was an "impossible" sum, which indeed did not exist in the whole world, and could not be counted even. "Why," the learned French advocate exclaimed, "if a man had begun counting at the birth of Christ, he could not up to this time have reached such an incredibly enormous total." Of course, M. Favre is no arithmetician, else he could not have committed such an egregious blunder. However, upon this point

Bismarck did not enter, but, following up Favre's remark, replied quietly, pointing to Bleichröder, "That is the very reason why I have brought a gentleman with me who counts from the Creation" (Bleichröder is a Hebrew).

Bismarck knew the enormous wealth and the immense resources of France, which at that time actually held one-fourth part of all the coin and bullion in the world!

As a curious illustration of the perfect mastery which Bismarck will occasionally show of subjects of a thoroughly technical nature, and altogether out of his own line, we will passingly refer here to a great speech of his, delivered in the German parliament in April, 1871, upon the most suitable site and construction of the building for the Reichsrath, in which the chancellor spoke like an expert architect, dealing not only with the subject at large, in its great outlines of conception and proposed execution, but entering into the minutest matters of detail connected therewith, which made Lasker remark, that the great architect of the German empire was clearly quite qualified also to be the architect of the German parliament-house.

As the proposed edifice could not well be taken in hand incontinently, and as it would take a long time to finish it, the erection of a temporary structure for the meetings of the German parliament was meanwhile resolved upon. This temporary parliament-house was to be erected on the premises of the great porcelain manufactory in the Leipziger Strasse. A mixed commission of members of the Reichstag and officials of the building board was appointed to examine the question of the said temporary erection, and whether it would be practicable to get the house ready against the time of the next meeting of parliament. The president of this commission was Director Weisshaupt, a gentleman made up of equal parts of red-tape and whalebone—a fine specimen, in fact, of the old Prussian bureaucrat. Under his guidance, the commissioners, all but one, decided that the building could not possibly be got ready in time.

The solitary exception was Deputy Römer, the member for Hildesheim. This one dissentient was just protesting against the resolution of the commission, when Bismarck, who evidently had got wind of the matter, entered the room, of course quite accidentally on purpose. The chancellor asked with apparent astonishment what Römer's protest meant. Whereupon Director Weisshaupt pompously informed the prince of the resolution which the commission had just passed, and proceeded to demonstrate the absolute impossibility of getting the projected building ready by the time fixed by the chancellor.

The first Napoleon used to say that the word "impossible" had no business in a French dictionary: Bismarck also objects very strongly to having asserted impossibilities thrown in his way. To the utter dismay, indignation, and horror, then, of the bureaucratic grandees around him, the chancellor dared argue the point with them, and he argued it, too, with such thorough knowledge of the subject that he completely dumbfounded Weisshaupt and his colleagues. He wound up by expressing his surprise that the "great architects" whom he had the honour and pleasure of addressing could possibly talk of impossibilities in the matter of a trumpery temporary structure. However, if they really believed the thing could not be done, or, he added, with a covert sneer, if they had made up their minds not to do it, they need only tell him so, and he would get an architect from London to show them that, and how, the thing could be done. The result of course was a general "caving-in," and the practical impossibility turned out after all a very easily practicable possibility.

Many a lance has Bismarck had to break with this same stiff spirit of routine and red-tape, which had so long been hanging as a dead weight on the otherwise so perfect state machine of Prussia.

The following striking instance of this may be adduced. After the capture of Strasburg there was found in the Strasburg branch of the Bank of France a sum of about £600,000, which Bismarck took to be state property, and accordingly laid hold of it. On the other hand the money was claimed as private property. Pending the decision of the question, Bismarck, wishing to hand over at once to the municipality of Strasburg some funds to be devoted to the commencement of the repair of the damage done by the bombardment of the city, with his usual rapid decision, took upon himself to have the money paid over to him against his own personal receipt, and to place it then in the hands of the German authorities at Strasburg, with instructions to advance the money on mortgage to the proprietors of the ruined or damaged houses for the rebuilding or repair of the same.

Months after, when he thought the matter had long since been settled, he learned, to his astonishment and dismay, that MM. Red Tape and Routine had not yet settled the delicate question of "competence" and "responsibility," and that the money remained still lying idle in the German treasury, awaiting the decision of the knotty question, which of the several governmental departments concerned had the greater claim to hand the money over to the parties for whose benefit it was intended.

Of course, the chancellor at once cut the matter short in his own sharp and decisive way. He telegraphed an order to the German authorities to hand the money over instantly to the municipality of Strasburg, and he left them to settle the question of "competence" afterwards at their own leisure. To the municipality he intrusted the task of using the money to the best advantage, and with all due precautions for the purpose for which he had originally intended it to be used.

Bismarck had taken the conduct of the Frankfort negotiations upon himself that all unnecessary delay might be avoided, and, indeed, the whole affair was concluded in a fortnight.

When the prince arrived at the Schwan Hotel in Frankfort, on the occasion of the peace negotiations, he was in mufti. The head waiter, who, indeed, knew the chancellor, but had never seen him dressed other than in his cuirassier's uniform, did not recognize the great man at first. "We had nearly made a mistake, your highness," he observed to the prince; "we at first did not know your highness, not being dressed in regimentals." "Well, if you had made a mistake," replied Bismarck, with a smile, "it would have been exactly like the French. They also did not know us till we had donned our regimentals."

When Bismarck was the Prussian representative at the old German Diet at Frankfort he was very intimate with Professor Jacob Becker, the well-known Frankfort artist, and with his family. On the occasion of these peace negotiations at Frankfort, the German chancellor had barely arrived in the old imperial city, and had only just got through the first and most arduous part of his heavy task, when he wended his way on foot to the domicile of his old friend, which he entered with a hearty " *Wie geht's, Kinderchen?* " A little trait like this shows the genial character and disposition of the man. There is, to use an expressive vulgarism, no " stuck-upishness " about him.

Another little anecdote in illustration of this may not be deemed out of place. The ancient township of Osterburg numbers among her citizens one Otto Bismarck, master shoemaker and member of the Rifle Association. In the summer of 1871 this good burgher had the skill and good luck of shooting himself into the highly honourable position of "King of the Rifles." Elated by his great success, he sent off the following telegram to Berlin, addressed to his illustrious namesake, the Chancellor of the German Empire:—"To his Highness Prince Otto Bismarck: Rifle-King Otto Bismarck of Osterburg sends his royal greetings, as fellow-countryman and namesake." The chancellor immediately sent the following cordial reply:—"I heartily thank my august namesake, Otto Bismarck of Osterburg, for his kind greeting."

At the banquet given by the Burgomaster of Frankfort in Bismarck's honour, after the conclusion of the peace, the chancellor proposed a toast "to the city" in a simple, hearty speech, winding up with the expression of his fervent hope that "the peace of Frankfort might prove also peace for and with the noble old city." This was received with thunders of applause, and the good Frankforters grew quite enthusiastic in their admiration and love of the man whom, only two short years before, they would have stoned to death had they had him at their mercy.

It is indeed surprising how the "brutal" Bismarck

(as the Berlin correspondent[1] of a great London paper called the chancellor some time since) has endeared himself to the people. The statesman they admire, but their love is all for the "man" Bismarck; and this love finds vent and expression occasionally in the strangest fashions and most extraordinary ways.

Thus, to give a few out of almost innumerable instances—when M. Schwenger, the patriotic Hamburg butcher, sends his majesty a fine 40 lb. sucking pig to grace the imperial table, he stipulates in his letter of consignment that Bismarck is to have a large slice of the roast, "with plenty of crackling, please your majesty, of which his highness is so very fond." All the famous breweries in the land are continually sending the chancellor barrels of beer of triple and quadruple extra strength.

A good citizen of Düsseldorf sends him a jar of table mustard of his own make, which he trusts will prove "as pungent to the palate as his highness's wit, and as genial to the stomach as the prince's good humour." An Oldenburg peasant, having heard that the chancellor has recently had a lot of plovers' eggs presented to him, sends him incontinently the largest and finest ham out of his larder, with a copy of

---

[1] There is reason to believe that the correspondent in question is not an Englishman. It appears, indeed, that he is a native of Prussia, but of French extraction, and that he belongs to a small knot of crotchety politicians, whose goodwill the chancellor is not likely ever to gain—which accounts for the milk in the cocoa-nut.

"home-made" verses in the broad Oldenburg dialect, in praise of a properly garnished breakfast-table set out substantially with those indispensable twin delicacies—ham and plovers' eggs.

The German railway companies join in presenting him with a complete saloon train, and a perpetual right of travelling gratis on all their lines. The learned Rabbis of Breslau claim him as a brother, bestowing upon him the high doctoral dignity of the "Mereine." The proprietor of a large Solingen cutlery house sends him a set of silver-handled razors for every day in the week, with a gold-handled one for Sundays, with hone and sharpening-strap, and oil and paste in small golden-stoppered crystal flasks, the whole in an elegant rosewood case. An enthusiastic Æsculapian apothecary of Magdeburg sends him, in a stand of solid silver, a dozen bottles of the famous "pepsined anti-dyspeptic digestive elixir," which, he calculates, will "last his highness fifty years" (six to eight drops in a thimbleful of cognac to be taken before dinner).[1]

Gifts flow in also from foreign and distant parts. Thus, for instance, the city of Moscow sends three magnificent white horses without a speck on them. The Germans of Milwaukie, United States, send him a pair of most "illigant" wooden shoes lined with the

---

[1] As regards the Solingen and Magdeburg gifts, the writer is not quite sure of the trustworthiness of the authority for the statements here made.

softest leather, and trimmed all round with the same material, and with the initials of the prince tastefully carved thereon. He is affectionately requested by the senders to wear them over his boots when travelling, as he will find them a great protection against cold, and a sovereign preventative to gout and rheumatism in the legs. The expression of a fervent hope is added, that he may live to wear them out, and a dozen other pairs after them!

The Germans of Sandhurst, Victoria, send him a splendid inkstand, with a most flattering address, expressive of the affection and admiration they feel for the great man.

This magnificent gift is made entirely of Australian materials, and is of Australian workmanship throughout. The basement or pedestal is of Australian black wood, covered on the top with a finely-chased plate of Australian silver. There is an inkstand on each side, consisting of an emu egg, covered with a richly-embossed, open-worked silver wreath. A silver emu, in a nest of silver fern leaves, forms the lid of each inkstand.

The centre of the pedestal, between the two inkstands, is occupied by a rock built up of a number of nuggets of gold quartz of the richest kind, taken from the Australian diggings. A silver windlass with bucket, placed on the left, is intended to show the way in which the quartz is raised. In front of the rock several aborigines of Australia are seen in the act of darting spears at some kangaroos. All the figures are made of solid silver. From the central portion of the rock rises a stately tree-fern, the stem or trunk of solid silver, and the leaves of Australian sovereigns. The workmanship of the whole is indeed exquisite, and it would be difficult to match so magnificent a gift. The inkstand is inclosed in a leather case made of kangaroo skin. The address is written on parchment by a German artist in Sandhurst, and it is ornamented with eight small medallion paintings representing the gradual progress of the colonies. And so the list might be extended almost *ad infinitum*.

Being on the subject of gifts of affection to great men, a little anecdote relating to Moltke, in which Bismarck also plays a part, may not here come amiss.

Some evil-disposed wags of Cologne had set a story afloat in the summer 1871, that the corporation of the famous city of the 288 different st—, well, that we may not offend delicate ears, let us say smells,—intended to present the great strategist with a splendid oak butt, magnificently carved and richly gilt, and divided into a multitude of compartments, each provided with a golden tap, to be filled with the contents of seven thousand bottles of Eau de Cologne, the genuine article, of Johann Marie Farina's manufacture. It turned out that the story was not true, and that the only "butt" in the matter was the corporation of Cologne. For the time, however, the story of the

Eau de Cologne presentation passed current. Count Itzenplitz, the then Minister of Commerce, having heard of it, asked Moltke to cede a few dozen flasks to poor Mühler, whereupon Bismarck observed, that if the intention of the gift solicited was to sweeten Mühler in the nostrils of the people, it would not be the slightest use, as seven thousand butts of the article would prove insufficient to accomplish that feat.

Mühler always was Bismarck's great aversion. Some two and a half years ago, Ludolf Parisius published a collection of Mühler's own convivial drinking and drunken songs, under the catch title, *A Prussian Minister of Worship who has missed his Vocation*. This incensed Mühler to a high pitch of fury, and the machinery of the law was soon set in motion to punish the audacious "libeller."

Bismarck, on his return from Gastein in 1871, during the brief stoppage of the train at the Berlin station in Leipzig, was accosted by the well-known newsvendor of that station, who presented to him a select collection of newspapers, magazines, and pamphlets, pleasantly remarking at the same time that their "business relations" dated from eight years back. "At that time your highness and myself," said the newsvendor, "were both beginners in our respective lines. Your highness, who was then passing through Leipzig on your way to Karlsbad, had only just taken to 'governing,' and I had made my first *début* in the news agency line."

The chancellor smiled, and took the papers, &c., offered. The sharp eye of the newsvendor having suddenly detected among the publications tendered to his highness the above-mentioned pamphlet, *A Prussian Minister*, &c., tried to take it away again, as he fancied the chancellor might be offended with the liberty taken with a colleague of his; but Bismarck, who also had just caught sight of the title, waved him off, saying, "No, no, my friend; please leave this with the rest. Railway travelling is tedious work. Let me have a little amusement at all events."

All the way to Berlin he perused Mühler's juvenile sins, and in consequence looked so pleased and beaming on his arrival in the capital, that it was believed for a time that he had succeeded in forming an alliance offensive and defensive with Austria.

In January, 1872, Bismarck succeeded at last in shaking off his "Old Man of the Sea," Mühler, and secured instead in Dr. Falk a colleague after his own heart. Already, in October, 1869, another man of the same congenial stamp had entered the ministry, Camphausen to wit, who had replaced Von der Heydt in the Ministry of Finance.

We shall see by and by how three more members of the old administration were finally got rid of in the course of another year, leaving Eulenburg behind as the only atom of the old leaven—Eulenburg, who would seem, however, to have turned of late remarkably pliant and plastic.

Here the writer craves indulgence for a slight digression, just to bring in an anecdote anent the tendencies of Eulenburg and the late Mr. Mühler, which will serve also as an illustration of the character of the man Bismarck.

Some years ago those Prussian Pharisee twins, Castor Eulenburg and Pollux Mühler, had comfortably settled between them a pretty little scheme of foisting upon the land a legislative act of sanctimonious Sabbath coercion that might in course of time have served, as has unfortunately been the case with us in England, for the thin end of the wedge to be ultimately driven home, even to the point mayhap of the most galling intrusion into the private habits and the purely personal concerns of the citizens of the state. The two concocters of this precious scheme took advantage of Bismarck's temporary absence from Berlin, to earwig the honest old king with their humming and drumming about the sacred duty of rulers to watch paternally over the morals of the people.

When the premier, upon his return to the capital, had the intended act submitted to him, he refused point-blank to have anything to do with it, and bluntly told his majesty that it was not the duty of rulers to thrust their paternal fingers into the pies of private life, but rather to attend to their own morals and habits, setting thereby a good example, as his majesty himself was so eminently doing by his own pure and blameless private life, and leave the people free to take care of theirs. The king was wise enough to see that the minister was right, and so the precious measure was shelved.

With the conclusion of the definitive peace with France in May, 1871, terminated another most important stage of Bismarck's political career. Up to this point he had proved himself to be the boldest as well as the most successful statesman the world had ever yet known. He had achieved many feats that were deemed impossible to accomplish.

Less than ten brief years before, he had been the most hated and the worst detested man in Germany; and he had succeeded in converting that hatred into affection, that detestation into respectful admiration, and he had attained a height of popularity unparalleled in history. He had overthrown the formidable power of the House of Hapsburg, and thrust it out from Germany. He had humbled in the dust the military and political pride and prestige of France.

He had throttled the hydra of the old Germanic Confederation. He had restored the old German empire, and accomplished the apparently impossible task of creating an indissoluble bond of union between the multitribed Germans of the north and the south, the east and the west, of the great Fatherland. He had gradually rid his cabinet—despite the stanchest resistance of King William—of the worst representatives of the rotten old "paternal" system, Bodelschwingh, Lippe, and last, but certainly not least,

Mühler, the Erymanthian boar who, conjointly with another equally horrid bore, Privy-Councillor Stiehle, of "Regulative" fame, had so long wasted the fair field of education in Prussia.

He had, if not actually slain, at least considerably fluttered the Stymphalidan birds of prey of Junkerdom and Saintdom, that would fain batten still as they did of old upon the bodies and the souls of the people. He had succeeded (almost) in knocking the old man out of even such as Eulenburg, and he had actually achieved the semi-liberalization of the great Conservative party in Prussia. He had defeated and upset every intrigue, every machination, every plot devised and hatched against him by the court and Camarilla clique, and the Junkers and the Pietists.

All these and other truly Herculean labours he had successfully accomplished. But another and infinitely more arduous task was now being set before him. He had to undertake to put down the arrogant pretensions of Rome. The task was not grateful to him; he certainly did not seek the struggle, but he boldly accepted it when it was thrust upon him.

He had foreseen from the beginning to what end the new-fangled dogma swere tending, which the most mischievous of all popes, set on and aided and abetted by the most crafty confraternity of cunning priests the world ever yet saw, was promulgating from the Vatican. He had done his best to nip the pernicious Papal Infallibility dogma in the bud.

Unhappily, the sensible section of the Œcumenical Council had proved to be in a lamentably discouraging minority, and the dogma had been promulgated from the Vatican, and the sensible minority of princes and leaders of the Catholic Church—Catholic now no longer, but simply Romish—had unfortunately thought fit to submit them to the decision of the blindly bigoted majority, bereft of all sense and reason.

With the exception of two bishops, Hefele and Strossmayer, they all of them had publicly proclaimed the monstrous infallibility dogma in their several dioceses, and had not scrupled to force the unhappy priests under their jurisdiction to profess a hollow belief in the gross and palpable lie, on pain of excommunication! Some of the German bishops, as Philippus Krementz of Ermeland, for instance, one of the sixty-seven bishops who had put their hands to a most solemn protest against the incredible papal pretensions to infallibility—God's own highest attribute—had set about with all the zest of neophytes to persecute the poor dissentient priests unhappily subject to their spiritual authority, and to coolly dismiss them from employment conferred upon them by the state.

It was high time, indeed, to put a stop to such monstrous arrogance. Rome, and the bishops who chose to go along with her, forced the struggle upon the state. Bismarck simply took up the gage of defiance of the temporal power insolently thrown down by the Romanists. He would have been a traitor to his country, to his king, and to his own old sturdy Protestant faith, had he allowed a set of rebellious Romish priests, mitred or otherwise, to ride roughshod over the laws and institutions of the land.

He accepted the combat after the maturest deliberation; for he was certainly the last man to embark in such a struggle without having minutely inspected and considered every feature of the position, and carefully weighed every chance and contingency, and without having counted the possible cost of the undertaking. Ay, he was well conscious that, just as Hercules had found the cleansing of the Augean stable incomparably his hardest task to achieve, so he himself was now entering upon the most arduous of all his labours—the purging of the Cloaca Maxima of Romish abominations, and he even felt that Hercules had a lighter task of it than himself. The Augean stable had been used by three thousand oxen only for the comparatively limited period of thirty years, whilst the unnumbered legions of Ultramontane black cattle had been at their dirty work for centuries.

He knew full well that in the gigantic struggle in which he was going to pit himself against the wily sons of Loyola and their Ultramontane followers and allies, he would require all his boldness and unflinching bravery; that it would tax all his energy, all his skill, all his astuteness; and that it would, indeed, need all his marvellous good fortune to lead him safely through to a triumphant end.

For it was perfectly clear to him that in this struggle he would find arrayed against him, besides the formidable phalanx of the foe he had to combat more directly and immediately, the fanatic feelings of the hopelessly ignorant and systematically priest-perverted bulk of the Roman Catholics in Germany; the unscrupulous intrigues of the Mucker Jesuits and Saints of the Protestant popedom, which up to a very recent period had arrogated to itself supreme sway over the minds and intellects of the Prussian people; the openly-declared hostility of the Junker party, and of a powerful section of the court and camarilla; the occult influence of the Queen Dowager Elizabeth; the secret sympathies of the Empress Augusta; the tender scruples of Lasker and other leading Liberals; the notorious strong reluctance of the Emperor William to wage war against the Church of Rome in the full sense and to the full extent contemplated by the great minister, and by all and every means even to the bitter end; and last, though, strange to say, not least, under the circumstances, the thinly-veiled and scantily-disguised perhaps, but none the less patent, ill-will of certain English professed *Protestant* journals and their accredited correspondents in the Prussian capital.

Now, it is precisely public opinion in this country that Bismarck has always most ardently wished and most strenuously striven to conciliate. He has declared over and over again, that he looks upon England as the truest and stanchest bulwark of civil and religious liberty, and that he sets the highest store by all and any manifestations of sympathy and encouragement that reach him from here.

The Jesuit Expulsion Law and the School Inspection Bill were the first great blows struck by Bismarck against the Ultramontanes and their adherents. Both these measures excited the unbounded rage of the Romanist faction.

The Romish bishops of Germany, of whom more anon in a special appendix to this memoir, assembled in council at Fulde, addressed a firm remonstrance to the imperial and royal governments of Germany and Prussia, in which the School Inspection Bill and the Jesuit Expulsion Law were set forth as the two chief grievances. No wonder, indeed, for these two measures dealt the heaviest blow and discouragement to the Ultramontane clique in Germany.

In all ages and in all countries the priestly caste has always made the most energetic and, unhappily, also the most successful efforts to secure in their own hands the education of the rising generation, that they might turn it to the perpetual enslavement of the mind of man in the bonds of ignorance and superstition.

Look at unhappy France. There the "Church" has for some twenty years past and more had it all its own way in the matter of education. The Jesuits and their kindred orders have kept a firm hold of the upper and middle classes of society, while the *Frères Ignorantins* and *de la Doctrine Chrétienne* have persistently guided the humble classes in the paths of densest darkness.

The lamentable want of genius or of talent of a conspicuous order shown by the French officers in the late war may justly be attributed, in a great measure at least, to the Bœotising influence of their Jesuit education; for the Holy Fathers of the Order of Loyola had somehow managed, under the empire, to gather the youth of the better classes of society almost exclusively in their own colleges, so that whilst the imperial lyceums and other secular educational institutions could barely number their pupils by tens, the Jesuit colleges numbered them by hundreds. Thus, for instance, the great Jesuit college at Metz, now happily done away with by Bismarck, had of late years never less than six hundred pupils, whilst the Metz Imperial Lyceum could barely secure fifty, with all the aid of its free scholarships.

Prussia, which people here have always been over-much inclined to look upon as the educational paradise of the world, has really and truly for the last thirty years or so, formed no exception to the general, not to say universal, rule of the fatal influence of the "Church"—no matter of what denomination or sect—upon the education of the people.

When Prussia, after Jena, found herself laid even much lower than France after Sedan, the chief of the phalanx of eminent men who then devoted themselves to the regeneration of the fallen nation, the great Stein, in his "Memoir on the Proper Organization of the Supreme State Departments, and the Provincial, Financial, and Police Departments in the Prussian Monarchy—1807," gave it as his deliberate opinion that the "ecclesiastical department, as such, stands in no natural connection whatever with public instruction; it can properly claim only the supervision over the churches and other ecclesiastical institutions.

"Schools belong to its province only in so far as the religious instruction therein is concerned; here it can accordingly never claim a right to direct, but simply to co-operate. As the direction of the elementary and the higher and scientific instruction of the nation is quite different from the supervision over public worship, and as each of the two branches demands and pre-supposes distinct and quite specific acquirements and views, a separation of the two is absolutely necessary. The position of a minister of public instruction requires a man of high scientific attainments, and one fully conversant with the state of science of his period, and familiar with the distinguished leaders and professors in every department of knowledge."

Although the narrow-minded king could not, after the Liberation War, be brought to consent to the carrying out Stein's programme to the full extent, and in the full sense in which the great minister had conceived it, more especially in the main and leading feature of a total separation of the two branches, Church and school, yet the new ministry of public worship, public instruction, and medical affairs, which was formed in 1817, was in a great measure organized upon the hints thrown out by Stein; and the first minister of public worship, &c., Baron Altenstein, who held the office for twenty-three years, till his death in 1840, acted in Stein's spirit as much as circumstances would allow. And it may be conceded that, up to 1840, the school system in Prussia was commendable at least, and might even in course of time have grown out of its imperfections.

It was at this period, unhappily, that Frederick William IV. came to the throne, and with him came the baneful, blighting influence of his wife, Elizabeth of Bavaria, who had been brought up a devout, if not actually a bigoted, Romanist. From the very commencement of her career as queen she exerted her all-powerful influence over the feeble, mediæval mind of her husband in favour of obscuration and retrogression, never once in the interest of enlightenment, progress, and freedom.

She found a fitting instrument to work her mischievous will in the notorious Eichhorn, to whom the ministry of public worship, &c., was intrusted in 1840, and who held the office till the March revolution in 1848, doing incalculable harm to the cause of education in Prussia, which his more liberal successors, Count Schwerin-Putzlar (March to June, 1848) and Jagetzow (June to November, 1848), had not the time allowed them to counteract.

Then came the reaction again; though it must be admitted that Ladenberg, Otto von Raumer, and more particularly Bethmann-Hollweg, tried at least to restore to public instruction a little of the healthy vigour of which it had been despoiled by Eichhorn in the interest of the set of Romish Jesuits and Protestant Pietists and Muckers who, under the inspiration and supreme guidance of the queen, held almost absolute sway over the mind of the king and over his resolutions, despite the strongest efforts of Alexander Humboldt, Bunsen, and other patriots to counteract their pernicious counsels.

It was thus that the most monstrous concessions were made to the Romish Church and hierarchy, and that a separate Catholic section in the ministry of public worship and public instruction was created, —fatal concessions that have led, as might have been foreseen, to the present Gordian entanglement, which there was nothing left for Bismarck but to cut with the trenchant blade of the most stringent coercive measures.

The reign of Frederick William II. is generally held to have been the most fatal to Prussia. Yet truly it was not so. The corpulent, un-Platonic lover of the daughters of Encke, the musician, the Countesses Matuschka and Lichtenau, was certainly not half so moral as the late brother of his present imperial majesty of Germany, nor possessed of one-tenth part of his mental accomplishments; but although his gross misrule prepared, in the largest measure, the way for the catastrophe of 1806, his influence upon the fate and fortunes of the Prussian monarchy was not one-tenth part so mischievous and pernicious as that of his grandson, Frederick William IV.

Even after the accession of the much stronger-minded present ruler, school affairs remained for a full decennium in the same unsatisfactory and dangerous state, owing chiefly to the pernicious action of the successor of Bethmann-Hollweg in the ministry of public worship and public instruction, the notorious Mühler, and his prompters and abettors Stiehle and Krätzig.

Under the baneful sway of this nefarious triumvirate of the densest obscurantists in the land, the schools in Prussia had at last become reduced to the most abject subjection to the arbitrary rule of a wretched set of clerical school inspectors, Protestant and Catholic, who, in the great majority of cases, unblushingly abused their official power and position to degrade education to an engine for crushing all mind, intellect, and independent free thought out of the rising generation. The clericals of both professions of faith were quite agreed in this, and walked their sorry way hand in hand in touching brotherly union. The war between them would of course inevitably have come so soon as their common enemy, instruction and enlightenment, should have been laid low.

Thus, when the Catholic priests in Posen and West Prussia grossly abused their position as school inspectors by banishing even the teaching of German from the schools under their sway, the Protestant priests held their peace with the most perfect equanimity. When, to quote one instance out of an innumerable host, one Schwalm, a Catholic chaplain holding the important office of inspector of schools in Dantzic, impudently dared to stigmatize the appointment made by the magistrate of a Protestant sewing mistress in the Catholic section of a suburban female school as a "monstrous and unheard-of" proceeding, and to cancel the appointment in the most arbitrary manner, without the shadow of a claim to the exercise of his self-arrogated power in the matter, the Protestant Pietists found this proceeding quite right and unobjectionable.

Of course they on their part arrogated to themselves the same right of the most arbitrary and tyrannical interference in the schools of their own profession of faith; and the Minister of Public Instruction himself, the late great Mühler, of drinking and drunken songs' authorship notoriety, whilst carefully abstaining from all interference with these arrogant inspectors of schools, devoted all the energies of his powerful mind to the absolute exclusion of the Jew element from teachership in "Christian schools."

Thus, shortly before his happy downfall, he peremptorily cancelled the appointment of a young Jewish master of mathematics to a corporation school in Westphalia, though the young teacher was thoroughly qualified in other respects, and of pure life and unblemished character. In this instance, however, the young Jew had his revenge: he wrote a public letter to the minister, in which he declared himself quite willing and ready to be received into the Christian community; only, that he might not simply exchange the old error for a new—perhaps worse variety of the same article—he asked Mühler, with childlike faith apparently, to be so condescending as to direct him to the proper selection of the branch or sect of the Christian faith to which he might with a clear conscience apostatize from the religion of his fathers. The minister returned no reply to this application; but the corporation were permitted for once to uphold the appointment made by them.

Now it was this very system of supreme clerical rule over the schools, so fraught with the deepest danger to the cause of education, to which Bismarck had put an end with the most able aid of Dr. Falk, the successor of Mühler in the ministry of public worship and public instruction, a man of large and liberal views, who comes fully up, in most respects at least, to Stein's *beau idéal* of what a competent minister of public instruction in Prussia ought to be.

The means by which this great revolution in the Prussian school system has been accomplished may look extremely simple, being only a bill providing that, whilst clergymen of all confessions shall remain bound to accept the position of school inspector of their district if offered to them by the state, they shall no longer be entitled to claim that position as a privilege *ex officio*, as most unhappily had been the case up to the time when the bill passed, to the grievous injury of, and sad detriment to, the best and truest interests of the state and the people. But, properly worked, this simple means will suffice to destroy the inordinate and dangerous influence of the "Churches" over the schools.

The considerable rise granted by government and parliament in the salaries of schoolmasters of every class and degree, cannot but powerfully contribute to raise the schoolmaster sufficiently high in the consciousness of his own worth and in the estimation of his fellow-citizens, to give him the will and the power to resist any act of tyranny which his self-arrogated clerical superiors may be tempted to exercise against him in future.

The municipalities and communes have also had conceded to them for the future a much more potent voice and determining influence in their own schools than they had for many years been permitted to have and exercise, more particularly during the ten years of Mühler's tenure of office, which saw sadder work done in the case of the densest obscuration than even during the time when the notorious Eichhorn swayed the destinies of the rising generation in Prussia. It was high time, indeed, that the government and the nation should return to the good old sound traditions of the Prussian state in church and school matters.

Who knows but that Bismarck and Falk, thoroughly trusted by the honest old emperor, and with the sympathies of the Crown Prince in favour of their views, may carry their school reform at no distant period, even to the extent of the absolute separation of Church and school?

But this very thing, in which every man of liberal mind in the land rejoiced, naturally filled the minds of the black gentry with dismay and rage, as they clearly saw the education of the rising generation slip away at last from their desperately tenacious grasp.

Hence the episcopal objurgations on the subject of the School Inspection Bill. To account for the episcopal rage anent the Jesuits Expulsion Law, it need simply to be borne in mind that, as the Jesuits are the black janissaries of the Pope, so the Romanist bishops are the violet janissaries of the order of Loyola. It was quite natural then, and should excite no surprise, that the Jesuit Expulsion Law should have been found figuring as the second chief count in the frenzied bill of indictment fulminated by the holy fathers of the Episcopal Council of Fulda against the imperial and royal governments and legislatures of Germany and Prussia.

When Loyola first bethought him of laying the foundation of what was so speedily to develop, under his much abler successors in the generalship of the Jesuits, into the most formidable politico religious order the world has ever known, the chief intent and purpose which he had more immediately in view was to stamp out the reforming movements in the Church of Rome, and to restore thereby the undisputed catholicity or universality of that Church, so grievously assailed and endangered at the time by the progress of that movement.

Those who came after him, more especially the consummate political generals who ruled the order from the first half of the seventeenth to the latter half of the eighteenth century, pursued much wider views and larger aims. They were unswervingly bent upon forcing the Christian world back some four or five centuries, and restoring the power and prestige of the Roman popedom to what it had been in the halcyon days of Gregory VII., Alexander III.,[1] Innocent III., Gregory IX.,[2] and Innocent IV.,[3] when the popes of Rome could proudly lord it over kings, emperors, and nations.

To the attainment of this end, happily impossible even in the seventeenth century, they devoted all their energies and all the vast resources of their deep priestcraft and statecraft; and they brought to bear upon it the whole formidable power of that numerous yet select society of men of higher intelligence and superior acquirements, whom a judiciously-conceived organization, based upon the principle of mute subordination and unquestioning obedience, had compacted as it were into a single body, every part

---

[1] A great man, and one of the very few worthy popes that have done honour to St. Peter's Chair.

[2] Count Hugolin of Signia, nephew of Innocent III. He was eighty years old at the time of his election (1226). Yet for full fifteen years the marvellous old man wielded, with undiminished vigour and preponderating success, the spiritual arm and the temporal arm of the Church of Rome against the second Frederick of the house of Hohenstaufen. He died in 1241, at the age of ninety-five.

[3] Sinibald Fiesco, Count of Lavagna, a Genoese lord. He was one of the most unscrupulous of men, even of popes. He practised through life the principle erected at a later period into an axiomatic maxim by the Jesuits, that the end justifies and sanctifies the means.

and member of which would blindly execute the orders of the supreme chief, in whom alone was vested the absolute command over the whole.

The pursuit of such an aim as this, which must necessarily involve in the end the subjection of the temporal power of kings and princes to the supreme spiritual authority of the Roman pontiff, could not but be attended with frequent collisions with the secular powers that were. So it came naturally to pass in the course of time, that even the most devout rulers of the most Catholic lands in which the Jesuits had at first been received more or less with open arms, were led to look with suspicion and dislike upon the order, whose intrigues and machinations, open and occult, threatened to undermine their legitimate authority, and to force the State into unworthy subjection to the Church.

Thus France was led to adopt stringent measures against the Society of Jesus. The great Pombal expelled the order from Portugal. The kings of Spain and Naples protested energetically at Rome against the subversive action of the Loyolites in their dominions; and at last the Emperor Joseph II. of Austria succeeded in inducing Pope Clement XIV. (Ganganelli) to decree the total abolition of the order by the famous Bull "*Dominus ac redemptor noster*" (23rd of July, 1773, promulgated the 19th of August of the same year).

It looked at the time as if this pestilent society

had received its death-blow; even the pious Maria Theresa, the Emperor Joseph's mother, who still continued supreme ruler in her own states, gave way reluctantly at last to the Pope's representations that she owed obedience to the commands of the Church, and consented to the expulsion of the fathers from her dominions.

But it soon turned out that the snake had not even been scotched. Poor Ganganelli had speedily to pay the penalty of his boldness. The enraged sons of Loyola had him removed by a dose of poison— a warning to all succeeding popes that might do aught to provoke their unscrupulous enmity.

Catherine II. of Russia and Frederick the Great of Prussia opened their states to the proscribed order, who soon found their way back again, however, under changed designations and a variety of spurious and lying pretences, to the lands from which they had been expelled; and when another infallible pope solemnly reinstated the order, it was discovered that it had never for the briefest period of time allowed its existence to be interrupted or suspended.

And so it has come to pass at last that the Society of Jesus is found in most countries of Europe, not excepting even the British Isles, to have obtained in this second half of the nineteenth century a wider and more dangerous influence than ever before; and everywhere it is pursuing the same pernicious aims by the same pernicious means as of yore.

"*Sint ut sunt, aut non sint,*" was the great Jesuit General Ricci's reply to the Pope's urgent prayer that he would allow the needful modification, however slight, of the organization and the avowed objects of the order. These men are unchanged, unchanging, and unchangeable. There can be no doubt but Father Bekx, the present general of the order, would return the same reply as Ricci if a successor of Pius IX. were to urge the same request upon him.

With such men then as these there is no possibility of coming to terms. War once declared against them, it must be carried on with unabating and unrelenting vigour and rigour, by all and every means, to their utter destruction and uprooting from the soil of the land as an organized body, just as the state would rightly crush out of existence any other band leagued against its peace and security.

It was in this light the great chancellor looked upon the matter, and it was in this spirit that the law expelling the order from the German empire had been conceived, and that it has been essential since, despite some weak, isolated attempts at resistance, which have simply tended to show the utter futility of all opposition to the law on the part of the holy fathers expelled, and of their aiders and abettors among the Romish clergy and laity in Germany.

In the Grand Duchy of Hesse, indeed, or rather

in Mayence, Bishop Kettler fancied himself so firmly rooted that even Bismarck could not remove him from his seat; and in this pleasing delusion, fostered by the peculiar circumstances in which the Grand Duchy of Hesse had found itself placed for many years past, he absolutely ventured to afford protection to the exiled Jesuits within the apparently charmed circle of his own diocese.

Certain English writers upon the subject, who would really seem never to be able to look beneath the surface appearance of things, went so far as to proclaim to the world that Kettler's stronghold in Mayence was impregnable. These gentlemen overlooked the important fact that Dalwigk, and his creatures who replaced him after his inevitable downfall, brought about by the late Franco-German war, had finally been kicked out from office and power, and that it had been entirely due to their and their master's most unpatriotic conduct and principles that William Kettler had ever been enabled to arrogate to himself the insolent sway which he had been so long permitted to exercise in a province of Germany which numbers more than two-thirds Protestants to considerably less than one-third Catholics.

Even in Alsace-Lorraine, where the peculiar situation of the country, and the exceptional circumstances and conditions of the case, had seemed to render the unsparing, rigorous execution of the new law extended to the new imperial territory a matter of extreme delicacy, if not actual danger, the thing has been accomplished with comparative ease and quiet.

In Alsace, Bishop Andreas Räs of Strasburg has for a great number of years held ecclesiastic sway over the Catholic portion of the population. He also is a member of the Jesuit body, though he craftily eludes pleading guilty to the soft impeachment. This worthy son of Loyola is not only a notable Jesuit himself, but he is the prime cause also of Jesuitry in the land.

Alsace-Lorraine rejoiced, up to two years ago, in the possession of three very large and most influential Jesuit establishments, of which the two principal ones were located respectively in Strasburg and Metz.

In the latter city there stood, more than twenty years ago, one of the greatest military establishments in France, the old Buanderie Militaire, or Military Laundry, and the vast storehouse of beds and bedding for the French army, which occupied the space of two entire streets. In olden times this extensive range of buildings had been a convent. Louis Napoleon, anxious to secure for himself the support of the clergy in France, ceded this splendid property to the Jesuits for the ridiculously small sum of £16,000. The fathers increased their new estate still further by the purchase of some land and buildings adjoining. Here the famous Jesuit college of Metz flourished for nearly twenty years, up to about two years ago, when Bismarck's measure bade the holy fathers remove to other quarters beyond the frontiers of Alsace-Lorraine.

The seminary in Strasburg was another important establishment of the order. A third was located at Issigheim, if I mistake not. Besides these three chief seats of the Jesuits in Alsace-Lorraine, a great number of larger or lesser so-called missions and stations of the society had been thickly strewn all over the land by the Bishop of Strasburg, whom they enabled to hold despotic sway over the souls and minds of the Catholic population.

All, or at least the immense majority, of these Jesuit establishments were creations, children, as it were, of the bishop, who accordingly bore them the most ardent affection. Judge, then, of the holy man's dismay when he found that the law which ordained the expulsion of his pets from the territory of the German empire had, by dictatorial decree, been extended over the newly re-annexed provinces.

He frantically rushed up to Berlin, where he craved and obtained audience of the Empress Augusta and the late Dowager Queen Elizabeth. His tearful representations made no doubt a deep and painful impression upon the minds of these august ladies, only too much disposed to sympathize with his grievances. But somehow the chancellor was on the watch, and, it is said, made effective use of the old Gregorian injunction, "*Taceat mulier in Ecclesiâ.*"

The bishop was subsequently called to Rome by his supreme chief, Father Bekx. Upon his return to Strasburg, he tried his blandishments and objurgations upon Chief President Möller, the then Imperial Governor-General of Alsace-Lorraine. He passionately pleaded with him to delay for six months the execution of the law. His excellency, one of the most kind-hearted and amiable of men, was weak enough to promise the suppliant bishop a certain respite, and also the widest possible indulgence in the execution of the law. Upon his return to his mansion in the Judengasse, Andreas Räs greeted his anxiously-expectant Jesuit brethren with the exulting shout, "*La victoire est à nous!*" He went about afterwards proudly boasting that his influence had actually paralyzed the chancellor's mighty arm.

A few days after his joy was turned to bitterest grief. Peremptory orders were received from Berlin to carry the law into effect without delay. Then, when he thus found the fox's brush had failed, he tried to don the lion's skin. He drew up a "petition" to the imperial government in bold and bombastic terms, more than verging upon the insolent and insulting, and sent copies of it to all the Catholic vicars, curates, and chaplains in Alsace, enjoining them to obtain the signatures of their parishioners to it.

He now reaped the reward of his twenty years' successful efforts *not* to educate his flocks; the petition showed a lamentably small number of genuine signatures to it; alas! the would-be petitioners were innocent of the noble art of writing. Not that it would have mattered much had every man, woman, and child in the land been able to sign it. When the bishop found all protests and supplications unavailing, he wisely submitted to the inevitable, and advised his brethren in the order to submit to it likewise. So the measure was carried out quietly and effectively.

In a few instances only there was a show of resistance made: thus, at one of the Jesuit stations near Strasburg, the head priest haughtily told the German official who came to signify the order of closing the house and chapel and leaving the country, that the chapel had been intrusted to his spiritual care by Bishop Räs, and that he declined to receive orders from any other authority except the bishop's own. The dull German simply shrugged his shoulders, intimating a hope that the holy fathers would spare him the annoyance of having to employ force for their removal. The head of the station then asked for a fortnight's delay, which was cheerfully granted.

Emboldened by the official's ready acquiescence,

he asked for permission also to continue saying mass in the chapel. This, too, was conceded without hesitation, only the awkward proviso was tacked to the concession, that the ceremony must be performed strictly in private, without the assistance of the usual congregation of the faithful. "For this, sir," exclaimed the irate priest, "we require not your permission." "Why did you ask me for it, then?" was the stolid German's reply.

This part of the chancellor's programme had now been duly accomplished. But it still remained for him to deal with the bishops, who coolly continued to set the law of the land openly at defiance. Here the struggle grew harder and fiercer than ever before. The consideration of this part of the question had, however, better be reserved for the special appendix to this memoir. For proper connection's sake, it may simply be stated here, that in the autumn of 1872 a most desperate effort was made by the wretched coalition of the court and camarilla clique, the priests and the petticoats, and the Junkers and the Pietists, to work upon certain pious scruples of the emperor, to induce him to withhold his sanction from the Catholic Church Affairs Regulation Bill then contemplated by Bismarck and Falk.

With his marvellous astuteness, the great minister, dreading lest his imperial master should be half inclined to hesitate, even after the eleventh hour, in his onward progress towards the final annihilation of Romish pretensions in the German empire ; and rightly judging how formidable the power of the hostile forces arrayed against him might prove in a supreme struggle on a field where he might hope only for a half-hearted support perhaps in the most important quarter, he, with his habitual masterly adroitness, quietly changed the venue, and forced his enemies to accept battle on a very different field, where he knew that the emperor-king would go frankly along with him.

Ever since 1866 the prince-chancellor had been hard at work to indoctrinate his royal master with the sound state maxim, that a nation which cheerfully bears the heavy burden of universal compulsory military service has the most indisputable right also to the fullest local self-government ; and that the feudal privileges claimed and exercised by a comparatively infinitesimally small caste, privileges dating from the darkest and worst days of the middle ages, are just as hurtful to the well-understood interests of the crown as to the general welfare of the nation at large.

Now it takes a long time indeed to teach old King William anything new ; but when the Prussian monarch has once thoroughly mastered a lesson taught him by his great teacher and guide, he may safely be relied upon to go in heart and soul for the new idea he has admitted into his mind.

This maxim proved to be true now ; and the result

was a project of law entitled the Kreisordnung, which was at the time variously designated in this country as the Counties Administration Bill, or the Districts Administration Bill, or the Local Government Bill, but which might have been more appropriately defined as the "Communal Self-government and Feudal Privileges Abolition Bill."

This bill was the most important measure submitted to the Prussian parliament since Prussia has had the grant of an embryo constitution bestowed upon her by the crown. It had been carried by a large majority in the Lower House towards the end of the preceding session. The Upper House had pleaded the near approach of the close of the session, and the ministry had consented to let the bill stand over till the next meeting of parliament in October, 1872.

Now, though the ministry might in a measure have been held committed to submit this bill as soon as practicable to the Upper House, yet it was not absolutely incumbent upon them to do so. They might, had they so listed, have opened the campaign in the Lower House with their Catholic Clergy Coercion Bill; and this would most likely have been done, had not Bismarck thought there were substantial grounds for dreading the fatal influence of the action that had been brought to bear upon the mind of the king during the parliamentary recess. So he craftily elected to open the campaign in the Upper House, where he might succeed in getting his most rabid adversaries of the combined clerical and Junker parties to run their heads hard against his majesty's declared will and pleasure.

For the king, once convinced of the necessity of the Communal Self-government and Feudal Privileges Abolition Bill, had taken the project of law under his own personal protection as it were, and had openly proclaimed his firm determination to see the bill carried, despite all factious opposition of the Upper House. And the Feudalists, with the usual blindness of their class, tumbled beautifully into the pit dug for them by the astute chancellor. They opened the old king's eyes to the true worth of their fulsome protestations of unswerving loyalty to the crown. They almost contemptuously disregarded the royal demands and representations, and, by an overwhelming majority, threw out a measure which their royal master had entreated them to pass. Henceforth, then, the old alliance between the crown and the Upper House might well be looked upon as dissolved.

Certain organs of the English press took the opportunity thus presented to them to criticise the position which King William seemed to have taken up in this matter. Up to that time our journalists had generally delighted in denying the existence in Prussia of anything approaching a constitution. Prussia, in their eyes, and in their double-leaded leaders, was simply an absolute monarchy, draped in the flimsy gauze of a sham constitution. Now they would suddenly turn round and cry, "Haro" upon the king for his "intended violation" of the "Prussian Constitution!"

One Tory organ sneeringly characterized the rejected bill as but a clumsy imitation of the English system, and an attempt to supersede the long-enjoyed privileges of the more opulent peasantry. According to the eminent politician who was thus airing his knowledge of Prussia and Prussian institutions, such a scheme might be successfully recommended to the country in due course of time; but for the time then being the tone of the Cabinet of Berlin was too high and mighty for any nation thinking itself independent to brook. Then followed some ravings about "virtual civil war," and other dreadful things to be apprehended from the threatened action of the crown. A well-known radical paper chimed in with these rabid denunciations, exclaiming about open violation of constitutional rights, extreme course of proroguing a parliamentary session, illegal adjournments of the Diet, and so forth.

These writers committed the fundamental error of confounding the Prussian Upper House with the British House of Peers. They ignored the fact that the Prussian Upper House is a creation, in a measure, of the crown; that there are comparatively few hereditary peers holding seats in it, and that the universities and larger cities and towns are represented in it.

Its re-organization, based upon a very liberal extension of the representative principle, would be perfectly legal, and certainly not one-tenth part so anti-constitutional as the swamping of the hereditary House of Lords would have been in the time of the Reform Bill, if carried out as then threatened.

These writers also strangely shut their eyes to the patent fact, that the Communal Self-government and Feudal Privileges Abolition Bill was the joint work of crown and commons. Now it is a self-understood axiom in all constitutional states, that whenever two out of the three great legislative factors are agreed, the opposition of the third factor can at the most retard but for a session or two the accomplishment of the joint will of the two other factors. Even tough William III. of England had to bow to this constitutional doctrine, and to change his sulky "*Le Roy s'avisera*" to a gracious "*Le Roy le veult.*" And it may surely be presumed that the Prussian Upper House cannot be held a more important and a more mighty factor in the constitutional system of Prussia than King William III. was in that of England at the end of the seventeenth century.

It was in this light that the Prussian people viewed the matter, and the nation at large would have been delighted if the "intended violation of the Prussian Constitution," so sternly and severely denounced by the constitutionalists of the British press, had been actually "perpetrated" by crown and country. But it was not to be so. Bismarck, indeed, counselled a radical reform of the Upper House, and a reform such as would rid him and the land of the coalesced clerical and feudalist opposition to all liberal progress.

Had the minister been able to be personally present in Berlin immediately after the rejection of the Districts Administration Bill by the Upper House, there can hardly be a doubt that he would have exercised his usual ascendant over the mind of Roon, and that the radical reform of that house proposed by him would have been voted by the cabinet. Unfortunately, illness detained him forcibly at Varzin, and his coalesced enemies had thus every opportunity afforded them to turn his absence from the scene of action at this critical juncture to the most effective use in the interest of the clerico-feudalist cause.

As the chancellor could not come to Berlin at the right time, his and the country's deadliest enemies, clerical and feudalist, had the rare chance afforded them of fighting the battle, so to speak, with united forces against the weaker wing of the army on the other side, and in the absence of its dread leader and commander-in-chief.

When Kleitz-Retzow and Senfft-Pilsach, and their tail of petrified mediæval Junkerdom, had, in contemptuous disregard of the king's wishes, and in cool defiance of his anger, thrown out the Districts Administration Bill—so warmly and specially commended to them on his majesty's behalf by Count

Eulenburg—his said majesty was very wroth indeed; and if anyone about his person had chosen at the time to work upon his ruffled feelings, it is by no means unlikely that the world might even have been startled by a decree of abolition of the Prussian Upper House, charmingly simple, without preamble or tag, issued from the king's private cabinet.

The proper course, which would have suggested itself at once to a truly constitutional sovereign, would have been to close the parliamentary session, re-open immediately a new one, pass the bill just rejected by the Upper House once more through the Lower House, and ask the lords again to deal with it; in the event of its rejection, to dissolve the Lower House, and appeal to the country. Then, as the result of this appeal could not be doubtful, crown and commons might, with perfect constitutional propriety, have united in devising effective means of reforming the Upper House altogether.

There is strong reason to believe that this truly constitutional course of action was actually recommended to the king by his great minister; but his majesty declined to act upon the advice, most probably for the very reason that it was sound constitutional counsel. Prince Bismarck then recommended an immediate large increase of the Liberal element in the Upper House—sufficiently large, in fact, not only to insure the passing of the Districts Administration Bill, but to carry the whole series of important measures which he and Falk had devised to break the power of Ultramontanism in Prussia and Germany. It was precisely at this juncture that his personal presence in Berlin would have been of the greatest importance. Yet, in the very teeth of this self-evident fact, we were repeatedly assured at the time by the Berlin correspondent of an influential London daily newspaper, that Prince Bismarck's late asserted illness was naught but sham and illusion; in fact, that the chancellor had never been better in his life than during this prolonged absence from the capital, and that his pretended sickness had simply been an "unworthy comedy!"

The Junkers had meanwhile seen the mistake which they had committed in rejecting the Districts Administration Bill. They began to discern clearly the threatening danger of their annihilation as a powerful political party. So did their clerical allies, who saw also that a radical reform in the organization of the Upper House would take away from them the last chance of resistance to the chancellor's projected coercion laws against their insolent pretensions and arrogant encroachments. They urged the feudalists, therefore, to avert the threatening blow by a timely submission to the king's will in the matter of the Districts Administration Bill. The advice was taken, of course, as the best thing that could be done under the circumstances.

Now certain august ladies had insidiously advised

his majesty not to decide in hot haste upon the steps to be taken, and to endeavour to soothe his ruffled feelings first by the excitement and pleasure of the chase. So the king went a-hunting, surrounded solely by the stanchest representatives of Junkerdom. Counts Stolberg and Münster got the monarch, as it were, absolutely to themselves. They were able to place before his majesty the Junkers' expression of deep regret that they should have offended the king, and their proffered humble submission to his majesty's will in the matter of the Districts Administration Bill. The king was artfully reminded of the days of the conflict, and how loyally the "nobility" had then stood by his majesty against the "arrogant pretensions" of the Lower House to interfere with the monarch's great military reorganization plan. They succeeded with the king—one feels almost tempted to add "of course," considering the Prussian ruler's temper and disposition. So his majesty's anger was appeased, and court and camarilla set to work to make the monarch relinquish the intended radical reform of the Upper House.

Count Roon also, who always had a considerable spice of the Junker in him, was hard beset by his colleagues of the Upper House to save their "time-honoured noble institution" from the "degradation" threatening it at the sacrilegious hands of the levelling chancellor.

Selchow and Itzenplitz, seeing how matters stood,

and how they were likely to go, suddenly took it into their heads to declare that they had themselves objected to the Districts Administration Bill, and that there certainly was no need, in their opinion, of a radical reform of the Upper House.

And so it came to pass that Bismarck's intended great measure, which would have thoroughly cleared the field for a truly liberal policy in Prussia and in the whole of Germany, was dwarfed down into a paltry creation of twenty-five life-peers, all of them, moreover, of a more or less Conservative complexion.

The chancellor of course felt deeply indignant, and he made no secret of his feelings upon his return to Berlin. It mattered little to him that the Districts Administration Bill had been voted at last by the lords, with some immaterial modifications. He clearly saw that his anti-Romish policy would be sure to meet with strenuous opposition in the Upper House, even should the king not explicitly withdraw his sanction from the projected measures, which there was but too much reason to fear, however, he might be prevailed upon to do by the incessant representations and petitionings of the Empress Augusta and the Queen Dowager Elizabeth.

There was one thing the chancellor was determined to insist upon, viz., unity of purpose and action in his own cabinet. His emphatic declaration to this effect led to the tender of Selchow's resignation, Itzenplitz expressing his intention to follow suit. Count Roon, who had really always shown the sincerest friendship and the most deferential esteem for the great chancellor, felt, most likely, secretly annoyed in his own heart that he should have allowed a set of designing men to use his power and influence against his friend and chief for their own somewhat dubious and cloudy purposes.

The count, an old man, by no means in the enjoyment of robust health, had for some time past been feeling the increasing infirmities of old age. It is no secret, that immediately upon the conclusion of peace he had begged the emperor to allow him to withdraw from the cares and labours of office. The emperor, however, who has the best reason to know that Roon is the greatest and most genial military organizer of the present age, would not comply with the request. Still, as the organization of the new German army was then nearly completed, it was thought that General Stichle, an officer of the highest merit, and second only to Roon for talent and power as an organizer, who has for some time past held the position of Director of the General War Department, might easily replace Roon in the War Office.

Such being the position of affairs, Count Roon tendered his resignation anew to the king, and there appeared thus for a time a fair prospect of the elimination of the Conservative element from the Bismarck ministry, and the importation into it of

Liberal blood instead. This would certainly have been the most natural and the most desirable solution.

It is one of the most strongly-marked, and, to speak the honest truth, not one of the least estimable features in the truly upright character of King William, that he will to the last extremity firmly stand by any and every old servant of the crown, even against his own better judgment. So it need not be marvelled at that it should have taken Bismarck so many years to purge his cabinet of the worst obstructives of the set—to wit, Bodelschwingh, Lippe, and Mühler. It may be easily judged, then, how his majesty was affected by the resignation tendered him by Selchow, Itzenplitz, and Roon.

Selchow is a man after King William's own heart. He is just the sort of respectable mediocrity in whose presence the monarch may feel perfectly at ease, in the clear consciousness of his own mental and intellectual superiority; and the history of all ages has demonstrated how highly kings value this qualification in their ministers. How many great statesmen have fallen, simply because the masters whom they served felt oppressed in their presence by the consciousness of their own inferiority to them!

Stein's vast genius was too much for poor Frederick William III. to bear. That king's son and successor, Frederick William IV., would never have men in his cabinet above the intellectual calibre of a Manteuffel or an Eichhorn.

It is one of the most convincing proofs of King William's immense superiority over both his father and his brother, that he has been able to go on so long with two such men as Bismarck and Moltke. This, however, certainly does not preclude his better liking for smaller men. So Selchow's tender of resignation affected his majesty rather unpleasantly than otherwise.

Still this might have been got over—as the event, indeed, has proved in the end. The king might also have spared Itzenplitz from his council. But Roon! the man who had so laboriously, so skilfully, and so patiently forged the exquisitely-tempered weapon with which the king had wrested supremacy in Germany from the grasp of Austria, supremacy in Europe from the grasp of France! No! the thing was not to be thought of. The king refused to accept the count's resignation, leaving Prince Bismarck thus to go on with the old cabinet unchanged as best he might, and thereby completely crippling him in his anti-Popish and anti-Feudalist policy—as the august ladies had foreseen, who had throughout the entire course of these wretched intrigues been the guiding spirits of this unpatriotic plot.

It was at this very juncture, it would appear, that the chancellor received trustworthy information that the highest ladies in the land were at the head of a female association for the protection of the Romish religion, and more especially to enable the Jesuit fraternity to set at defiance the law of expulsion passed against them. He also learnt that one of the queen's chamberlains, Count Schaffgotsch, was reported to have been contributing largely to the Romish agitation fund, established for waging war against the best and truest interests of the land, the nation, and the Crown; also, that the said nobleman had quite recently paid the fine inflicted upon a Polish-Romish agitator for treasonable practices.

The prince made a report to his majesty upon the subject. He did this in his capacity as minister-president of the council, with a view most likely to open the monarch's eyes to the pernicious effects of these vile popish leanings in the highest quarters. In the eyes of King William, domestic quiet would appear to be a blessing that cannot be purchased too dearly. So the petticoats got once more the better of the great minister, his majesty contenting himself with recording on the chancellor's report some vague intention of "looking into the matter at some future time."

It was in his capacity as premier of the Prussian Cabinet that Prince Bismarck experienced this semi-defeat. He clearly foresaw that other, perhaps more striking and bitter, defeats might soon be in store for him, should his duty as premier compel him to place certain other pregnant facts before his majesty, and advise appropriate action thereon.

This was a short time before the latest Papal Allocution, when the Romano-feudalist reaction was in full flow, and when there was reason for the gravest apprehension lest the king should be driven, by the fatal influence of his own wife and of his brother's widow, into a positive withdrawal of his sanction from the projected anti-clerical measures. Nay, there seemed but too much reason then to fear lest the presumably most effective of these intended laws, and therefore also the most objectionable to the Romish crew—the Civil Marriage Act—had been smothered even ere its birth.

Prince Bismarck was holding three distinct offices, to wit, the chancellorship of the German empire, the premiership of the Prussian Cabinet, and the Prussian secretaryship for Foreign Affairs. Each of these three offices entails upon the holder an amount of actual hard work more than sufficient to tax the utmost energies of even a great statesman. Bismarck, the hardest worker of the age, somehow managed to bear the combined burthen of the three without sinking or even flagging under its weight.

The most arduous task which the premiership entailed upon him was certainly the necessity of having to explain and defend his progressist home measures, first in a more than semi-Conservative cabinet, then to convince the king of their absolute necessity, and obtain his sanction to them in the teeth of the formidable opposing influences of court and camarilla, priests, petticoats, Junkers, and Muckers. It is a wonder how even the Titan Bismarck could so long have sustained the incessant fierce struggle which this involved, and the harassing stretch on which it must have kept his mind.

If the prince were an ordinary statesman he would certainly have retired in disgust from a task seemingly growing more and more impracticable the nearer it was being pushed towards the ultimate goal he was striving to attain—the creation of a socially, politically, religiously, and intellectually free constitutional German empire.

But Bismarck is a man of a very different stamp. His burning patriotism can only be extinguished by the cold hand of death. So when he found himself thwarted in the highest quarter in his wisely-devised home policy, he bethought him that there remained much for him to do also in the equally important foreign branch of his gigantic plan, and that he might, if pushed hard for it, safely leave perhaps the realization of his views and aspirations on the inner political and religious field to time and to the *altera spes Germaniæ*, the Crown Prince. So the prince resolved to tender to the king his resignation of the post of premier of Prussia.

We were told at the time by the self-same high authority of the British press who had asserted

Bismarck's unbearable brutality of manner, and poohpoohed the statement of his illness with such charming assumption of exclusive knowledge on the subject, that the prince, with his habitual brutality of course, had rushed into the presence of the emperor, and had endeavoured to frighten his majesty into submission to his own imperious will by threats of resignation, and that his majesty had thereupon coolly and quietly taken the overbearing minister at his word.

A statement of the kind could only demonstrate most convincingly how very little the imaginative gentleman who indulged in it did know of the character of the king and of that of Prince Bismarck; besides that, it argued the deepest and densest ignorance of the relations actually subsisting between King William and his great minister and friend. However, it is barely worth while to refute such pure imaginary sensational statements that bear their refutation in their own patent absurdity.

The real truth of the matter was, that the king was very considerably taken aback and disquieted by the prince's resolution, and that it took all the marvellous powers of persuasion of the latter to reconcile his majesty to the notion.

It would not be going too far even to assert, that had the Papal Allocution, which dropped in immediately after, come in just a little sooner, there would have been no change in the presidency of the council. As it was, the king consented, only most reluctantly, in the end to relieve Prince Bismarck of the over-onerous burthen of the premiership of Prussia.

There can be barely a doubt that the king at first fully believed the change effected to be merely nominal. In one of the illustrated comic papers of Berlin there appeared at the time an excellently-conceived double cartoon of a sledge (stated to be the imperial governmental chariot), with the driver sitting in front in number one, behind in number two; the respective legends stating severally that it might be very pleasant to occupy the driver's seat in front, but that there happened to be the trifling inconvenience of not being able to discern what the party in the sledge might be concocting behind the driver's back; whereas, on the other hand, the driver, though seemingly simply occupying a seat behind, could always keep his company in full view under his eye—and that the guidance remained after all the same, no matter where the charioteer might elect to take his seat.

It was clearly under something like this impression that his majesty consented to relieve Prince Bismarck of the nominal presidency of the council, which would, as the king thought, devolve (nominally) upon the senior minister of state—Count Roon. In this little calculation the king had counted without Count Roon, who is the very last man in the world to accept a merely nominal position.

We have spoken at length of Count Roon in his

memoir. We will therefore content ourselves here with remarking once more, that he is the greatest and most genial organizer, and the most able army administrator of the present age. He is more than this. He is not only field-marshal, but also doctor; and he does equal honour to both the military grade and the academic degree. It would perhaps be going too far to call him a brilliant orator, but everyone must admit, at least, that he is a sharp and skilful debater, and a clear, terse, fluent, and pleasing speaker. He certainly is not a statesman of the very highest order, yet he ranks vastly above the common run of the article as it goes in these degenerate times.

To ask a man of this high stamp, and one so thoroughly conscious of his own merits as Count Roon is, to accept the merely nominal position of head of the ministry without the actual rank and title, was truly a most grievous blunder to commit for such an adept in kingcraft as King William.

It was but natural then, under the circumstances, that the count should decline complying with his majesty's wishes, and maintain the tender of his resignation of the Ministry of War, the burthen of which was really weighing too heavily upon his shoulders.

Here was an awkward dilemma for the king. He wished to retain both Bismarck and Roon, but he did not see how it was to be done, and how the equally just claims of both were to be reconciled and satisfied. The expedient of appointing Roon premier, and bestowing upon the prince-chancellor of the German empire the chancellorship also of the Prussian kingdom, suggested itself no doubt, but this looked at the best but a doubtful expedient. There is reason to believe that the king, finding himself in this embarrassing position, referred the whole matter to Prince Bismarck, asking for his guidance and aid in devising the most suitable course of action under the circumstances.

It would appear that just about this time the chancellor had strongly inculpating proofs placed before him that Count Eulenburg, the Home Secretary, whom he had fondly flattered himself to have brought over to his own liberal ways and convictions, had been mixed up with the wretched anti-national camarilla, popish, and feudalist intrigues of the preceding three months; that he had, in fact, played a false and treacherous game against him.

The writer of this memoir of the great chancellor received at the time a letter from a well-informed Berlin politician, a member of the Reichstag and of the Prussian House of Commons, an extract from which he ventures to subjoin here, as best calculated to show how the case really stood at the time, and what were the opinions entertained upon the subject in Liberal circles in the German capital.

"You are aware how, in the olden days, Eulenburg and Mühler were always named together as the chief pillars of Junkerdom and Muckerdom in the cabinet.

Recently, however, the chancellor had seemingly succeeded in making a semi-Liberal, at least, of Eulenburg. Now it would appear to turn out that the Home Secretary has been trying his hand at a little intrigue of his own against his trusting chief, with an ambitious view—most likely to the premiership. Well, the chancellor has found it out, and there is excellent reason to hope now that the days of the count's ministerial life are numbered. The Paris or Vienna embassy will surely afford greater scope and a more genial sphere for the count's diplomatic *penchant* and talents than the Prussian Home Office.

"At any rate, the chancellor has opened the campaign against his doubtful and slippery colleague in the columns of the *Kölnische Zeitung* in a slashing article inspired by Lothar Bucher, and written, it is averred by some, by Privy Councillor Wagener, whilst others name Professor Aegidi as the author. I have reason to believe the latter to be the real Simon Pure.

"We have got rid at last of Selchow. It has been a hard tussle. At first the king would not hear of it. In the end he has given way, however. Königsmark, the late president of the province of Posen, takes Selchow's place. He is a first-rate administrator, and possesses a thoroughly practical knowledge of agriculture in all its branches. He has made the improvement of land, cattle, and horses his special study. In politics I have reason to believe him a Liberal Conservative, with every disposition to go along with the times. I will venture to assert that he will prove a great acquisition to Bismarck, and I am almost sure that the chancellor was the man who advised the king to call him to his council.

"Our stiff friend Itzenplitz will go next, and, I repeat it, Eulenburg will follow. The chancellor will take care, it is to be hoped, to have these two Junkers replaced by men whose political views shall be more in harmony with his own. Even as matters stand, the chancellor may be considered to command a majority in the cabinet, reckoning General Kamecke as a voter on the other side, which I, for one, am by no means sure about as yet. Königsmark, I repeat, will go along with Bismarck, or I am much mistaken.

"Were there two additional Liberals in the cabinet, Roon would have no choice left but to follow the chancellor's lead, or send in his resignation to the king. This is my view of the matter. I am quite aware it is not shared in by many just now. On the contrary, I am sorry to say a feeling of deep despondency is, so to speak, creeping over the minds of all liberal men in the land.

"I must admit, for my own part, that there seems to be very good reason for this feeling. The king is passing through one of his periodical fits of 'concrete piety,' as poor Kalisch used to have it, in which his majesty will occasionally indulge when the Grace-of-God notion waxes strong within him, and he devoutly believes himself to be a chosen vessel and a special favourite of Providence. This disposition of the royal mind is not favourable, of course, to the growth and development of liberal ideas and tendencies. Roon also has strong pietistic leanings, and Eulenburg is a rank Mucker.

"Our Protestant popedom is also looking up, and taking to persecuting liberal-minded clergymen, which, with us, is always a sign of the triumph of reaction. Eulenburg has been initiating another of his wretched attempts at Sabbath legislation, which he durst not have ventured upon under Bismarck's premiership. All these are very bad signs, I admit. Still my faith in Bismarck remains as firm and absolute as ever. *I do not give Roon three months' hold of office as premier.* Should the reaction prove successful, however—which God forbid!—we may expect the resignation of the chancellor and his Liberal colleagues. King William and his misleaders will then speedily find that times have vastly changed since the days of the conflict, and the nation will soon impose its own sovereign will upon the crown. Heaven grant there may be no need for this; but should the necessity unhappily arise, I, for one, have not the slightest fear of the result."

This extract was published in the *Morning Advertiser* of the 25th of January, 1873. Attention may be invited to the fact that the writer proved singularly correct in his estimate of Roon's chances of the retention of the premiership.

There can hardly be a doubt that the revelation of the Eulenburg intrigue must have powerfully influenced Prince Bismarck in arriving at a decision in the matter referred to him by the king. Bismarck and Roon had worked pretty harmoniously together for ten years, and the Minister of War had always ultimately deferred to the premier's guidance. The chancellor might therefore reasonably hope that he should retain his old ascendency over Roon's mind, and thus continue to be able to carry out his own policy, though the ministry would no longer bear his name.

At this juncture came the Papal Allocution already alluded to, which roused the indignant wrath of the king, giving great offence also to Roon and other stanch Protestant members of the Junker party. Had this allocution been delivered a few weeks sooner, the opposition would certainly not have prevailed against the chancellor.

Taking the circumstances altogether, there would seem to be very good reason for the belief that it was with Prince Bismarck's full sanction, and even in a measure upon his advice, that the king finally appointed Roon minister-president of the council, throwing the grade of field-marshal in by way of make-weight, to prove his singular regard for the great organizer of his hosts. Upon Prince Bismarck the monarch bestowed at the same time the singularly exceptional honour of the knighthood of the highest order of the Royal Hohenzollern House, to wit, the Black Eagle, set in brilliants.

The prince's enemies tried hard to maintain that this most rare distinction was meant by the king as a parting gift to his great minister, and that it might thus be considered to herald his imminent dismissal from the councils of the crown. Of course those who could argue thus knew not the king's character.

The question of the presidency thus settled, there still remained some minor arrangements to be made. Count Roon had to be relieved of the burthen of the War Ministry. This apparently easy task was found beset with considerable difficulties. It seemed quite simple, if not almost a matter of course, to appoint to the vacant office General Stiehle, the actual director of the General War Department, a man of the highest merit, and second only to Roon as an organizer and in administrative talent.

Here, however, an unexpected difficulty presented itself at the very outset. Roon, who would not consent to accept a merely nominal position, objected just as strongly, it would appear, to allow his successor in the War Office that absolute control over his own department which he himself had exercised for some thirteen years. And as General Stiehle is just as stiff-starched in this respect as Roon himself, the negotiation came to naught. General Bose, to whom the office was tendered next, proved as impracticable upon the same point as Stiehle had done.

General Kamecke, one of the youngest generals in the Prussian army, showed himself more accommodating, and was accordingly appointed Minister of War. This General Kamecke is the officer who began the famous attack upon Spicheren on the 6th of August, 1870, which broke up Frossard's corps, and did more to demoralize the French army than even Weissenburg and Wörth. Kamecke is unquestionably one of the best generals in the Prussian service.

Poor Roon had barely had time yet to get firmly fixed in the saddle of his new supreme position in the Prussian cabinet, when Edward Lasker,[1] one of Bismarck's most brilliant and most potent allies in the National Liberal camp, sprung a highly disagreeable surprise upon the ministry. He laid bare a system of deep official corruption which had for some years past unhappily obtained in the Ministry of Commerce—more especially in the matter of railway concessions.

When Lasker made his first move in this ticklish affair with all his habitual skill and caution, a wise president of the Council of Ministers would at once have divined the full scope and bearing of the "mild" attack made upon the Minister of Commerce by the leader of the Liberal majority of the commons, and he would have endeavoured to take the sting out of

[1] A brief memoir of Edward Lasker will be found at page 1 of vol. ii.

the affair by instituting at once an efficient inquiry into the matter, suspending meanwhile the parties most strongly implicated, and inviting Itzenplitz to resign.

Instead of which, Count Roon must wildly rush into an assumption of something like solidarity with his impeached colleague, committing the egregious blunder into the bargain of making an utterly groundless and gratuitous *tu quoque* thrust at Lasker, which that gentleman could afford to treat with contemptuous indifference, and for which the premier had to apologize humbly almost immediately afterwards. Blunders of this kind it is next to impossible to retrieve in Count Roon's position and at his age.

Then the mild attack developed into a most scathing denunciation of the ministerial misdeeds of Itzenplitz, and the matter expanded into the great official corruption scandal. Itzenplitz had to give way, and his majesty had to yield, however reluctantly, to the inexorable logic of facts. Roon had found out that he was really not strong enough for Bismarck's place and Bismarck's work; and the chancellor, who vigorously reassumed on the occasion his full power and action as the virtual chief of the administration, at once enacted a cabinet regulation which, by requiring all grants, concessions for railways, &c., in future to be submitted to the sanction of the whole council of ministers, must necessarily render altogether impracticable all attempts to indulge in corruption.

Itzenplitz was replaced by another Bismarckian minister, Achenbach. Count Roon soon followed the Minister of Commerce in his retirement; and the great chancellor had played and won his return match to the apparently successful move made a few brief months before by the court and camarilla, and the Jesuit, Junker, and Petticoat Coalition, which had then terminated in his retirement from the presidency of the Prussian council, and seemed to threaten to inaugurate a new era of reaction in Germany. In Bismarck's new cabinet Eulenburg was the only minister left of the old set of the year 1862; and so far, it would appear, he has become as pliant and plastic as ever in the hands of his great chief.

The ecclesiastical policy of the chancellor was once more in the fullest ascendant. Falk proposed and carried a series of laws, in May, 1873, exacting from and enforcing upon the Romanist clergy obedience to the laws of the land, and leaving the bishops ultimately to choose between frank submission to the laws of the state and painful severance from their sees and their dearly-beloved loaves and fishes.

The "Civil Marriage Law," which followed, wrested from the grasp of the black crew the most formidable weapon of resistance and obstruction in their armoury; and to conclude this branch of the subject, the subjoined new supplementary and complementary law—passed by the Reichstag at the end of April, 1874, to wit:—" 1. Ecclesiastics or other Church servants dismissed from office by sentence of a tribunal, may be prohibited from residing in certain districts or places, or may be assigned a residence by the police authorities of the state. In case of resistance to such order of the police authorities, or the continued exercise of religious functions by disqualified ecclesiastics, the central authorities of the state shall have power to declare such ecclesiastics deprived of their nationality, and to expel them from federal territory.—*N.B.* An appeal is allowed to a superior tribunal. (Amendment by Reichstag.) 2. The provisions of Clause 1 are also applicable to persons who assume ecclesiastical functions, or have such functions transferred to them, contrary to law, and to those who have been legally condemned to punishment. The police authorities may prohibit or assign to the accused residence in certain districts or places after the commencement of a judicial inquiry and until the termination of legal proceedings. " 3. Persons who, according to the provisions of this law, have been deprived of their nationality in one federal state, lose that nationality in every other, and cannot be naturalized in any other federal state without the sanction of the Federal Council "—will speedily take away from renitent and recalcitrant bishops and other ecclesiastics the power of continuing to set the state and its laws and decrees at defiance, after having been duly and legally deprived of their offices and functions by sentence of a properly-constituted tribunal.

In the early part of the present year (1874) Bismarck was struck down by a painful and wearying malady, from which he has now happily recovered. His illness happened at a most inopportune time. The Army Organization Bill had to be submitted to the Reichstag. The emperor-king and his military advisers were of opinion that, in the peculiar position in which Germany was placed, threatened by a possible coalition of three military powers against her, it would not be wise to leave the efficiency of her army to the very precarious chances of budgets voted from time to time, and that the only prudent course to pursue would be to have the "effective" fixed once for all—in downright defiance, of course, of the sound constitutional maxim, that the representatives of the people should always have and hold the control of the purse-strings over the government.

Had Bismarck been able to plead the cause of the government personally before the Reichstag, he would most likely have carried his point; but in his compulsory absence, an important section of the National Liberals, with Lasker at their head, expressed a strong dislike to grant the government such a very extensive vote of confidence as that implied in the Army Bill.

The clericals and feudalists were at once on the *qui vive:* they scented another conflict between parliament and crown, like that which had been so happily settled in 1866. They tried to get round the king. They talked largely of Roon for vice-chancellor and representative chief of a new anti-parliamentary government. Even the ominous and ill-omened name of Manteuffel cropped up. Happily the great chancellor recovered in time, sufficiently, at least, to nip all such pretty schemes in the bud. He suggested a sensible compromise, which was cheerfully accepted by the crown and the Reichstag, and he is now once more to the fore as vigorous and as powerful as ever.

The ecclesiastical laws of May, 1873, have meanwhile removed Ledochowski from the archiepiscopal seat of Gnesen and Posen: the same fate threatens speedily to overtake the great Paulus Melchers of Cologne, who is already in prison, Dr. Förster of Breslau, Dr. Eberhard of Treves, Dr. Martin of Paderborn, and other high dignitaries of the Romish Church in Germany, if they do not repent them in time of the error of their ways, and frankly acknowledge the supreme authority of the state over all subjects alike, irrespective of creed.

Another law will speedily provide for the filling up of vacant episcopal sees and Catholic Church offices.

Early in this year, as we have said, Prince Bismarck suffered most severely from a fierce and protracted attack of his old enemy—neuralgia in the lower extremities, which prostrated him for months, and necessitated an almost absolute cessation from work. Towards the end of May he left Berlin for his Varzin seat, to recover health and strength in the retirement and quiet of country life.

By the advice of his physicians he went afterwards, in July, to Kissingen, for the completion of his cure. There a vile assassin—a wretched, ignorant, fanatical, Romish-Catholic journeyman cooper, named Kullmann—made an infamous attempt upon the great man's life—*ad majorem Dei gloriam.*

But the Almighty would have none of such "glory." The instigators of the crime—the intellectual authors of it, as the Germans have it—had badly chosen their instrument. The would-be assassin was no Clément, no Ravaillac. He was only a bungler at his murder-trade. The vile attempt failed—the bullet intended for the heart simply grazing the chancellor's wrist.

God willed it not that His own chosen instrument should be removed from this sphere in which there remains still much for him to do.

The joy of the German people over the chancellor's fortunate escape exceeded even, if possible, the fierce, deep indignation felt in every part of the great fatherland at the monstrous attempt, and thousands upon thousands of congratulatory addresses came pouring in upon the beloved man from all quarters.

The chancellor has now (August) left Kissingen, re-invigorated for the arduous struggle which awaits him again in October, and for which the attempt and its failure have placed new and formidable weapons in his hands. Mayhap it will soon become evident and manifest to the world that Kullmann's bullet, which only grazed Bismarck's wrist, has struck to the heart the Romish Church in Germany.

For the clearer comprehension of the great Church question in Germany, a few brief remarks upon the Romish episcopate and the Old Catholic movement in Germany are added in a special appendix to this memoir. A few personal and family notices of Prince Bismarck, and we have done.

The physical conformation of the great minister is in rare harmony with his moral, mental, and intellectual organization. His frame is powerful and well-knit, his figure tall and commanding, his chest broad, his head massive, his face compact, with the unmistakable stamp of the man's mighty mind imprinted upon it.

Bismarck married, on the 28th of July, 1847, Johanna von Puttkammer, by whom he has issue two sons and one daughter.

The daughter, Countess Marie Elizabeth Jane, was born at Schönhausen on the 21st of August, 1848.

Count Herbert (Nicholas Henry Ferdinand) was

born at Berlin on the 28th of December, 1849. He is a lieutenant in the 1st Regiment of Dragoon Guards.

Count William Otho Albert was born at Frankfort-on-the-Main, on the 1st of August, 1852. He is a lieutenant attached to the 1st Regiment of Dragoon Guards.

The prince is proprietor of the lordships of Schwarzenbeck and Friedrichsruhe, in the Duchy of Lauenburg; Schönhausen, in the Province of Saxony; and Varzin, Wusson, Puddiger, Misdon, Selitz, Chomitz, Nakel, and Rheinfeld, in Pomerania. He is thus one of the largest landed proprietors in the German empire.

In the army he has attained the rank of lieutenant-general (*à la suite* of the Magdeburg Cuirassier Regiment No. 7). He is chief also of the 1st Magdeburg Landwehr Regiment No. 26. He is of course a member of the Prussian House of Lords. As regards orders, collars, medals, and ribbons—why, he has enough of these articles to cover himself all over with them if he felt so disposed.

This brief memoir of the great minister may most fitly be concluded with an anecdote in illustration of one of the chief guiding principles of his life.

Count Enzenberg, late Hessian minister, now ambassador of the German empire to the republic of Mexico, is a most passionate autograph hunter, who has succeeded in collecting one of the most copious and interesting autograph albums in the world. About two years ago, when this gentleman left for his ambassadorial post in Mexico, he had to present himself to the prince-chancellor of the German empire. He eagerly seized this opportunity to hand his autograph album to Bismarck, expecting, of course, a new and important contribution to its contents. The prince, however, simply glanced at the album, then handed it back to its grievously disappointed owner, who bitterly bewailed his ill-luck to privy councillor Lothar Bucher, Bismarck's right-hand man. Bucher, who, by the by, was once upon a time a political refugee in London, on account of his subversive tendencies, took compassion upon the poor man, and promised him to place the album once more before the chancellor with a view to obtaining the great man's autograph.

A few days after the album was duly returned to the delighted owner with Bismarck's autograph added. The chancellor had written it on the same page which bore already two inscriptions—one by Guizot and one by Thiers. Guizot's lines were as follows:—"*Dans ma longue vie j'ai appris deux sagesses: l'une est de beaucoup pardonner, et l'autre de ne jamais oublier.*" (In my long life I have learnt two maxims of wisdom: one is to forgive much, and the other never to forget). Beneath this Thiers had written:—"*Un peu d'oubli ne nuit pas à la sincérité du pardon.*" (A little forgetting does not lessen the sincerity of the forgiveness.) And beneath this again Bismarck had written:—"*J'ai appris dans ma vie à moi de beaucoup oublier, et de me faire beaucoup pardonner.*" (For my part, I have learned in my life to forget much and to have much forgiven me). Highly characteristic indeed of the statesman who, from the most hated and best-abused, has succeeded in becoming the most popular and best-loved man in Germany.

THE ROMISH EPISCOPATE AND THE OLD CATHOLIC MOVEMENT IN GERMANY.

(SPECIAL APPENDIX.)

THESE papers were written two years ago. No material alterations have been made in them, however, as they are chiefly intended to explain and elucidate the question of the desperate struggle between Church and State in Germany.

There is now only a Romish episcopate left in Germany. The two evangelical Churches, the Lutheran and the Reformed, have no bishops. Superintendents-general, consistorial directors, and so-called prelates, are the highest dignitaries recognized in them, although the courtesy title of bishop (without a see attached to it) is occasionally bestowed by the state upon eminent churchmen, such as the late Bishop Westermeier, Bishop Dräsecke, and others. To call the actual occupants of the episcopal sees Catholic bishops would be a misnomer.

In the course of a discussion before the Reichstag in 1871, Bishop Kettler of Mayence broke a lance with Blanckenburg, then a leading Conservative Liberal with Bismarckian proclivities, whom the clericals hate with intensest Christian love. Blanckenburg had asked the bishop to give the house the benefit of his experience of the working of the principle of *dictatorship* in the Romish Church (the discussion had arisen in the course of the debate upon the imperial dictatorship in Alsace-Lorraine). The bishop replied that Blanckenburg by his question showed that he had not the slightest notion of the constitution of the Catholic Church. "I did not say the *Catholic* Church; I said the *Romish* Church," replied Blanckenburg calmly, amidst shouts of laughter from all parts of the house except the centre. The bishop was too indignant to pursue the subject further; so he contented himself with darting at the profane Protestant one of his most potent excommunicating glances. Since the German bishops have tamely, nay, cravenly, submitted to swallow the monstrous dogma of papal infallibility, they are simply servants of the Pope of Rome, and absolutely dependent upon their infallible master.

Never before in the history of the Church had the German episcopate submitted to such fearful degradation as this. There was a time, indeed, when a synod of German bishops would claim and exercise the power of deposing popes—the Synod of Worms, for instance, January, 1076. Even so late as the end of the last century, in 1784, a number of German archbishops held a council at Ems, to deliberate upon the expurgation of the spurious Isidorian decretals[1] from the ancient genuine collection, and upon the

[1] In the first centuries after Christ, even up to the ninth century, the Bishop of Rome had no actual supremacy conceded to him, no power or authority superior to that of the other metropolitans and bishops. He simply enjoyed a certain prestige as successor of St. Peter. The synods, or general assemblies, of the bishops alone were considered supreme and infallible, and the Bishop of Rome was subject to their authority just as all other bishops were. Still, the occupant of St. Peter's chair was treated with a certain amount of deference by his episcopal brethren, and he was often consulted on disputed points, or called on to arbitrate between contending prelates.

His counsels and decisions were generally made public, and forwarded in writing to the several sees. This gave rise to the collection of the so-called papal decretals, which Bishop Isidor of Sevilla made in the seventh century. This collection soon acquired great fame and authority in the Church. In the ninth century, when the Romish bishops began to try their hands at subjecting the temporal power to their spiritual sway, they hit upon the notable plan to base their pretensions upon the semblance of acknowledged ancient practice and historical right.

This they effected by forging a certain number of such decretals, antedated by several centuries, and with the names of former Roman pontiffs affixed to them.

In these spurious decretals the supremacy of the Bishop of Rome over all other metropolitans and bishops was boldly assumed, all dignitaries of the Catholic Church, without exception, being declared to be simply officers of the supreme Pontiff of Rome, who had power and authority vested solely in him to guide, direct, and watch over the performance of the ecclesiastic functions of the metropolitans and bishops; to decide all disputes in the Church, finally, and without further appeal (thus shelving the supreme jurisdiction of the synods); to create new bishops and found new sees; to ordain bishops in cases of hindrance or refusal of the metropolitan; to grant or to refuse, as he might list, the bestowal restoration of the old supreme authority and jurisdiction of the synods over all bishops alike, the Roman pontiff included.

Both these points—the expurgation, to wit, of the spurious Isidorian decretals, and the restoration of

of the pallium upon the metropolitans, the symbol and condition of their high dignity; and last, but not least, to make and promulgate new laws and regulations for the Church.

In the matter of this last and most important assumption of the spurious decretals, the co-operation of the synods was not expressly excluded: it was even declared desirable in important cases, but as it was declared at the same time that no synod could legally be held without the sanction of the Pope of Rome, the decision was left substantially in the hands of the latter.

These spurious decretals were most industriously propagated and most successfully smuggled into the old collections, so that in course of time their absence from certain collections was actually looked upon as an accidental omission, to be supplied as soon as it was discovered. So Pope Nicholas I. († 867) could already boldly venture upon appealing to the pseudo-Isidorian decretals in support of his asserted supremacy over all other bishops of the Catholic Church. True, the French bishops of the period looked through the infamous swindle with Gallic acumen, and told Nicholas their candid opinion about it. Unhappily they had themselves appealed to the authority of the self-same decretals in certain cases when it had suited their purpose to do so, and the Pope could therefore afford to disregard their objections.

It was upon this foundation that the seventh Gregory and the third and fourth Innocent afterwards reared the stupendous structure of papal pretension and spiritual tyranny. And it is upon the self-same foundation of these base forgeries, so impudently palmed upon the Catholic world, that Pius IX. and his Jesuit masters would fain base their present monstrous attempt to bend rulers and peoples abjectly under this vilest and most odious of all yokes.

the old supreme authority and jurisdiction of the synods over all bishops alike, the Roman pontiff included, and some minor points in the same sense and direction were carried, and the resolutions of the council were submitted to the Emperor Joseph II. of Austria. They are known in history as the Punctuation of Ems.

Joseph, unfortunately, in the conceit of his fancied omnipotence, foolishly disdained availing himself of the efficacious aid thus tendered him by the highest dignitaries of the Catholic Church in Germany, and the Punctuation of Ems was quietly strangled by a committee of the Aulic Council. Afterwards the emperor would only too gladly have retraced this false step, but it was too late then. The golden opportunity had passed by to effect a radical reform in the Church of Rome.

And now, in this nineteenth century of ours, in this age of universal enlightenment, we have to taste the bitter humiliation of beholding an entire body of most highly-educated men—for such the German archbishops and bishops unquestionably are—swallowing the whole nauseous dose of the spurious decretals, with all the later corollaries tacked to them, the monstrous infallibility dogma included. We do not wonder to see a Cullen gorge this vile stuff—it is somehow his natural food. We can understand a Manning pretending to prefer it to more wholesome doctrine—to him it is simply one of the means to his own ambitious ends. But it is melancholy to find a Hefele, a Krementz, and others of the same high stamp of intellect browsing upon the same weeds along with the common herd.

To show how fully and acutely conscious these men must feel of their self-degradation, the merest reference to the protest issued in the last stage of the late Vatican Council by sixty-seven bishops of the opposition will suffice. In this protest, which bears the signatures of many German bishops, among others, and more conspicuously, those of Krementz and Hefele, there occurs in this protest the following passage, among others equally strong and significant :—" There is, then, nothing left for us now but to protest against the said proceeding (the elevation of the papal infallibility pretension to the dignity and power of a sacred dogma of the Church), which, in our conscientious opinion and belief, is highly detrimental to the Church and the Holy Apostolic See; by this our solemn protest we repudiate and cast from us, before man and before the awful judgment of Almighty God, all and every share in the proceedings, and in the responsibility for the disastrous consequences which will inevitably spring therefrom, and which are even now already beginning to manifest themselves. Whereof this present solemn protest shall be an everlasting witness!" Yet some of the very same men who signed this solemn protest and repudiation are now among the foremost champions of papal infallibility and other perilous doctrines of the Neo-Roman Church, and actually do not blush to run emulative excommunication races, as it were, among them, visiting with the heaviest curse of the Church their infinitely more honest and upright dissentient fellow-priests who are unhappily subject to their spiritual authority, and whom they would fain force to submit abjectly to the grossest ecclesiastic tyranny ever yet attempted.

What are clear-sighted, straightforward men to think of the honesty and uprightness, for instance, of Bishop Krementz of Ermeland, who, after affixing his signature to the above strong repudiation of the papal infallibility doctrine, is now found one of the foremost and most forward among the prosecutors and persecutors of those Catholic priests who sturdily refuse to descend to the same low depth of wretched tergiversation and base compliance with Romish pretensions as he and his fellow-bishops have not scrupled to do?

Among these honest Catholic priests Professor Michelis occupies a high rank. He is one of the most learned and deservedly most highly esteemed champions of the Catholic faith against Romish innovations. In the beginning of 1872 he started a religious journal at Königsberg, in Prussia, called

Der Katholik. Hardly had the first number of the new paper been issued, when the bishop (Krementz) betook him in hot haste to address the subjoined ukase to the deans of his diocese:—

"Whereas it has come to our knowledge that the unhappy priest, Professor Michelis, who, in shameful forgetfulness of the duties of his holy calling, is seeking only how to bring scandal and vexation into the Christian world, and how to destroy the Church of God, has his pestilent organ, which he publishes at Königsberg to the aforesaid end, and which he impudently calls '*The Catholic,*' distributed gratis through the Post Office, which forwards the same more particularly to teachers in the elementary schools, and to certain influential laymen in the country,—now we herewith enjoin it upon all parish priests and all other ecclesiastics in this diocese, as a most sacred duty, to keep strictest watch and ward that this pestilence of the soul be kept away from their flocks; also, and more especially, to warn all under their spiritual guidance and teaching against receiving and accepting from the Post Office all and every and any such missives and papers as may be forwarded to them free of charge, and to return the same at once unopened to the senders. We invite your reverence to give this present pastoral the promptest and fullest circulation among the parish priests, &c., in your deanery; also, on your own part, to bring all the means at your command to bear upon the faithful execution of the instructions therein contained.

"The Bishop of Ermeland,
"PHILIPPUS."

"FRAUENBURG, *Jan.* 18, 1872."

The right reverend father in God did not, however, take much by this move of his. The professor simply replied to it by the publication in the third number of his paper of the most salient and telling paragraphs of the episcopal protest, to which Krementz had affixed his name; and by putting it to the common sense of his readers whether the man who had thus appealed to the awful judgment of the Almighty, in his solemn repudiation of the detrimental doctrine of papal infallibility, could, in justice or in common fairness, claim the right of excommunicating and grossly persecuting him (Michelis) and others for simply continuing to retain the same opinion which he (the bishop) had himself been among the foremost to hold and profess.

Archbishops Scherr of Munich, and Freising and Melchers of Cologne, are of the same stamp as Krementz. It is generally believed that they have been prevailed upon to submit to the obnoxious dogma by the tempting promise of the cardinal's hat.

There has been found among the whole batch of these protesting bishops only one true man who has kept faithful to his avowed Old Catholic and anti-infallibility creed—Bishop Strossmayer, the Demosthenes of the late Vatican Council.

The continued sturdy opposition of this man to modern papal pretensions seems to act upon his holiness's mind as the presence of the non-bowing Mordecai acted upon Haman of old. Blandishments and threats alike have been resorted to in vain to shake his resolution.

In January, 1872, he was specially called to Rome to afford his holiness a final opportunity of trying once more the effect of his personal power of persuasion upon the stanch defender of the Old Catholic faith. The Jesuits could not contemplate the possibility of the bishop being able to resist the passionate appeal of Pius IX. The Ultramontane press triumphantly announced beforehand that the bishop would declare his readiness to recant his heretical errors, and to kiss the papal foot-covering henceforth as an infallible slipper. It turned out no go, to use an expressive vulgarism.

On the occasion of the last audience given to the bishop, Pius placed the declaration of adhesion to the Vatican decrees before him, adjuring him most urgently and most solemnly to affix his signature thereunto; but Strossmayer remained as firm as a rock, and left both document and pen untouched in the hands of the Holy Father, steadfastly declaring it to be his final and unalterable resolution never to submit to the spurious dogma. He would abstain from ostentatious doctrinal professions, and from agitation against the authority of the Holy See; but he would and could go no further.

The Pope was much chagrined of course; but it is reported that he for once used very mild language to the recalcitrant bishop, whom he simply informed that he felt grieved he could no longer look upon him as a member of the true Catholic Church, and that he was quite sure now, to his deep sorrow, that he (Bishop Strossmayer) would not die as a Catholic should. So they parted; and, although the eloquent tongue of the Demosthenes of the Vatican Council has remained mute since then, the bishop rejects the infallibility dogma to the present day as firmly as ever.

It has lately been pointed out in English journals, as a significant sign of the times, that Bishop Strossmayer holds aloof from the Old Catholic movement. The simple explanation of this, however, would seem to be, that the bishop may perhaps not have entire faith in the soundness and efficacy of that apparently somewhat lukewarm and neutral-tinted movement of semi-secession from Rome, and may see reason to misdoubt the earnest singleheartedness of purpose of some of its leaders. It will be shown hereafter that this would not be quite a fair view of the matter, and that the Old Catholic movement in Germany is, with all its grievous shortcomings, still an immense step forward in the path of Church reform.

The Catholic portion of the population of the German empire numbers about fourteen millions to twenty-eight million Protestants.

These fourteen millions enjoy the diocesan ministrations of twenty-seven princes of the Church of Rome, of whom five are archbishops, one prince-bishop, nineteen bishops, and two titular bishops *in partibus*. The five archdioceses in the empire are those of Cologne, and of Gnesen and Posen, in Prussia; of Bamberg, and of Munich and Freising, in Bavaria; and of Freiburg, in Baden. The prince-bishop is he of Breslau, in Prussia. Of the nineteen bishops, two fall to the share of Alsace-Lorraine, to wit, the Bishops of Metz and Strasburg; nine hold sees in Prussia, to wit, the Bishops of Culm, Ermeland, Fulda, Hildesheim, Limburg, Munster, Osnabruck, Paderborn, and Treves; six in Bavaria, to wit, the Bishops of Augsburg, Eichstaedt, Passau, Ratisbon, Spire, and Wurzburg; one in Hesse, to wit, he of Mayence; and one in Wurtemberg, to wit, the Bishop of Rottenburg. The two titular bishops are Monsignor Namszanowski, Catholic Chaplain-General of the Prussian army, now suspended from the exercise of his ecclesiastic functions, and Monsignor Forwerk, Apostolic Vicar-General in the kingdom of Saxony (which numbers about fifty thousand Catholics out of a population of two millions and a half).

Most of these high dignitaries of the Church of

Rome were at one time, seemingly, stanch opponents of the modern monstrous pretensions of the Vatican. Many of them figure as signataries of the famous protest of the sixty-seven. They are all of them now, without exception, the professed humble servants of Rome, although comparatively a few of them only venture to put themselves prominently forward as militant champions of the Vatican.

Among these may be mentioned more particularly Archbishop Paulus Melchers of Cologne, Archbishop Gregory von Scherr of Munich and Freising, Bishop Andreas Räs of Strasburg, Bishop Philippus Krementz of Ermeland, Bishop Henry Hofstaetter of Passau, Bishop Pancratius Dinkel of Augsburg, Bishop Ignatius Senestry of Ratisbon, the Prince-Bishop of Breslau, Dr. Henry Förster, Bishop William Emmanuel von Kettler of Mayence; and Monsignor Namszanowski of Agathopolis.

The names of Kettler (or Ketteler, for fame spells the pious syllables both ways), Krementz, and Andreas Räs have already occurred in these pages. It needs simply be added here that Kettler is the most dangerous Jesuit of the order. He was the prime mover and the soul of the Fulda Council. It was he who conceived the notable plan of welding together into one compact body the forces of the two detrimental bands—the black crew of his own Jesuits and the red crew of the International; and he has for years past used his utmost endeavours to make the German workmen believe in his truly brotherly sympathies for their sufferings. It is a pity, too, that it should be so, for Kettler is a superior man—a man of the highest intelligence, and there really was the stuff in him for a patriarch of the new German Church of the future. Unluckily, he has gone too far in his open hostility to the new German empire, and has been too insolent in his opposition to have much chance left him now of such an elevation, unless he should very suddenly and unexpectedly turn his coat the right way.

Anent the German patriarchate here alluded to, the subjoined extract from a letter written by the same high parliamentary authority already quoted in these pages may not be altogether without interest :—

"Bismarck and Falk have elaborated a measure which, it may safely be predicted, will very considerably astonish the whole brew (*Gebräu*) of rebellious Roman bishops and Church dignitaries in Germany. If the Prussian government should be ultimately compelled by the blind obstinacy of Rome to act in bitter earnest, the world may rest assured that the 'man at the helm' will be found fully equal to the height of his mission. . . . I know I am not going too far if I declare to you that this said measure will prove the first step towards a total separation of Catholicity in Germany from Rome, and the ultimate establishment of an independent German primacy. This may seem to you a Utopian dream; yet I am convinced the result and issue of the present struggle will fully justify my prevision. You know that I enjoy the rare privilege of being permitted an occasional peep behind the curtain of the great *theatrum mundi*."

To return once more to Dr. Krementz. That prelate is one of the leading episcopal "excommunicators." In the earliest stage of the struggle between the infallibilists, and anti-infallibilists, he took upon himself to excommunicate Dr. Wollmann and Professor Michelis, against the express provisions of the Prussian law, which demand the previous explicit sanction of the government to the exercise of the power of excommunication. All efforts on the part of the Prussian government to induce the prelate to cancel this most illegal step have hitherto proved unavailing.

The bishop, who is strongly suspected of belonging to the Society of Jesus, and who is at any rate a most accomplished Jesuit in his casuistry, has always pleaded for excuse his inability to disobey the law of God, as he is pleased to call the will of the Pope. Where this clashes with the law of the land, he sees himself, however reluctantly, compelled to disobey the latter.

He does not exactly go quite so far as openly to avow the monstrous doctrine proposed by Pope Boniface VIII., in the famous bull *Unam Sanctam*, that the oath taken to the constitution, as well as that taken by the servants of the state to the ruler or the legally constituted authorities of the land, is always subject to the reservation of the supreme authority of the laws of God, and of all laws, decrees, rules, and regulations of the Church of Rome. Bishop Senestry of Ratisbon has done this; but Dr. Krementz is too Jesuitical, and therefore too clever, to commit himself to so uncompromising a profession of faith. He simply urges that the law of God must be obeyed in preference to the law of man, and that the infallible pontiff of Rome is the only authority empowered by the Almighty to declare the true law of God—which, though a little milder in expression, is much the same in substance as the Bonifacean doctrine. Pius IX. of course holds this doctrine, and so did his two predecessors—the eighth Pius and the sixteenth Gregory.

When the late Count Leopold Sedlnitzki, who was at the time Catholic Prince-Bishop of Breslau, professed his inability to obey certain injunctions of the latter Pope which ran directly counter to the bishop's duties to his country and his sovereign, and to the oath taken by him to the latter and to the constitution of the land, the pontiff insolently told him that it was his (the Pope's) prerogative to define the limits of the binding power of an oath taken to a secular authority, and that the bishop had only to follow unhesitatingly the dictates of his supreme ecclesiastical chief, all oaths and scruples of conscience to the contrary notwithstanding. Sedlnitzki, a most exceptional instance of uprightness and loyalty in the episcopate, preferred finally the resignation of his high dignity to disloyal submission to Rome : he did not even stop half-way, as the Old Catholics would fain attempt to do in these present times, but he abjured the monstrous errors of the popish Church altogether and turned Protestant. In his last will and testament this truly noble man bequeathed his fortune to Protestant schools—not one farthing to a Catholic institution.

After this slight illustrative digression return we to Bishop Krementz. This prelate then had, by his refusal to obey the law of the land in preference to the dictates of the Pope, broadly avowed that he looked upon himself, not as a servant of the Prussian state, but as a simple dependant of the supreme hierarch of the Romish Church. Bismarck and Falk considered it only natural therefore, under the circumstances, that the very handsome allowance paid by the state to the occupant of the Frauenburg see should be stopped until the right reverend father might see the error of his ways. The high provincial authorities at Königsberg were therefore instructed by Dr. Falk, with the full assent and sanction of the whole ministry, and with the special approbation of the chancellor, to stop payment of the bishop's income.

Now his episcopal lordship of Ermeland has, like most priests, a very strong affection for his temporalities. When he saw himself threatened, therefore, with the deprivation of his beloved loaves and fishes, he sent up acute cries of distress to Queen Elizabeth, and also to the Empress Augusta, with whom he had been on most friendly terms at Coblentz in times gone by, when Prince William of Prussia was governor-general of the Rhenish provinces.

The two august ladies thereupon advised an appeal to the emperor direct, and the bishop, who had openly demonstrated his disloyalty to the state, had the cool assurance to entreat his most gracious majesty's intervention to set aside the threatened stoppage of his episcopal pay. This appeal of the bishop was of course craftily seasoned with a long string of hollow professions of profound personal devotion and reverence.

The kind-hearted monarch, instead of leaving the matter in the hands of his advisers, or inviting Dr. Krementz to prove the sincerity of his professions by frank submission to the demands of the law of the land, thought fit to intervene personally in the affair by ordering the payment of the quarter due of the bishop's income. In his anxious desire to avoid if possible recourse to extreme measures against the Church of Rome, and to afford the recalcitrant prelates of that Church in Prussia, even at the eleventh hour, a *locus pœnitentiæ*, the emperor-king chose to disregard the fact that this somewhat arbitrary revocation of a ministerial resolution and rescript must necessarily deal a heavy blow to the authority of his own government, and tend to encourage rather than otherwise the stubborn resistance of the Catholic bishops and Church dignitaries in Prussia.

As soon of course as the bishop had touched his quarter's income, he reiterated to the ministry his profound regret that he should continue to feel constrained to decline complying with the ministerial order to reinstate Wollmann and Michelis in the Catholic community of his diocese.

About this time came the intemperate outbreak of the Pope against the German empire and emperor (in his allocution on St. John's Day, 1872), by which his majesty was most painfully affected.

Bismarck, with his habitual skill, availed himself of the opportunity afforded by the insolence of the papal allocution to invite the king's special attention to a kindred papal missile hurled at Prussia by Pope Clement XI., on the 18th of April, 1701, in which that other pink of popedom informed the assembled cardinals, that "the Margrave of Brandenburg had, through a barefaced sacrilege almost unheard of among Christians, dared presume to bestow upon himself the name and style of a king of Prussia—in the very teeth of the holy canons, which command heretical princes to lay down their powers, instead of daringly aspiring to still higher honours. This shameless and godless crime he (the Pope) had duly denounced to all Catholic princes."

Now, as the Emperor William knows that the said "holy canons" are in force to the present day, and as Bismarck took care to show him how to read this papal allocution on St. John's Day by the light of the Clementine fulmination of a hundred and seventy-one years ago, he submitted once more, as he had done over and over again already, to the chancellor's will, and he promised accordingly not to intervene again between his minister and the Bishop of Ermeland, or any other prelate against whom it might be necessary to take coercive measures.

So when, emboldened by his former success, Dr. Krementz ventured to ask the emperor-king to be permitted to present himself before his majesty on the occasion of the emperor's recent visit (1872) to Marienburg, he received his answer from the chancellor, who told him, in so many dry words, that the emperor would not receive him unless he would previously renounce his insolent pretensions to act independently of, and even against, the law of the land. In reply to this, the bishop, trusting to the "ladies' party" at court, unreservedly adhered to the position assumed by him on the question of excommunication. The result has been that the holy father, to his most bitter and intense grief, has seen his episcopal pay stopped at last.

Of Bishop Andreas Räs it may be permitted to tell a characteristic trait, taken from Abel Pilon's great work on the late Œcumenic Council, one of the greatest curiosities in the way of books ever published. This work consists of eight large volumes. It is richly illustrated, chiefly with portraits of Pius IX. and the other eleven popes who have held councils, the sixty cardinals then living (in 1870), the five hundred fathers who attended the late Vatican Council, fac-similes of their signatures, &c. Among these latter figure the autograph and signature of the Very Reverend Father in God, Andreas Räs, Bishop of Strasburg. The sentiment of the autograph, which bears date Rome, 16th of May, 1870, is rather curious, and at least highly characteristic of the man. It is written in Latin. The English version is as follows: "Wherever thy fatherland be, it is a valley of tears. It is ridiculous to cling to it with such obstinate affection as men will do. One's country matters naught for good nor for evil." (*Nullum patria bonum, nullum facit malum.*) It must be admitted that the right reverend bishop is candid, at least. He unblushingly gives expression to the most pernicious of all the pestilential principles of Romanism. True, such as he and his fellows are the "dead-souled" men who acknowledge no ties of country—who are simply and solely, and exclusively and absolutely priests, not of the living God, but of the Baal of Rome.

Archbishop Scherr of Munich and Freising is one of the leading excommunicators. In his blind, frantic, infallibilist zeal he will stop short at nothing. One of the most earnest rejectors and denouncers of the papal infallibility dogma is a certain Mr. Bernard, parish priest of Kiefersfelden, near Kufstein (Tyrol). Having tried mild remonstrance and harsh threats—both alike in vain—to induce Mr. Bernard to submit to the supreme authority of the Romish Church, Archbishop Scherr resolved at last to cast out the black shepherd from the fold. To impart a deeper solemnity to the ceremony, his grace went in his own most reverend person to dispossess the recalcitrant priest of his cure of souls.

So, one fine day he appeared suddenly in the Otto chapel, near Kufstein, in full archiepiscopal canonicals and paraphernalia, to curse poor Mr. Bernard in the well-known style of Romish cursing. He declared that renegade priest cast out from the blessed community of the Church of Christ, and by that fact deprived of his cure of souls, and dismissed sempiternally from his sacred office.

The congregation, who, like that of Father O'Keeffe, the parish priest of Callan, happened to dearly love their spiritual guide, listened to the archbishop's cursing in mazed silence. When the archiepiscopal performance was over, however, Scherr found himself suddenly confronted, from the stone pulpit in the gallery running round the chapel, by the excommunicated man himself, also arrayed in full canonicals, who protested in temperate but firm language against the *illegal* interference of the archbishop with his (the parish priest's) flock, and boldly told the prince of the Church to his face that he was firmly resolved to continue to act as parish priest, just as he had done up to that time, and without paying the slightest heed or attention to the archiepiscopal performance his flock had just been compelled to witness, to the grievous offence and injury of Christ's own true Church.

The archbishop was taken completely by surprise. Fancy Paul Cullen to be tackled in a similar manner by Father O'Keeffe in the chapel of Callan! He—Scherr, not Cullen, of course—shouted to the congregation, at the highest pitch of his voice, not to listen to the excommunicated and expelled priest of Belial. But his shouts were treated with cool, contemptuous derision by the congregation, who lovingly gathered round their own pastor, solemnly vowing to stand faithfully by him, in spite of all bishops and archbishops, and even of the Pope himself.

The poor discomfited archbishop then tried another tack. He betook him to blessing the congregation in the loudest way; but this also remaining without the least impression upon their hardened hearts, his most reverend lordship at last made up his mind to go away considerably chopfallen.

He was fain to rest content with appointing a red-hot, infallibilist zealot, one Father Stangl, *vicarius in spiritualibus* of the parish of Kiefersfelden. As there happened to be a few, a very few, Neo-Catholics in the Kiefersfelden commune, Mr. Bernard, who is naturally of an amiable and conciliatory disposition and temper, permitted this man to officiate in his parish church for the very small minority of Neo-Catholics of his flock.

But give the devil even the tip of your little finger, and he will use his utmost efforts to drag your whole body down to hell. Master Stangl would not long rest content with this kind concession, but resolved to try a *coup d'église*.

So one fine day, when the parish priest was just in the midst of the celebration of high mass, this worthy son of the Romish Church entered the sacred edifice in lay attire, and loudly called upon the congregation, in the name of the Archbishop of Munich, to leave the church, which he declared desecrated by the ministrations of an excommunicated schismatic. No one paid the slightest heed to his vociferations. He then addressed himself specially to the children present, who, however, remained also perfectly unmoved, most likely because the dear innocents did not even clearly understand what the brawling zealot meant by his virulent denunciations of their beloved pastor.

To put an end to the scandal, Mr. Bernard at last, after all his exhortations to the man Stangl had proved unavailing, bringing on simply fresh fits of cursing, felt compelled to use his right of master of the premises; and so Master Stangl was bundled out neck and crop by a couple of strong-armed Kiefersfeldeners, who, it is averred, instead of honouring the mild instructions of their pastor in the observance, preferred honouring Stangl in the breech with a few vigorous kicks, just by way of a gentle caution not to come there again. Besides which, the poor man had to answer Mr. Bernard's complaint to the Civil Court for brawling in a place of public worship.

Another of the most rabid section of archiepiscopal and episcopal excommunicators is the Most Reverend Father in God, Paulus Melchers, by Divine Mercy and the Grace of the Holy Apostolic See Archbishop of Cologne, one of the most shining lights now (*à non lucendo*) of the darkest and densest Ultramontanism. (Archbishop Melchers is now in prison, and will soon be deprived of his see.)

In one of his latest pastorals (1872), this Paulus of our days delivers him of an elaborate treatise on the necessity of faith, as *he* understands it—to wit, absolute unreasoning, unconditional belief in all and everything that Rome may choose to teach. He calls upon his flock to cling to this blind faith, which he dubs the most precious gem bestowed upon man by God's mercy.

"This pious, absolute faith is the light," he exclaims, "without which we cannot discern the right way to our eternal destination: it is the root and origin of all Christian virtues, the one thing needful, without which we cannot hope to attain to eternal bliss. 'He that believeth not shall be damned,' sayeth our Divine Lord (St. Mark xvi. 16), and again, 'He that believeth not is condemned already' (St. John iii. 18). 'Without faith it is impossible to please God,' says the Apostle (Hebrews xi. 6)."

It is said a certain dark personage is rather given to quoting Scripture to suit his own purposes. The Romish hierarchy would certainly seem to take after this personage in this respect.

"This faith," continues the archbishop, "is indispensable, not simply because the Lord Almighty has commanded it, and that it behoves man to unconditionally accept and hold for true all that God, who is truth eternal, has revealed to him, but also and chiefly because our fallen nature, our feeble intelligence, impaired and obscured by the act and influence of original sin, is no longer able to understand and comprehend of itself divine things and eternal truths in the way requisite for salvation. True, a few of these eternal truths, such as the existence of a Supreme Being, for instance, and the Immortality of the Soul, our human reason may still be able to conceive. But the history of all ages has sufficiently shown how difficult it is for man to conceive these truths without admixture of gross errors."

Here our worthy archbishop has unconsciously stumbled upon a great truth; what, indeed, is the entire Romish Church system but a grain of eternal truth buried and stifled under a heap of the grossest errors?

"Things divine," continues Paulus, "and the great truths of eternity are so sublime, and lie so far beyond the perception of our senses and our natural ideas, that we can only believe in them as mysteries. As the sailor cannot trace his path across the immense ocean without the aid of the compass, as the astronomer cannot measure the stars of heaven and their orbits without the aid of the telescope" (rather awkward illustrations these, my lord archbishop!) "so man, without the light of faith to aid him, is unable to find, in his pilgrimage through this life on earth, the right path to the Heavenly Fatherland. Therefore has the Love of God revealed to man all that is needed for his eternal salvation, and has commanded him to believe in it, on forfeiture of his hope of eternal bliss."

And now comes the gist of the matter. "This faith," says Paulus of Cologne, "without which we cannot be saved, is a supernatural, divine virtue, whose germ and essence is imparted to us by divine grace in the holy sacrament of baptism. It consists in the persistent will and faculty to believe implicitly in all and everything the Holy Church represents to us as of divine origin and revelation. Divine belief consists not in a mere tacit assent, a vague supposing or taking for granted; it is an implicit conviction, an absolute, undoubting, and unconditional assurance of the truth of the thing which forms its subject. And naught can ever form the subject of this divine belief but what the testimony of the Holy Church affirms to rest upon Divine revelation. We have superabundant proof of the infallibility of the Holy Roman Church."

This the archbishop then proceeds to demonstrate at great length, in the approved Romanist fashion, by bold assertion, gross perversion of facts, and still grosser twisting of biblical texts. Not content with demanding of the faithful believer tacit assent and obedient submission to all and every and any thing Rome may choose to proclaim to the world, he absolutely requires of him the sincerest internal conviction of the truth, the divine truth, of Rome's teachings! "Every conscious doubt," he says, "of the truth of what the Holy Roman Church affirms to be true, is rank rebellion against the divine authority with which the Almighty has endowed His Church. The believing Christian must submit his intelligence to the infallible authority of Holy Church, even though the mysteries of the revelation proclaimed transcend his reason."

Regarding the papal infallibility dogma, the great

Paulus has the brow to declare that "this dogma rests, equally with all other dogmas and tenets of the Church, upon divine revelation (!). It has, in fact and truth, always existed in the traditions of the Church, and has at all times been held as an article of faith, although it had not before this been solemnly proclaimed to the world. The late Vatican decrees are founded on Holy Writ and unassailable tradition!"

In what passage of Holy Writ the slenderest foundation even can be found for the late Vatican decrees, the great Paulus of course leaves us to find out for ourselves.

Having thus assigned with almost incredible assurance a divine origin to the papal infallibility dogma, and claimed for it the unimpeachable authority of Holy Writ, Archbishop Paulus Melchers proceeds in this marvellous pastoral of his to make a fierce onslaught upon what he is pleased to call the "conceit of knowledge," which he contends is the bane of this unbelieving age. With fiery zeal he denounces all systems of education that are not based exclusively upon the tenets of the Church of Rome, which said Church is proclaimed by him to be the only safe shield and protection of Christian belief and true morality!

He then comes down with thundering eloquence upon those abominations in the sight of the Almighty —mixed marriages and civil marriages. He winds up ultimately by hurling a complete armoury of the choicest anathemas upon the devoted heads of the men of the fourth estate, whom he brands as the pestilential propagators of so-called Liberal ideas. He implores his flock not to let their eyes be blinded, their intellects dazed, their minds destroyed, and their souls killed by the deadly poison of un-Catholic and anti-Catholic journals. He tells them to apply to their parish priests and chaplains for advice and instruction in the selection of proper reading for them. He warmly urges them to subscribe largely and liberally to the Romish papers, such as the noble *Germania*, the *Vaterland* of Dr. Sigl, the *Vaterland* of Count Leo Thun, the Munich *Volksfreund*, the *Volksbote*, the *Deutsche Reichszeitung*, and other—well, let us say famous publications of the same "high" moral stamp.

He also strongly advises them to read the *Lives of the Saints*, and other good books, such as the popular translation of the renowned *Pietas quotidiana erga beatissimam Virginem Mariam*, printed in the original Latin for the special use of Jesuit schools, *cum facultate superiorum* on the title-page.

This fine work, so particularly suited for the religious instruction and moral guidance of ingenuous youth, and so specially calculated to nurture and develop the noblest gifts of God to man—the mind and intellect—gives for every day of the year the narration of a remarkable event in the life of one of the saints, the said event being intimately connected with the adoration of the Holy Virgin. A few instances, taken at haphazard out of the collection of three hundred and threescore odd wondrous narrations, will suffice to show the character and tendency of the book.

Thus, the story for the 9th of April relates how "Holy William"—not he whose praises Burns has sung so sweetly—had so much loved the Virgin Mary, that after his death there grew out of his mouth a miraculous lily, with "*Ave Maria!*" stamped on it in golden letters. That for the 6th of August, how St. Gigistenus, the holy shepherd— who may have been a most pious Mariolater, but would certainly seem to have been a most unfaithful shepherd—used to attend assiduously to his devotions at all and any time of the day, piously intrusting the tending of his flock meanwhile to the loving care of the Virgin Mary, who, the story gravely informs us, always sent down an angel on this special service. That for the 5th of December, how St. Abbas could never touch an apple, nor even sit by to see other people eat apples, as it always reminded him of Eve's shameful fall.

Then there is a story, gravely told, of another holy man, who was so modest that when they came to wash his body after his death, the corpse was seen three distinct times to wave off the women charged with this office. Is not this rich, and is it not singularly calculated to cultivate modesty in young lads and lasses? It need hardly be added that the book abounds in tales of seduction, some of them indecently prurient, just the sort of thing to raise a blush on the cheek of innocence, or even, as poor Paul Bedford used to say of certain stories he had had to listen to occasionally in the experience of his life, to make vice sick.

If the wretched panderers to vice in the obscene literature line had but known what a mass of bestiality might be dug out of this class of Romish educational learning, what a good thing they might have made of its importation, mayhap without incurring the risk of so many months of forced seclusion from the outer world as some of them have had to suffer! Even in Bavaria, where a great deal in this way can be put up with, the minister of public worship has been compelled to prohibit, for decency's sake, the use of this precious "Holy Virgin adoration" production in the public schools and gymnasiums.

I will now give a few quotations from the pious columns of the *Volksfreund* and of the renowned Dr. Sigl's *Vaterland*, which may serve to show the true character of the journalistic literature so warmly and urgently recommended to the faithful by the great Paulus of Cologne and his episcopal brethren of Munich, Passau, Augsburg, Ratisbon, and Mayence.

Some time ago a Bavarian gentleman happened to die, one who had grown grey in the service of the state, a man of unblemished reputation, of most amiable disposition, esteemed by every good and honourable man in the land, and a pious Catholic too, though not a thick-and-thin supporter of Romanist errors and pretensions. Well, Dr. Sigl, the pet of the episcopate, thought he could not turn the occasion to better account than to call upon the readers of his precious *Vaterland* " to rejoice with him that another enemy of the Holy Father had been carried by the devil down to hell and eternal perdition ! "

The Munich *Volksfreund* some time ago had a remarkable article, in which the sad falling off in the reverence and submission due to the "source of all light"—to wit, his holiness the Pope—was attributed simply to the working of the coal mines! "Know ye not," said the learned editor of this so-called friend of the people, "that it is written in the Holy Book, 'And darkness was upon the face of the deep; and God said, Let there be light, and there was light?' Now, whither did that darkness go which had thus been expelled by the new light created? It was precipitated into the depths of the earth—in the form of coal (!)—and ever since, presumptuous man has been digging up again this *condensed darkness;* the reign of darkness has returned to the upper world, where it wars against the light of our holy religion ! "

The schools in Bavaria have for long years been absolutely and exclusively in the hands of the Romish priesthood. To what low depth of condensed darkness must the teachings of that priesthood have reduced a people that can be made to swallow such nauseous trash !

The writer Sigl, of the *Vaterland* of Munich, is the most vituperative of the Romish journalists in Germany. He beats Veuillot and Majunke hollow, and he certainly could give points to the worst specimens of the transatlantic editor. Of late he had grown so outrageous in his language, that even his warm protectors, the Archbishop of Munich and his chapter, deemed it imperatively necessary to remonstrate with him, and to counsel a little moderation, whereupon the worthy doctor coolly writes in his journal :—

" The *Vaterland's* mode of fighting the enemies of the Church seems to displease some people. We should like to know what these squeamish people would have. *Beasts*, gentlemen who remonstrate with us, must not be laved with Eau de Cologne, or propitiated with buttered buns and gingerbread. They must be hit hard over the snout, to make them roar again with the smart. And it is with *beasts*, in sober truth, that we Catholics have to contend in this new-fangled empire ! " Considering that the Bavarian and imperial German ministers and the Bavarian king and the German emperor are the parties here so elegantly qualified as "*beasts*," it is truly astonishing how people in this country can still pretend that there is no liberty of the press in Germany.

What the teachings of such pastorals as those of the Archbishop of Cologne, and certain kindred productions by some of his most and right reverend brethren in the Pope of Rome are calculated to lead to, the writer had an opportunity of witnessing on the occasion of a late visit to Elberfeld. Elberfeld and Barmen are twin cities in the so-called Wupperthal, or valley of the river Wupper, better known as the Muckerthal, the chief seat of the rankest pietistry of Protestant Germany. Of the 150,000 inhabitants possessed jointly by the twin cities, nearly 140,000 are Protestants, and only about 12,000 profess the Catholic religion. Elberfeld more particularly is the centre of the stiffest Protestant orthodoxy.

Well, the writer had occasion, through the kindness of a friend, a sincere Papist with anti-infallibilist leanings, to assist at a select meeting of gentlemen of the Romish Church, which had been convened to consider the probable effect of a late gathering of Old Catholics in a great German city which has long been the seat of Roman Catholicism. Whether the fact that this meeting was held in an ultra-Protestant town may have had something to do with the matter, the writer will not undertake to say, but he found that the speeches made and the expressions used were singularly moderate, not to say benevolent, towards

Döllinger, Schulte, Reinkens, Michelis, and the other leaders of the secessionist movement, who, it was to be most deeply regretted, it was averred by some of the leading speakers had unhappily been misled by the "conceit of knowledge," as Dr. Paulus Melchers, the Archbishop of Cologne, had so appropriately and felicitously defined the cause of the aberration and deviation from the right path of these formerly great Catholic doctors.

Such was the general tenor of all the speeches made, with the exception of one delivered by a young chaplain who had been brought up in a Jesuit college, and who was more than suspected of being one of the secret members of the Jesuit fraternity.

This son of Loyola spoke in a very different strain indeed. He declared he could not sit by and listen calmly to attempts to plead excuses for such monstrous arch-heresiarchs as the men whose demoniac spirit of rebellion would not let them stop short even of loading the most atrocious parricide upon their sin-burthened souls (!), for it was no secret that the Most Holy Father had been struck to the heart by their revolt against his supreme authority, which revolt he (the speaker) could only compare to the rising of Lucifer against the Most High, or to the rebellion of Korah against Moses, and to the attacks made upon the Holy Catholic Church of Rome by Savonarola, Arnold of Brescia, Wycliffe, Huss, Jerome of Prague, Luther, and a host of other "pestilent devils!"

The Most High had thrust Lucifer and his seditious following from heaven down into the deepest pit of hell. He had made the earth open her mouth and swallow up Korah and all that appertained unto him. He had sent fire from heaven to consume Dathan and Abiram and all that appertained unto them!

In the good old days (!), when faith still held supreme sway over the Christian world, and the adversary of God and man had not yet stirred up in the congregations of believers that most detestable and most sinful spirit of doubt and inquiry which blabbering fools called reason, the Church used to proceed in faithful imitation of the Most High—it lopped off its rotten branches. So long as it did this there was no danger that damnable heresies would ever obtain a firm hold on any considerable portion of the Christian community. Most unhappily, however, a foolish, nay, a sinful spirit of indulgence and forbearance had replaced the rigid old sternness of principle.

Had Luther, Melancthon, Zwingli, Calvin, and the rest of the devil's band of so-called Reformers been burnt at the stake, or hanged on gallows, the Church would not now have to witness this sedition of Döllinger and his following of wretched "reasoners," who in the blind conceit of their so-called knowledge would fain oppose the placing the keystone in the great arch of all saving faith—the acceptance of the divine dogma of papal infallibility, emanating from the direct inspiration of the Holy Ghost!

Yes, Dr. Melchers was quite right to call it the conceit of knowledge. What was the real nature of this knowledge of which these poor fools were so proud, and for the sake of which alone they were forfeiting their eternal welfare? Had they not read their Bible? Did they not know that it was by Satan's counsel that man was first beguiled to taste of the pernicious fruit? Yea! with knowledge came sin into the world!

So the good young man raved on, quoting Scripture passages by the yard to prove that no mercy should be shown to Döllinger and his co-rebels, who were liberally compared to the fruitless, leafy fig-tree which Christ cursed, and to the offending eyes and limbs which He commands His followers to pluck out and cut off, and cast from them.

All this was delivered with most impressive intensity of intonation and zest; and the young speaker seemed to be terribly in earnest.

At last he branched off into a fierce denunciation of the notorious wine-bibbing and beer-guzzling of the good Elberfelders, which, considering the protuberant corporations and the copper-noses of most of the elder Catholic ecclesiastics present on the occasion, seemed rather impertinent and perhaps slightly out of place. Upon this subject he waxed so eloquent that it would truly have rejoiced the hearts of Dr. Manning, Sir Wilfrid Lawson, and others of that class to hear him, and would have made their eyes overflow, albeit not with crusty old port and double-distilled cognac.

How the sermon ended, and whether any of the elder priests present rebuked their young brother's fiery zeal afterwards, the writer cannot tell, as his friend and guide, who averred that he knew the young champion of fire and water to be himself much given to Bacchus and Gambrinus, and that he had good reason to misdoubt his actual soberness then, declared he could not stand the hypocritical rant any longer, and insisted upon leaving.

His good episcopal lordship of Augsburg, the learned Doctor Pancratius von Dinkel, is another most determined champion of excommunication, interdict, and suspension under the provisions of the precious "Apostolicæ Sedis" constitution of the firebrand Pope Pius IX. But, like his episcopal brethren of Munich, Cologne, Breslau, Ermeland, &c., he has been but moderately successful in his crusade against the anti-infallibilist clergy of his diocese.

There is notably the case of one Renftle, a recalcitrant parish priest in his diocese, who has excited the head shepherd's most holy anger and most pious grief. This God-abandoned man had presumed to reject the dogma of papal infallibility in the teeth of the sternest and most peremptory episcopal injunction to believe in it himself, and make his parishioners believe in it, for which gross and glaring act of contumacy the bishop dismissed him of his own sole authority from his sacerdotal office. The hardened sinner flatly refused to part with his living, and the Bavarian government, impiously professing to act in strict conformity with the letter and spirit of the constitution of the land, declined sanctioning the episcopal decree of dismissal, which they had the hardihood even to qualify as "an act of usurpation of the power and functions of the state."

It was not of course likely that the bishop would submit to this audacious interference with his rights, powers, and privileges; so he addressed a formal complaint to the Bavarian chambers, that the government had illegally obstructed him in the free exercise of his spiritual authority.

Now the anti-German and anti-Liberal coalition of the two sections of Ultramontanes and Particularists formed at the time the undoubted majority in the Bavarian Lower Chamber. So victory was confidently anticipated by the infallibilists; and, indeed, they gained the first step. The bishop's complaint was referred to a committee, which decided that it should be taken into consideration by the house. A sharp and keen debate ensued. Ministers were strongly attacked and bitterly reviled by the leaders of the two coalesced sections. But they replied with spirit and effect. In the division which took place at the end of the debate, the Ultramontanes carried in a gouty canon in an armchair, that they might benefit by his precious vote.

The Liberals, not to be outdone, had poor Müller, one of the deputies of the palatinate, who had had the misfortune of sustaining a bad fracture of the thigh, brought all the way from his home in the palatinate up to Munich, with his broken limb firmly imbedded in a plaster of Paris casing. Mind, this was in the winter, and the patriotic man ran thus the most imminent danger of paying dearly for his unswerving loyalty to his country and his party.

Three members of the Particularist section let themselves be gained over by ministerial eloquence and common sense, and ratted from the coalition. Thus it came to pass in the division that the numbers were equal on both sides—76 to 76; and the episcopal motion was lamentably lost.

Dr. Senestry, the Romish bishop of Ratisbon, of whom I have had occasion to speak before, has also had to deplore, in his excommunication campaign against "apostate" priests in his diocese, the unreasonable and impious opposition of the temporal authorities. This man is certainly the boldest of the violet janissaries of Jesuitry, even Kettler of Mayence not excepted. It is this Dr. Senestry who openly avows and proclaims Pope Boniface VIII.'s monstrous doctrine, as laid down in the famous *Unam Sanctam* bull, which would subject all ordinances of the temporal power to the supreme and divine authority of the laws, decrees, rules, and regulations of the Church of Rome!

There can hardly be a doubt that the other Romish bishops in Germany hold pretty much the same view of the divine supremacy of Rome, only they are not quite so boldly outspoken as Dr. Senestry is; and, for the matter of that, our own Cullens and Mannings are just as decided "suprematists" as their German brethren in the Pope, only that they are too wily to pluck at unripe pears.

Mayhap the time may come sooner than expected when these gentlemen also will drop all disguise, and unveil to the bewildered gaze of the Protestants of England the hidden charms of the Church of Rome in all their mediæval beauty. A sad look-out for our country! Happily there is this great consolation, that all lies, however huge, are doomed to perish in the end, vanishing in the light of all-conquering truth, the same as the hardest-frozen icebergs will melt away in the rays of the sun.

Dr. Henry Förster, Prince-Bishop of Breslau, is another star of the first magnitude in the bright constellation of excommunicators. This gentleman passes, and not unjustly so, for a deeply-learned ecclesiastic. In the great controversy which preceded the final decision of the Infallibility Council, he brought all his learning and acute reasoning powers to bear against the Vatican demands; but at last he "caved in" like the rest, and took with extraordinary and most fiery zeal to cursing those honest men who faithfully stuck to their colours and boldly continued to avow their anti-infallibilist convictions in the teeth of the spurious decision of a packed majority of sham bishops.

He showed himself the bitterest of the bitter in the feud with these honest men, more particularly with Dr. Reinkens, one of the leaders of the Old Catholic movement—a man of still deeper learning than is possessed by Dr. Förster. Dr. Reinkens, who is now the first bishop of the Old Catholics of Germany, is, indeed, barely second in ecclesiastical lore to even the great Döllinger himself, and almost rivals Professor Schulte in extensive and profound knowledge of the canon law. He is a man still in the prime of life, of most amiable disposition and conciliatory manners, and gifted with rare eloquence, enhanced by the charm of a most pleasing and flexible organ. In the *annus mirabilis* 1866, the writer enjoyed the rare privilege of passing many happy evenings at the Zwinger in Breslau, in the society of Dr. Reinkens, then Rector Magnificus of the Breslau University; and he has the most pleasing recollection how he, in common with all around, used to hang rapt and entranced upon the sweet suasion flowing from the honeyed lips of that Gamaliel.

Upon the devoted head of this man the prince-bishop poured more especially the full vials of his wrath, exhausting the whole armoury of suspensions, interdicts, and excommunications. He cursed him with a grievous curse indeed, but apparently with no great effect, Dr. Reinkens remaining as stout as ever in his thorough repudiation of Romish error and popish presumption, and drawing more and more disciples to follow in his wake.

Seeing which, and appreciating the fact at its true value and import, Henry Förster, who is by no means a fool in his generation, has of late (1872) been skilfully preparing a strategic movement to the rear, with a view, clearly, to an ultimate backing out in the event of the Ultramontanists being finally worsted in the present struggle.

Through his own special organ, the *Schlesische Volks Zeitung*, he has lately once more proclaimed to the world his real views on the papal infallibility dogma, which the episcopally-inspired writer in that paper declares to have been "concocted by its authors, and passed through the council in a manner most objectionable, that has left a biting sting behind in the minds of many good Catholics, a sting which in German minds means something very different from what might be the case with other nations."

"How many Catholics," continues the inspired writer, "are there in Germany who are no longer Roman Catholics? and how many who have hitherto remained Roman simply because they could afford to continue to be so without grievous disadvantage to their interests, but who will speedily talk in another strain when heavier times shall come, and who will cheerfully rat to the secessionist movement so soon as the state shall put on the screw with full force?" He warns his readers not to indulge over freely in uncalled-for dogmatic utterances anent "doctrinal divergences of opinion, which can only tend to alienate honest men of all parties from the cause of the Catholic religion."

True, Bishop Förster does his best to keep his rear quite clear in the matter, so that he may be free to act in any way and direction events and circumstances may point to. No one need wonder that he should anxiously and ostentatiously repudiate all and every solidarity of opinion with his own recognized organ, stoutly averring that he has nothing whatever to do with the articles therein appearing. This may do for outsiders, but those who are in a position to take an occasional peep behind the scenes know full well that, though another hand may have guided the pen, it certainly was Dr. Förster's brain that guided the hand.

There remains now only one more of the more prominent members of the Romish episcopate in Germany of whom a few words have to be said, to wit, Monsignor Namszanowski, Bishop of Agathopolis *in partibus infidelium*, late Catholic Chaplain-General of the Prussian army.

This man is one of the most rabid "Piononists" of the bunch of Romish priests in Germany. After a long course of most patient and forbearing endurance of his haughty contumely of the state and its laws, the Prussian government saw itself at last compelled to suspend him and his vicar-general, a mere subservient tool of his, from the exercise of their ecclesiastic functions in the army.

In the very teeth of this suspension the contumacious priest persisted in acting as if the state and its authority and laws had no actual tangible existence for him. He continued to hurl anathemas by the dozen upon the devoted heads of Old Catholic army chaplains, and to direct the Neo-Catholic chaplains to set openly at defiance the orders of the military authorities in all church matters. In the free distribution of his thunderbolts of suspension, interdict, and excommunication, this fiery zealot did not restrict himself to those among his clergy who simply reject the infallibility dogma; but he liberally bestowed these bounties upon all breakers of the disciplinary laws of the Church.

Like Paulus of Cologne, he entertains the deepest aversion to mixed marriages, contracted without the proviso of the rearing of the children in the tenets of the Romish creed. Formerly, before the Civil Marriage Act was passed, the law in Prussia required that the Catholic ecclesiastic authorities should sanction the celebration of mixed marriages without insisting on any such proviso. This was the theory; but practically every imaginable obstacle was thrown by the high Catholic clergy in the way of such marriages without the Catholic proviso, and law-abiding Catholic priests who celebrated a marriage of this kind without the special sanction of their diocesan were often visited with all the high penalties of the Church. Some two years and a half ago (15th of November, 1869), Prince Charles of Roumania, who belongs to the Catholic branch of the Hohenzollerns, married a princess of the Protestant House of Neuwied. The marriage was celebrated in strict obedience to the law of the land, by Dr. Kaiser of Düsseldorf, who then held the position of Divisional Catholic Chaplain in the Prussian army. The wrathful Monsignor of Agathopolis suspended him at once from his functions, for "a gross breach of the disciplinary laws of the Holy Roman Catholic Church." Some time after, when the exigencies of the war then raging between Germany and France made it slightly unsafe for the Chaplain-General of the Forces to indulge in the luxury of a tyrannous exercise of an unlawful authority, this suspension was removed. After the war, Namszanowski suddenly took it into his head to renew it, declaring it final at the same time, and irrevocable but by the supreme head of the Church of Rome,—the poor divisional chaplain being coolly told to go to Rome "on his knees," and at the feet of holy Pius IX., with "a contrite heart and a crushed soul," crave remission of his " gross sin," and forgiveness of his " monstrous crime !"

Such and their like, as it has been endeavoured to sketch them here in brief outline, are the men who stand banded together against the authority of the state and the supremacy of the law in Germany, and whom the government of the land sees itself at last, however reluctantly, compelled to put down by the strong hand.

And when a foreign government finds itself thus driven, very much against its will, to take legal measures, in conjunction with the representatives of the people, for the protection of all citizens of the state alike against the most monstrous tyranny ever attempted since the dark days of the Middle Age, our blessed Catholic Unions of Great Britain and Ireland must impertinently and insolently take upon themselves to send sympathizing, encouraging, and congratulatory addresses to the worst Romish contemners of and offenders against the law of a land whose affairs certainly are no legitimate concern of British citizens.

And the pragmatical old *Spectator* must, forsooth, descend to treat its readers to twaddle like the following :—" The Prussian Liberals despise the toilsome way of undermining the foundations of the great authoritative Church (!), and prefer to resort to the old-fashioned method of persecution (!). They will reap what they are sowing. The freest private thought in Europe has been hitherto that of Germany, but it will not long survive this shameful confession of weakness (!), this spasmodic terror of the Church of Rome. The State which authoritatively persecutes an authoritative Church will find itself cutting its own ground from under its feet, and leading impartial German citizens to suppose that there must be truth behind a system so formidable as to call for state aid to assail it (!). It is an ill omen for the infant empire of Germany, that in its very earliest days it is abandoning the sober traditions of that free thought and free religious combination from which the intellectual influence of Germany has sprung, and substituting for it a principle of dictatorial scepticism and jealous domination."

One would barely think it possible to cram so much ignorance of the real facts of the case, combined with such gross presumption of criticism, within so limited a space.

It now only remains to show the true nature and scope of the Old Catholic movement in Germany, which is but imperfectly understood in this country.

Never before in the world's history has there been a reform movement of such magnitude and importance so fiercely assailed by enemies, so hesitatingly, lukewarmly, and half-heartedly supported by friends and sympathizers, as the present so-called Old Catholic movement in Germany.

This is the third great secession movement from

Rome which Germany has witnessed in the course of the last four hundred and seventy years.

The first strong effort to check the audacious encroachments and repel the monstrous pretensions of Rome was initiated at the beginning of the fifteenth century by John Hus of Hussinec (the Czech way of spelling the name). Properly speaking, this was not a German movement. John Huss, who strangely enough is spoken of by many historians as one of the leading German reformers, and a man of singularly large and liberal mind, was a Czech, and most unfortunately, one of the densest and intensest Czechs of his time, and the blindest and fiercest foe to everything German.

When this unhappy man began his truly fatal career upon the religio-political stage, Germanization had made very considerable progress in Bohemia, and the Czechian part of the population of that land had been impelled to make large strides forward on the road to civilization. The German University of Prague, founded in 1348, was then one of the chief seats of learning in Europe. At this University Huss held the divinity chair.

The man was thoroughly honest and sincere in all his acts and intentions; but his intense Slavism, and his fierce, unreasoning Germanophobia clouded his mind and dwarfed his understanding. The preponderance, nay, the mere presence, of the German element at the Prague University filled his soul with bitter envy and hatred, and, naturally despairing of all chance of accomplishing aught against German intellectual superiority in the legitimate field of fair competition and emulation, he set himself to work, with the unswerving pertinacity of Czech malignancy, upon the very poor mind of the indolent and incapable Wenzeslas, until he finally succeeded in obtaining from that worst scion of the bad house of Luxemburg the expulsion of the Germans from their legitimate position in the University of Prague.

This was in 1409. With the king's decree in his pouch, he triumphantly mounted the pulpit to call upon his dearly beloved Czech brethren to join with him in thanks to God for His signal mercy just vouchsafed unto them. "Praise be to the Almighty, my children," he fervently exclaimed, exultingly waving the decree high over his head,—"Praise and glory be to Him who has so graciously helped us in our arduous efforts to expel these hated Germans from our (!) University, and has given us the victory at last!"

Zisca subsequently completed this victory of the Czech over the German element in Bohemia.

Look at that unhappy country now, and behold the sad results! An ancient sage held that the most formidable punishment inflicted hereafter upon mischievous busybodies and ambitious wrongheads, would be to compel them to look on, helpless and hopeless, whilst the natural consequences of their bad and wild acts and deeds were inexorably developing their inevitable results before their spell-bound eyes. If there be truth in this strange speculation, how bitterly Huss must feel to the present day the fruits of the " glorious " victory so blasphemously celebrated by him at Prague more than four centuries and a half ago!

This unhappy Germanophobia of the Bohemian professor proved in the result also the most fatal hindrance to the full success of his earnest labours for a radical reform of the Church of Rome, which but for this might have had a very different issue. Hatred begets hatred. What wonder, then, that the Germans, so blindly and malignantly persecuted by Huss, should have learnt only too well the evil lesson taught them by their Czech enemy, and should ultimately even have bettered the instruction!

Huss first began his reformatory work about 1402. Long before this, in the second half of the fourteenth century, three of the most enlightened men of the age—Stickna, Milicz, and Janow—had prepared the way in Bohemia for the coming reformer and his new gospel, by teaching the people the doctrine and tenets of good John Wicliffe.

At the beginning of his reformatory career Huss stopped, far short indeed of the demands of his great predecessors. Nay, when certain English students who were then attending his divinity lectures at the Prague University, urged him to read the works of the great proto-reformer Wicliffe, he declined at first, with every sign of pious horror, to read the "blasphemous heresies of that pernicious Anglican schismatic." At last, however, he was prevailed upon to read, and, behold! he found the doctrine of Wicliffe in singular accord with his own latent views and opinions. From this time forward his onsets upon the errors of Rome grew bolder.

Still for years the dispute between him and the Pope was carried on with much courtesy on both sides, and even with singular forbearance on the part of Rome, the Pope hesitating a very long while before he could make up his apostolic mind to hurl the bolt of excommunication at the Prague professor.

Even after the publication of Huss's book, *De Ecclesiâ*, in which the reformer sturdily maintained that the true Church was truly spiritual, and had nothing whatever to do with temporal power and authority; that Christ alone was the head of the Church, and the pretended vicegerency of the Bishop of Rome a monstrous lie, which it was sacrilegiously sought to maintain in the very face of the opposing authority of Holy Writ; and that the Bible knew nothing of popes and cardinals,—Rome still continued to evince an earnest desire for conciliation, which actually induced Pope Johannes XXIII. to repeal the excommunication bull on the occasion of the reformer's citation to appear before the council at Constance (1414).

Nay, the Pope's judge of heretics in Bohemia, Nicolas, Bishop of Nazareth, solemnly certified before a notary public that he had many times and oft conversed with Master John Huss, had eaten with him and drunk with him, and attended his preachings, yet had never detected error or heresy in him, but had always found him, in all his words and acts, a true and sincere Catholic. Pope Johannes even joined in the Emperor Sigismund's safe-conduct granted to the Bohemian schismatic.

And truly it was not Rome in this instance that could justly be accused of the horrible murder of the unhappy man. There was no pope at the time of his trial. It was a concatenation of fatal circumstances, independent of Rome's will and interest, that led to the final catastrophe which made a martyr of Huss and covered the great Council of Constance with indelible disgrace.

The moderate reformers, with Johannes Gerson and Peter of Ailly at their head, regarded the Bohemian as an impracticable firebrand, and as the greatest obstacle in the way of a moderate, practical reform of the Church of Rome, such as they themselves were bent upon imposing upon the council.

Then there were Huss's deadly enemies, Stephen Palacz and Michael de Causis, who unhappily wielded a most formidable influence in the council, which they used most unscrupulously to work his ruin.

Then all the rich prelates were deeply embittered

against the reformer for that he had dared to counsel the confiscation of their accumulated vast wealth and their rich livings for the benefit of the state.

And lastly, and most fatal of all, there was the bitter enmity of the Germans, who refused to see aught in poor Huss, delivered at last into their hands, but the man who had all through life been their irreconcilable and victorious foe.

It has thus been shown how Rome treated Huss, for some twelve years at least, with comparative tenderness.

Luther, also, who yet showed himself from the very outset of his reformatory career a much more uncompromising and determined foe to Rome than poor Döllinger and most of his followers can be said to have done as yet, was not, for nearly three years after the publication of his famous ninety-five theses against papal absolution, treated with a tithe even of the virulent animosity that we see displayed by the Jesuits and Ultramontanists of our day against the leaders of the comparatively very mild anti-infallibilist movement.

No terms are deemed too opprobrious, it would appear, to apply to such men as Döllinger, Huber, Michelis, Friedrich, Reinkens, Schulte, Zirngiebl, Maassen, Keller, Anton, and a host of other eminent Catholic professors who repudiate the late Vatican decrees.

Thus that brilliant Ultramontanist organ, the

Donau Zeitung, asserts, for instance, that the faces of these secessionists are such awful libels upon the Aryan race, that they ought to be "confiscated" for the honour and in the interest of that race!

Another clerical scribe will have it that Satan has so unmistakably set his mark upon "Döllinger and his crew," that the kindest angel of salvation cannot fail to see it! Is it not truly astonishing how men with such truly patibular and "hell-marked" countenances as these unhappy Döllingerians are now declared to carry patent in the light of day, could ever have succeeded in attaining to high ecclesiastical dignities, and could so long have been held up before the world as the only lights and oracles of the most orthodox of all Roman Churches?

Nor would it appear that the Döllingerian professors have fared much better at the hands of the more liberal section of the Catholics in Germany. Many years ago the late Heinrich Heine applied to poor Döllinger, then the biggest canonic gun and the most ardent and uncompromising champion of popery in Germany, the opprobrious epithet of "archinfamous" (*der erzinfame Pfaffe Döllingerius*). It is strange how this epithet seems to stick to him to the present day, and how even many of the most sincere among the secessionists, who are now apparently marching under his banner, continue to look upon him as naught but an inveterate Catholic priest with strong Romish leanings!

Nay, there are some who go so far as to doubt the sincerity of this man, and believe him to be simply a crafty tool of Rome. Others, less prejudiced, are ready to concede his honest adhesion to the present movement, into which he has been forced, however, they maintain, simply by the monstrous excess of Romish pretensions.

One of these semi-pro-Döllingerians will have it that the Rector Magnificus of the Munich University should be regarded as a man cheerfully willing to believe and to teach that two and two may fairly be held to make five, but sternly refusing to have the five turned into six.

Now, all these liberal Catholics will be satisfied with nothing less than an openly-avowed secession from Rome, and the initiation of an independent German Catholic Church.

They insist upon the absolute abolition of the celibate of priests, which they contend is clearly an offence against the laws of God and of nature.

They insist equally upon the total abolition and prohibition of all conventual orders and communities, whatever deceiving name they may bear, and under whatever specious pretext they may hide the real purport and object of their institution.

They will have no more auricular confession, no more pretended remission of sins by a set of men at least equally sinful with the penitents who confess to them.

They demand that civil marriage shall be made obligatory, not simply optional.

They will have no hierarchy in the Church of God, which they maintain is the most hideous excrescence of the second and third centuries after Christ. The priest shall be dependent on his conscience alone, and shall teach the Word of God such as he himself sincerely believes it, free from all dogmatic trash and popish perversion. Every member of the flock shall freely exercise the right of independent thought and inquiry, to enlighten and thereby purify and strengthen his faith.

The monstrous priestly tyranny of the arbitrary refusal, on any pretence whatever, of the sacraments of the Church to any member of the congregation shall absolutely cease. To the whole congregation alone, in its collective capacity, it shall appertain to judge whether a member has fallen away from it beyond the possibility of re-entering within the pale.

These and a few other demands of the same stamp and in the same direction constitute the leading part of the programme of the most advanced section of the secessionists from Rome. Upon the granting of these demands, which they declare to be the minimum that will satisfy them, they insist.

They say they will not allow themselves to be cajoled by the craft of a set of priestly professors of the Döllinger stamp into the acceptance of a few futile concessions; they will have a true radical reform of the rotten system, which has too long been permitted to stand in the way of all progress and improvement of the human race. What use is the expulsion of the Jesuits to us, they say, which our Döllingers, our Schultes, our Michelis would throw to us as a sop? The Jesuits are only the carbuncle that shows the foulness of the body on which it grows. It is no use to cut the carbuncle off: the body must be cleansed of its foulness. The Church of Christ must be purged altogether of Rome, and of all that appertaineth thereunto.

It must certainly be confessed, that between the two—the Ultramontanists and the Free Catholics—Döllinger and the other leaders of the more moderate sections of the anti-infallibilists are by no means in an enviable position.

The programme of the more advanced of the two moderate sections of the secessionists is scarcely a shade less radical.

The constitution of the new "Old Catholic" Church contemplated by this section goes back to the second century after Christ, and somewhat resembles Presbyterianism in its leading features. The presbyter, or priest, is to be elected freely by the community. He is to receive a fixed salary, amply sufficient for the proper maintenance of himself and his family and the education of his children; for this section of reformers also has inscribed on its banner the abolition of Gregory VII.'s monstrous law of the clerical celibate among the chief and most indispensable conditions and demands of its programme.

Professor Huber of Munich has recently called attention to the curious circumstances attendant upon the promulgation of the Gregorian clerical celibacy law in 1074. It is a well-established historical fact, that the humbler clergy more especially received with angry indignation the tyrannical and infamous papal command to put away their wedded wives, and that the wretched law would never have been carried into execution had it not been for the gross ignorance and correspondingly blind bigotry of the miserable mob in those dark times, and in a measure also, to do due homage to the truth of the matter, to the dissolute habits to which the clergy were even then addicted.

Pope Gregory, with his habitual consummate craft, made the people believe that his decree was directed against these notorious dissolute habits.

"*Si qui sunt presbyteri, diaconi, vel subdiaconi qui in crimine fornicationis jaceant, interdicimus eis ex parte Dei Omnipotentis et Sancti Petri auctoritate ecclesiæ introitum, usque dum pœniteant et emendent,*" says the text of the law. But the true purport and scope was speedily made apparent through the sweeping interpretation put upon it by the authorized legates and messengers of Gregory, who everywhere sternly and inexorably insisted upon all presbyters, deacons and sub-deacons, putting away their wedded wives.

In Siegebert of Gemblours' *Chronicles* ad annum 1074, the real purport of the Gregorian decree is plainly stated :—" *Gregorius Papa celebrata Synodo Simoniacos anathematizavit, uxoratos sacerdotes à divino officio removit.*"

It seems certainly a curious way of breaking the black sheep of the clerical flock of their vicious and dissolute habits by absolutely forbidding all priests to marry, in contempt of the plainest laws of God and nature. But Gregory of course used this ostensible motive simply as the specious pretext for his iniquitous enactment. What he wanted, was to sever the clergy from all the tender ties of family, and from all connection with true citizenship. The Pope and Rome were henceforth to be the sole family and country of the Catholic priesthood.

Professor Huber, indeed, does not explicitly join in the demand of the more advanced sections of the secessionists, that the Gregorian Decree of 1074 should be absolutely repealed and annulled; he, like his Döllingerian fellow-professors, takes his stand upon the so-called Trentine Symbolum,—rather a narrow platform of reform, it must be confessed. Yet he clearly feels much inclined to travel considerably beyond the limits fixed by Döllinger; and the world need not be surprised in the least to see

Huber and many others of the school of restricted reform go over with arms and baggage to the camp of the more radical sections. As regards the clerical celibacy question more particularly, Huber, at least, may be said to stand already more than half-way over the Döllingerian boundary line.

Another demand of the programme is the dissolution of all chapters. Here, again, the reformers go back to the institutions of the Christian Church such as they were in the second century after Christ, when the Church knew only presbyters and bishops; before the latter, who were originally intended simply to act as superintendents over the former, had yet succeeded in usurping a self-arrogated authority and grafting an unwholesome, hybrid, semi-monarchical, semi-aristocratic constitution upon the healthy tree of the Democratic Christian Church as founded by Christ.

The celebration of mass and of all other acts of public worship in the vernacular of the country, forms another leading item in the programme of this section of reformers.

It is also demanded by them, that all ministerial functions be performed without additional fee or reward in future, the priest's pay by the community being held to cover the whole remuneration for his labour.

"Equality of the grave" forms another leading demand. Death levels all ranks and all social distinctions, these reformers argue. Let us abolish, then, all paltry funeral pomp. Let men's good deeds and the true grief of sincere mourners follow them to the grave. One priest should suffice to deliver the funeral oration over the grave of the highest and wealthiest and the poorest and lowliest parishioner alike.

No more auricular confession, no pilgrimages, no processions, no adoration of saints, relics, or images. These, and a few minor demands, fill up the sum of the programme of the more moderate reform section.

We now come to the demands of the Döllingerians proper—that is to say, of Döllinger himself, Reinkens, Schulte, Langen, Huber, Friedrich, Maassen, Zirngiebl, Froschammer, and other Old Catholic professors.

The chief points of the programme of this, the most conservative section of the Old Catholic secessionists, may be given in a free version of their own words as follows :—

"1. In the full consciousness of our religious duties, as members of the true Church of Christ, we hold fast by the Old Catholic faith, based upon the unassailable Divine authority of Holy Writ, and borne witness to by the irrefragable testimony of sacred tradition.

"We hold ourselves, therefore, true members of the Catholic Church, and we are determined to strenuously resist all attempts to drive us out of the community of that Church, and to despoil us of any of the ecclesiastic and civic rights vested in us by virtue of our membership in that community.

"We declare the ecclesiastic censures, suspensions, and excommunications launched against us by Rome, and by bishops acting under the inspiration of the Roman See, to be utterly arbitrary and groundless, and therefore of no avail or force.

"We are not troubled in our conscience thereby, nor feel ourselves in any way hindered from active participation in the community of the Catholic Church.

"Taking our stand with full confidence in our right, upon the confession of faith as contained in the so-called Trentine Symbolum, we reject and repudiate the dogmas enacted under the pontificate of Pius IX., in opposition to the true doctrine and tenets of the Catholic Church, and to the sound principles that have guided that Church since the days of the Council of the Apostles. We reject, more especially and explicitly, the dogma of the infallible ministry, and the supreme, ordinary, and immediate jurisdiction of the Pope.

"2. We hold fast by the ancient constitution of the Church.

"We declare our deliberate and resolute opposition to all and every attempt to oust the bishops of the Catholic Church from the immediate and independent guidance of the Church in their own dioceses.

"We firmly reject and repudiate the false doctrine

laid down in the Vatican decrees, to the effect that the Pope is the sole and only divinely appointed representative and head of all ecclesiastical power and authority—a doctrine running counter to the Trentine canon, which pronounces the existence of a divinely appointed hierarchy of bishops, priests, and deacons.

"We acknowledge the primacy of the Romish bishop in the duly restricted sense in which it was acknowledged, upon the authority of the sacred Scriptures, by the fathers and councils in the days of the old undivided Catholic Church of Christ. That is to say, we declare that points of faith cannot be defined and settled solely and simply by the decision of the Pope for the time being, not even with the explicit sanction or tacit assent of the bishops, who are bound by their oath to yield obedience to the supreme pontiff. To be of force and avail, such decision must absolutely be in full conformity with Holy Writ and with the ancient traditions of the Church, as handed down to us through the channel of the recognized fathers of the Church and the Œcumenical Councils.

"We maintain even beyond this, that the council of the Church, even with the fullest attributes of Œcumenicity, which were so lamentably wanting to the late Vatican Council, cannot, even with the unanimous assent and sanction of all its members, claim the power of upsetting the foundations of the Church and the traditions of the past. It cannot issue decrees binding upon the members of the Church. To invest decisions and decrees of councils in matters of faith or points of theological doctrine with force and effect, binding upon the conscience of Catholics, it is an indispensable and precedent condition that such decisions and decrees should be clearly proved to be in strict conformity with the original belief of the Church and the traditions handed down to us.

"In all matters relating to the laying down and passing of rules and precepts of faith and belief, we claim not only for the Catholic clergy and those learned in divinity, but for the Catholic lay world as well, and as fully, the unrestricted right of giving their assent to such precepts and rules, or of protesting against them and refusing to be in any way bound by them.

"3. We aspire to effect, with the co-operation of theological and canonic science, a reform in the Church of Rome which shall, in the true spirit of the Old Catholic Church, remove the present abuses and defects, and accomplish more particularly the legitimate wishes of the Catholic laity to have their due share in the management of the affairs of the Church, at present most wrongfully usurped by the clergy.

"We declare that there is no ground whatever for imputing the taint of heresy to the Church of Utrecht, and that no actual dogmatic antagonism can be said to exist between that Church and ourselves.

"We fervently hope in a reunion with the Greek-Oriental and Russian Church, whose separation from the great Catholic Church was not compelled by constraining causes, and is based upon no essential dogmatic difference.

"With the accomplishment of the reforms we are striving to bring about in our own Church, and by continuing resolutely our forward movement on the path of knowledge and science, and of progressive Christian culture and moral improvement, we hope to attain at last, however gradually and slowly, to an ultimate understanding and full agreement with all other Christian confessions, more especially with the Protestant Churches of Germany and the Episcopal Anglican Church of England and America.

"4. We hold the due study and cultivation of science an indispensable element in the education of the Catholic clergy. We consider the artificial exclusion of the clergy from the intellectual culture of the age, such as we see unhappily practised in boy seminaries as well as in the higher clerical schools under the one-sided guidance of bishops, to be most dangerous and pernicious, considering the high pedagogic importance which these institutions possess for the proper education of the people.

"We desire and court the co-operation of the secular authorities in the education and training of a morally-pious, scientifically-enlightened, and patriotically-minded clergy.

"We demand for our parish priests and the so-called lower clergy an independent, honourable position, protected against any and every attempt at arrogant hierarchical dictation and tyranny. We protest most energetically against the wretched custom of arbitrary removal and translocation of pastors of communes—the so-called *amovibilitas ad nutum*—one of the most pernicious importations from France, which has of late been much practised by German bishops.

"5. We stand firmly by the constitution of our country, which secures to us civic freedom and humanitarian culture, and we reject and repudiate for this reason, as loyal citizens, the new-fangled dogma of papal supremacy, which threatens the very existence of the state. We vow to stand firm and true to our government in the struggle against the Ultramontane pretensions dogmatized in the Syllabus of Pius IX.

"6. Whereas it is notorious that the present disastrous distraction in the Catholic Church has been caused mainly by the so-called Society of Jesus—a religious order which has grossly and perversely misused the undoubted power to spread and foster among hierarchy, clergy, and people tendencies inimical to civilization and progress, anti-actional and dangerous to the state ; and whereas their said society professes and teaches a false and corrupting moral, we declare it to be our sincere conviction, that peace and prosperity in Church and State, harmonious action in the Church, and the due cultivation of proper relations between the latter and civil society, will be possible only when an end shall have been put to the pernicious action and influence of this order.

"7. As members of the Catholic Church such as it existed in its purity, before the attempted innovations of Pope Pius IX., culminating in the late Vatican decrees, had essentially altered and sadly marred its original character—of that Catholic Church accordingly, upon which alone the state has bestowed political recognition, and to which alone public protection has been guaranteed—we maintain and reserve to ourselves all and every and any rights, claims, and titles to our legitimate share in all real property and possession of the said Catholic Church."

It must, indeed, be confessed that the programme of the Döllingerian section of the German secessionists from Rome moves on a very narrow platform. In truth, it would have been difficult to hit upon a less satisfactory basis whereon to rest the confession of faith of the Old Catholic Church than that contained in the Trentine Symbol.

Of the several synods held in the course of the last eight centuries or so, for the avowed purpose of reforming the more glaring defects in the institutions of the Church of Rome, the two most important and, in their earlier stages at least, most promising were the Council of Constance and the Council of Trent.

The Council of Constance, which sat from October, 1414, to May, 1418, was, properly speaking, a revival or continuation of the Council of Pisa. This latter had been held in 1409, to effect a radical reform of the Church of Rome, and to settle the dispute between the two anti-popes, Gregory XII. and Benedict XIII.

The fathers of this council had unhappily allowed themselves to be duped by the Ultramontanist party into beginning their work at the wrong end. They had deposed both anti-popes, and elected in their stead Alexander V. as sole head of the Church. Immediately upon his election the new pope adjourned the discussion of the reform question for three years, and dissolved the council.

The fathers of the Council of Constance, which was professedly called to take up again the reform question dropped at Pisa, declared their firm determination to act with more wisdom, and to enforce a partial and moderate reform, at least, of the Church of Rome. Yet they allowed themselves to be duped once more by the cunning of the Romish party.

The new pope, Martin V., whom the council elected in the place of Pope Johannes XXIII., and the two anti-popes, Gregory XII. and Benedict XIII., proved just as crafty as Alexander V. All that the fathers of the council succeeded in accomplishing was the base butchery of poor John Huss and his friend and fellow-reformer, Hieronymus Faulfisch—better known in the history of the great Reformation as Hieronymus of Prague; but the Church of Rome was left pretty much in the same rotten state as before.

The Council of Trent was called some hundred and thirty years after, in 1545.

The Emperor Charles V. had for a long time tried hard to have a general council of the Church summoned by the Pope, but all his efforts and endeavours had proved unavailing against the obstinate opposition of Clement VII.

However, after the death of the latter (25th of Sept., 1534), the Conclave had elected a member of the house of Farnese, one of the astutest politicians of the age.

The new pope, Paul III., instead of opposing, like his predecessor, the convocation of a general synod, professed his eagerness to submit to the examination and decision of an Œcumenical Council the dispute between the Court of Rome and the Lutherans in Germany.

He admitted also that the Church stood, indeed, in the greatest need of reform, and solemnly promised to do everything in his power to contribute to a satisfactory settlement of this and of all other matters that were "unsettling men's minds, and disturbing the peace and concord of the Church of Christ."

The astute Pope used his utmost endeavours to cajole the German Protestants into an active participation in the council which he proposed to convoke.

He sent a special legate, the accomplished and eloquent Paul Vergerius, to Germany to persuade the Protestants of Rome's sincerity in the church reform question.

The legate sought and obtained an interview with Dr. Martin Luther, whom he treated with singular deference. The arts of Vergerius failed, however, in overcoming the reluctance of the Protestants to send delegates to the council.

Pope Paul had signified his intention to have the council held at Mantua; the German Protestants, on the other hand, insisted upon the selection of a city in Germany for this purpose, and demanded guarantees also for the absolute independence of the council.

Luther himself remembered too well how well-nigh Miltitz had succeeded once in cajoling him clean out of his reformatory intentions and designs, and he was on his guard, therefore, against the sweet suasion of Vergerius. Still, when the synod was actually convoked by the Pope to meet in Mantua, the great reformer expressed his opinion that it would be better for the Protestants to attend the council than keep away from it.

He freely expressed his belief also that the Pope was not sincere in the matter, and that he only wished to put the Protestants in the wrong, by showing the world that it was not he who objected to submit all disputed points to a general synod, but that the Protestants refused to join in the projected work of conciliation. It would be better, therefore, to go to Mantua, said Luther, in his advice to the Elector Johann Friedrich of Saxony.

The council, adds the plain-spoken man, would, after all, in the position of affairs then, turn out to be a "contemptible, lousy" council. Moreover, it should be borne in mind also, that a hostile decision of the council could not do the Protestant cause any great harm, as it was a well-established fact that general synods were not by any means held to be infallible; so far from it indeed, that the resolutions and decrees of one synod had often been set aside by another synod.

However, the elector and the other Protestant princes of the empire, and the delegates from the Lutheran free cities and towns, declined the Pope's invitation, to Paul III.'s intense satisfaction.

Meanwhile, a very strong and earnest desire for a thorough reform of the Church of Rome had arisen among the very princes of that Church, which gave the Pope considerable uneasiness. At the head of these threatening reformatory movements stood Cardinals San Marcello, Caraffa, and Contarini.

The last-named of the three, more especially, was truly a sincere reformer. He was a man of great erudition, intense earnestness, and unblemished character. To get rid of him, Pope Paul sent him to

Ratisbon, in 1541, as legate to preside over the negotiations opened in that city between the Church of Rome and the Lutherans, in obedience to the desire of the Emperor Charles V., who was truly anxious to restore the unity of the Catholic Church, and fully convinced that Rome ought to make considerable concessions and introduce sweeping reforms to accomplish this great end.

These negotiations were conducted by Johannes Eck, Julius Pflug, and Johannes Gropper, for Rome; Melanchthon, Martin Bucer, and Johannes Pistor for the German Protestants. Julius Pflug and Johannes Gropper were much inclined to conciliation, and the legate himself, who presided over the discussions, was bent upon making the largest concessions to the Lutherans. So it came to pass, to the joyful surprise of the latter, that the leading articles of the Lutheran faith were fully adopted by the Catholic doctors and the papal legate.

The joy was of short duration, however. The Pope repudiated the doings of honest Contarini, and the entire attempt at conciliation fell through—every concession that had been made at Ratisbon being ultimately formally withdrawn by the Court of Rome.

After the peace of Crespy, concluded between Francis I. and the Emperor Charles V., the 18th of September, 1544, the emperor induced the Pope once more to convoke a general synod for 1545.

This was the famous Council of Trent, which, repeatedly suspended and adjourned, and once (in 1547) actually translated to Bologna, lasted altogether some eighteen years. It was ostensibly called, of course, to effect at last a satisfactory settlement of the differences in the Church.

But Paul III. soon showed the true nature of his aim and intentions. He openly avowed that the council was called to condemn solemnly the "Protestant heresy," and he concluded an alliance offensive and defensive with the Emperor Charles, whom he promised to aid in his intended war upon the Protestants in Germany, not only with subsidies in money, but also with an auxiliary corps of 12,000 foot and 500 horse. On the 15th of July, 1546, he issued a bull, in which he ordered prayers and general confessions and fasting, to propitiate the Almighty in favour of the war undertaken by pope and emperor for the destruction of the heretics, and the restoration of the peace of the Church.

When, after repeated adjournments, a new synod was finally convoked for 1562, to meet in the city of Trent, there seemed for a time to be some slight chance of an ultimate agreement between Rome and the Protestants, and of a satisfactory reform of the Catholic Church.

Among the leading proposals of the Emperor Ferdinand I., figured the celebration of all religious services in the vernacular of the country, the admission of the laity to the chalice in the Holy Communion, and the abolition of the celibate of the priesthood.

The Pope and his followers rejected, of course, all these demands, and the great Council of Trent came at last to its final termination, leaving the Church pretty much in the same state and condition in which it had found it at its first sitting in 1545.

With the exception of passing a few high-sounding but unmeaning resolutions and decrees, the great council had positively nothing whatever to show in the way of a tangible result of its labours.

It cannot, then, but be considered a most unlucky thing for the true interests of the great German secessionist movement from Rome, that Döllinger and his more immediate followers should have elected to take their stand upon the narrow basis of the Trentine Symbolum and the canon which pronounces the existence of a divinely appointed hierarchy of bishops, priests, and deacons, instead of going in boldly at once for the still sufficiently moderate demands of the less radical of the two other sections of secessionists.

But whilst fully admitting that the confined view thus taken by Döllinger and his fellow-professors of the church reform required cannot but be held matter of sincere regret, the justice of the strictures passed in this country upon the Old Catholic movement in Germany cannot be admitted.

An opinion has been expressed here, that never before in the world's history has there been a reform movement so hesitatingly, lukewarmly, and half-heartedly supported by friends and sympathizers as the Old Catholic movement in Germany. Strange to say, this remark would seem to apply with special force to the reception which the movement has had to meet at the hands of English churchmen. With the exception of a very few instances of Anglican bishops and deans having shown warm and hearty sympathy for the movement and the man at the head of it, no very cordial welcome has been given in this country to the reformatory efforts and aspirations of the German Old Catholics.

In fact, the movement clearly has not been properly understood and correctly appreciated in this country. The strangest notions would seem to be entertained about it, even by leading Protestants. Dr. Littledale, who has published a most valuable article upon the subject in the *Contemporary Review*, is about the only man of authority who shows an intimate knowledge of the question, and treats it with becoming justness and true appreciation of its real scope and import.

With the known Ultramontanist influences at work in many of our leading organs of the press, it is not to be wondered at that but scant justice should be extended to the German secessionists from Rome in the columns of the organs in question.

Still it cannot but seem strange that so much cold water should have been thrown, and such severe strictures passed upon the movement, as we have seen in the columns of certain English journals.

"The Old Catholics," says one of these high authorities, "are a small, weak sect, having no state or empire particularly their ally." (This latter statement lies certainly open to the objection of being slightly contrary to fact.) "Distinctive tenets, moreover, have they none. They reject papal infallibility, but in every other respect they are as papal, as Roman, as the Pope and Rome themselves!"

It seems hardly credible that a statement so utterly opposed to the true facts of the case should have been permitted to appear in a professed Protestant journal.

Let any man of fair understanding and impartial mind carefully peruse the programme of even the "excessively moderate" Döllingerian section of the German secessionists, and then let him judge for himself whether even Döllinger and his followers can possibly, by any stretch of the imagination, be held to be "as papal, as Roman, as the Pope and Rome themselves."

It may be permitted to call special attention to the second section of the Döllingerian programme, which claims, in unmistakably clear and precise terms, for all Catholics, both the clergy and the laity, the freest exercise of the right of independent judgment in all matters of faith and belief. "Neither the Pope by himself, nor even with the fullest and most unanimous concurrence and sanction of an Œcumenical Council of the Church, can issue decrees binding upon the members of that Church. In all matters relating to the laying down and passing of rules and precepts of faith and belief, we claim, not only for the Catholic clergy and those learned in divinity, but for the Catholic lay world as well, and as fully, the unrestricted right of giving their assent to such precepts and rules, or of protesting against them, and refusing to be in any way bound by them."

Let this doctrine once be admitted in the Church of Rome, and the most deadly blow will have been dealt to that Church. It is the thin end of the wedge which, properly driven home, must shiver to pieces the encroachments and pretensions of the Pope and of Rome.

END OF VOL. I.

www.ingramcontent.com/pod-product-compliance
Lightning Source LLC
Chambersburg PA
CBHW030326240426

43673CB00040B/1285